K.E.S.S.
THE STORY OF
A SCHOOL

THE HISTORY OF KING EDWARD'S SCHOOL STOURBRIDGE

R. L. Chambers MA

Mark and Moody

Copyright © 1988 R. L. Chambers, M.A.
First impression 1988
Second impression 1988

First published in Great Britain in 1988 by
Mark and Moody Ltd., Publishers, Stourbridge,
West Midlands, DY8 1DQ.

All rights reserved. No part of this publication
may be reproduced, stored in a retrieval system
or transmitted, in any form or by any means,
electronic, mechanical, photocopying, recording
or otherwise, without the prior permission of the
copyright owner.

ISBN 0 9506 4396 3

Printed and Bound in Great Britain
Mark and Moody Limited
Established 1840
Stourbridge

FOREWORD
BY
PROFESSOR I. M. KENNEDY

(Professor of Medical Law & Ethics at Kings College, London)

There has been a school in Stourbridge on the same site for 557 years. Such continuity of occupation and existence, you would say, would make history writing relatively simple: all the materials which go to make up a history would be around somewhere although it may be a bit of a chore finding them. But, you may go on, Stourbridge is a small provincial town with nothing much to tell us. A history of its School seems like an excess of local pride, or enthusiasm for the politics of the parish pump.

You would be wrong on both counts. As regards the second point, the history of the School comes alive in the hands of R. L. Chambers and has so much to tell us at a number of levels. We see Tudor England with magic and mystery, fear and irrationality driving the actions of men, always close to violence. The age of Shakespeare, who lived little more than 20 miles away, makes sense as it is brought to life. We see also what Mr Chambers calls the age of Pope in the early eighteenth century when the gavotte of political and social intrigue had replaced the invocations of the astrologer and the hand on the dagger. Then, we see a Dickensian Dotheboys Hall as the school slides into neglect and for more than a decade seems to have no pupils at all.

These are major themes but there are others. We see the comings and going of a local bourgeoisie, scheming, plotting, being idle, being benevolent and, above all, keeping and enjoying power. We see the tide of the industrial revolution sweeping over the town and school and washing away the old curriculum of the classics (and only the classics), and bringing in a curriculum which was more relevant to local needs and changed attitudes. Shades of the present! And there is much more.

Returning to the first point, was the history simply a matter of gathering the materials together, as some may think? Certainly not. The first chapter has all the mystery and breathless pursuit of a first rate detective story. Mr Chambers is the detective, bringing the combined gifts of analytical rigour and creative imagination to bear on the treasures which luck keeps putting in his way. Luck, as any historian knows, is usually the hero of the piece, and certainly it plays its part here, but Mr Chambers makes his own luck. He rejects old theories, asks hard questions and infects the reader with the love of the chase. When he describes how he sat down to examine his latest hoard of materials and notes, en passant, that it was Christmas Eve, I for one can understand him.

The result more than repays the effort and dedication. This is not just a story of a school. It is a sensitive and informed piece of social history, treating of both local and national issues. It is a model of how to write local history. We learn about the school, the officers, the governors, the town and its 'dynasties', and the wider social and political structures. The Foley family, for example, allows us glimpses into divisions between Whigs and Tories, conservatives and reformers, which make theory come alive. We watch Mr Chambers picking his way through the law of property and untangling the way land was held. We see him poring over accounts to discover not just the finances of the school but also such things as educational policy. An item in the accounts of 1627 shows the usher being reimbursed for the purchase of a 'dixonary' and other books. This allows Mr Chambers to remark on one of the sadnesses of the history, that "in the whole vast array of the school archives we find practically no references at all to the scholastic matters which were the real business of the school and the cause of its being. Teaching and learning, the work and tools of the classroom, even the books without which the school could not have functioned at all, were conspicuous only by their absence in the records".

As I say, this is a sadness. The sounds of the boys repeating their lessons, the games they played, the imprecations of their masters, are all lost to us. The burghers who kept the books were interested in more substantial stuff. But, then, we are carried off again as Mr Chambers traces the seal of the founders of the School to the Wool Staple of the City of Lincoln and analyses who really was the donor of the School's library in the mid-seventeenth century. It is hard not to be at once impressed by Mr Chambers' scholarship and intrigued and delighted by what you read.

And what of the author? I knew him as my headmaster: at first a forbidding figure, but later a warm and dedicated teacher. My memories, for example, of being invited on Saturday evenings to his house for play-readings are some of the happiest of my youth. (Will these evenings be known to Mr Chambers' successor poring over the archives in the year 2,400 AD?) Mr Chambers' record as a headmaster and teacher was outstanding. Thousands like myself will vouch for that. What now is clear is the range of his abilities and his extraordinary dedication to his School. We could not appreciate this as pupils. It is not too late to acknowledge it as ex-pupils.

This history of our School is written with love and yet with the detached rigour of the true scholar. Mr Chambers frets in his first paragraph that histories of schools "are almost bound to be dull". This is the exception. With it, Mr Chambers has earned himself a place in the pantheon of headmasters which must exist somewhere. His history does his school and him proud and I salute him.

IMK
December 1987

Contents

	Page
Foreword	v
List of Illustrations	x
How it all Came to Light I	1
How it all Came to Light II	32
How it all Came to Light III	40
Origins and Mysteries	48
The First Phase	53
The Seventeenth Century I Peace in Time of Conflict	57
The Seventeenth Century II Conflict in Time of Peace	79
The Early Eighteenth Century Thomas Wentworth	87
The St. Thomas's Period and the Dead Hand	112
Endpiece to Joseph Taylor	150
An End and a Beginning: Giffard Wells I	158
An End and a Beginning: Giffard Wells II	171
Over the Threshold	192
The Last Phase I	199
The Last Phase II	226
Finale and Dedication	253
Index	257

List of Illustrations

Between pages 118 and 119

I   Portrait of Edward VI
II   Deed of Gift
III   Quitclaim
IV   The School Seal
V   The Black Box
VI   Nash's view of Stourbridge
VII   The School Front 1868 and The School Houses c. 1700
VIII   Portraits of four headmasters 1833 – 1934

How It All Came To Light
I

The trouble with histories of schools is that they are almost bound to be dull. We need not go into the reasons for this. The reader can supply his own, but equally, since no one in his senses would willingly set out to be a bore, the reader may well ask, "Then why start? Why not let the dull past slumber in its dulness?"

That is what I too was ready to ask myself, and that is why I was very reluctant, and genuinely so, to start on the history of King Edward's School, Stourbridge. But I remembered two things. One was that school histories are only *almost* bound to be dull, and (as a pendant to that) that the characters who are going to turn up in the history of this particular school will certainly turn out in many cases to be such extraordinary people, recorded in such extraordinary detail, that boredom cannot live with them. (I know this, because I have lived with them and wondered at their antics for more than thirty years.) The other thing is that the story of how this school's history came to be unearthed is in itself a strange tale and well worth the telling. It is almost as if the oddballs and eccentrics who wove their strange courses through the school's four centuries and more of accumulated records must surely have cast their spell over the staid and normal researchers of our present time (those, that is, who dared to cast an enquiring eye over the story of their activities) and must in some way have confounded their judgments and touched their reasons with a predisposing bias towards the loss of logic and the rule of fantasy.

So it was even in the year 1951, when it all first began. That was the year when I first came to Stourbridge, as headmaster of its grammar school. It was also the year immediately preceding the 400th anniversary of the school's Edwardian foundation. The two facts were merely coincidental, but the coincidence was not without its importance.

I vividly remember the opening scene, as it were, of the play. I had come to Stourbridge in the summer term, several months before I was due to take up my new office, in order to interview thirteen-year-old boys for the purpose of a new entrance examination, whose birth coincided with the time of my arrival. I was in the middle of my interviews, sitting in my new study and asking myself, as one tends to do on such occasions, whether all this was a good idea, when, in an interval between two of the thirteen-year-olds, there came an unexpected knock on the door. Wondering who had the nerve to interrupt on such an occasion, I pressed the 'Come in' button, the door opened, and in came an odd little procession — four boys, evidently sixth-formers, and a visibly excited master shepherding the party. I had already met a number of my new colleagues, and I recognised in this one the tall figure of my senior history master, Mr George Burley — Old Boy of the school, distinguished history graduate of Birmingham University, and, as I had been told, expert and enthusiast on the history of the school, and author in recent years of a pamphlet on that subject which the governors had published.

At this stage it has to be recorded that I cannot be sure how many of these details I consciously knew or consciously remembered on that June day. I can say, however, that that did not really matter. What I established at once was the reason for the invasion and for Mr Burley's excitement. The boys in his party were carrying between them two tin deed-boxes, of the type used by solicitors — one of them black, the other a rather obtrusive bright brown. Mr Burley explained that these had been sent down to school from the offices of Harward and Evers (Mr Bryan Evers, the principal of that firm, was our Clerk to the Governors) and that we had found 'The Black Box', containing the school's long-lost ancient records. I gathered also that the tradition of the lost records, lurking in the fabled Black Box, had long been current, but until this glad day no one really knew for certain whether it was to be taken seriously. But now the doubts were resolved: the tin boxes were full of a great mass of papers and books, some of them clearly as old as the school. The tradition was verified. The Black Box was found!

I have to admit that I did not really share to the full in Mr Burley's excitement. For one thing I had not yet got the feeling that this was my place, the heart and centre of my life (as it was certainly afterwards to become). For another thing my attention was totally committed in quite a different direction. The thirteen-year-old boys whose educational future it lay in my hands to settle were clearly of far more importance than any records from the past, however valuable for the disinterested pursuit of pure knowledge they might prove to be. I can remember also even now after thirty-five years the persistently recurring thought that the ancient tradition of the Black Box had found an odd justification, to say the least, in the discovery of two boxes, one black but the other bright brown, and neither of them, quite obviously, very old. However, Mr Burley seemed very sure, and he was certainly very happy, about the discovery, so I stilled my doubts and ushered out my visitors, so that I could get back to the thirteen-year-olds.

That was my first introduction to the world of the Black Box, and in the fullness of time my slight but persistent doubts settled into much more demanding questions and found for them some quite startling answers. It was to be some years into the future before I discovered the real Black Box, and some years again before the Harward and Evers offices began to prove themselves a positive cornucopia of school archives — and archives, what is more, which when actually worked on yielded real information about real people and real events. In the meantime I was aware only that the so-called Black Box papers were undergoing the lengthy and time-consuming process of being calendared — numbered, listed and entered onto sheets of permanent record. It became clear that they comprised an accumulation of over two thousand items, many of them mere scraps of paper containing almost meaningless notes, but at the other extreme very substantial items — including two leather-bound folio volumes which contained the governors' minutes of their proceedings, apparently consecutive and complete over a period of 150 years. While the calendaring process was going on I was myself no more than a detached spectator on the side lines, for this was not really my world. I did, I remember, ask myself on many occasions what was the real importance of the calendar, compiled with such elaborate care, when the documents which were its elements seemed to be yielding remarkably little in the way of real information about the past. I was told that it was of crucial importance to record the two thousand items not only in themselves but in their relationship to each other according to their precise location in the two deed-boxes. This, I suspected at the time, and I am now sure, was a mistake: it was due to a failure to recognise the true nature of the Black Box hoard. The collection in fact was not a collection in any real sense of the word: it bore all the marks of an entirely haphazard accumulation. Some one at some time — probably a lawyer's clerk — had gathered up these masses of papers and books and, to put it crudely, had just bunged them into the boxes to get them tidily out of the way. Whether a seventeenth-century note from one of the school's tenants at Evesham or Worcester happened to be packed with other notes from the same source and period, was entirely a matter of chance.

However, the historians were certainly happy, and it did not become the new headmaster, raised in the foreign discipline of the ancient classics and in any case a stranger to the school and town, to put his oar in. Even so, the new headmaster noticed one or two strange things as time passed. One came in the course of the 400th anniversary celebrations of 1952, to which I have referred. The Black Box discovery was, of course, a pure godsend from the point of view of the creation of a celebratory programme. There was a grand exhibition of historical records, mounted at the school and attended by hundreds of visitors. It must have become clear even at that early stage that the school now possessed a quite unusual volume of records from the past. At the time, of course, they were merely 'quaint' — bits of old letters, ancient account books — one with an entry written "at the very moment when the Spanish Armada was making for our shores" — builders' bills, annual income and expenditure accounts, governors' minutes of their proceedings, instructions to foreclose on poor devils of defaulting tenants, and so on and so forth. The strange thing to which I have referred cropped up in relation to the two volumes of the governors' minute-books. There were displayed in a glass-topped case, one of many, in the art-room, and in common with the dozens of other exhibits they bore, each one of them, a neatly typed explanatory label. I still possess those two labels, and the strange thing, which I noticed at the time but was tactful enough to keep to myself, was that one label described the minute-books as *'Covering the years 1688–1838'*, while the other referred to the *'Minutes and accounts of the Governors for 1689–1837'*. Clearly someone had blundered, for the two pairs of dates could not both be right. Imagine my surprise, on referring to the minute-books themselves, to find the correct dates were 1688 and 1849. The historians had not only produced two mutually incompatible pairs of dates, but only one of their four dates was in fact correct.

I began to think that there was some sort of hoodoo on the investigation of our ancient records. The logic of clearly incompatible pairs of dates was of the same order as that of identifying one traditionally lost and ancient Black Box with two newly discovered modern lawyer's deed-boxes, one black and one bright brown.

Perhaps this is a good place to tell the story of how the true Black Box came to light. This happened in 1954, three years after the discovery of the documents, but several more years than that before I was to find myself being drawn into the world of the Black Box almost, as it were, against my will. The great 'age of discovery' in the field of the school archives was not to come until the years 1959 and 1960. Meantime the work of calendaring the Black Box documents went, imperceptible and unperceived, upon its way, and there was little to draw attention to what lay concealed in Harward and Evers' archives. It was still assumed that the Black Box had been found.

I cannot pretend to remember precisely every detail of what happened. But certainly it happened one afternoon, when the boys had gone home, or most of them, and the caretakers and cleaners had taken over the school. At that time the head caretaker was named Charlie Hough. He and his wife lived in an apparently Victorian house on the High Street front next above the Assembly Hall. Here they provided dinners for a small number of boys and masters under a system of private enterprise. Charlie Hough had succeeded his father as head caretaker, and memories of 'Old' Hough still survived. One of my colleagues used to say that he was known to the boys as Arbin. The explanation of this was that his conversation constantly began with the words "Arbin thinkin'." Be that as it may, Arbin's son — himself now well on in years — was now in charge, and his domain, while its headquarters were situated in the stokehold below the back of the library in the A Block, included also various outposts in other parts of the buildings. One of these outposts was a cupboard — a walk-in cupboard — under the staircase on the ground floor of the P Block. This formed a repository, and quite a capacious one, for various cleaning materials, brooms, mops, and so on. Here on that afternoon in 1954 I came looking for the caretaker for some purpose long forgotten now. And here, as he came out of the broom cupboard to see what

I wanted, I caught sight of an interesting object in the shadows behind him. It proved on investigation to be an oak chest, quite clearly ancient and quite black with time. It had three bands of iron encircling it, and three gaping lock-holes roughly carved out of its side, empty now of their original locks but undoubtedly intended to accommodate them. I was naturally fascinated by this discovery, and lost no time in questioning Charlie Hough to find out what I could. The whole history of the chest very quickly came to light — astonishing, you might think; but the explanation of that was that by an extraordinary piece of luck the Hough family went back in the history of the school as a sort of caretaking dynasty for three generations. Charlie had followed his father: 'Old' Hough had in his time followed his mother. Down the years from Old Hough's mother came the word that this chest was once 'Mrs. Rupert Deakin's blanket-box'. Now Rupert Deakin had been headmaster from 1885 to 1905, in the days when the head lived in the old headmaster's house, next adjoining, in fact, to the present caretaker's house and on the site of the assembly hall. So the chest went back the better part of a century, and had in that time degenerated in its function from that of 'Mrs. Rupert Deakin's blanket-box' to that of the caretaker's repository for electric light bulbs and toilet rolls!

The next thing was to get the chest expertly photographed and prints sent to the furniture department of the Victoria and Albert Museum. The specialists there expressed themselves satisfied that this was an English chest of Midland oak, probably 15th century. So much for 'Mrs Rupert Deakin's blanket-box'. This was in fact the original muniment chest of the Tudor foundation, and, as it turned out, of the Tudor foundation's predecessor, the original 'chantry chapel' of the year 1430. These conclusions did not, of course, emerge all at once, but the emergence of the chest itself from the P Block glory-hole was a most significant incident, the trigger, as it were, which set off a train of enquiry and discovery in a process which gathered momentum over the years and which is still, in a sense, going on.

I cannot recall how long it was before it dawned upon us that Mrs Rupert Deakin's blanket-box was the true Black Box. But if one had to create a model in the mind of what the Black Box ought to have looked like, here in every detail it was. It was of the right age, certainly of the right colour, and with its three iron bands and its three locks it was entirely typical of the English muniment chest of the fifteenth and sixteenth centuries. In other words, if the school archives really had been in a black box, and if this chest had lain concealed on the school premises for the better part of a century, it would be quite astonishing if the blanket-box and the fabled Black Box were not one and the same. But if they were, how had the Black Box become 'Mrs. Rupert Deakin's blanket-box'?

These are the sort of questions which will not rest in the mind until they have found an answer. In this case the search entailed an enquiry into the whole history of the school's business management over the centuries. It became clear that originally the governors nominated one of their own number to be their representative and agent for a period of two years. Incidentally, they paid him an honorarium sometimes out of all proportion to his labours, and certainly out of proportion to the total income of the foundation. Then later on, in the early eighteenth century, they changed the system: they continued to elect one of their own number to be what they called 'the Collector', but they appointed as a paid official a permanent 'Deputy Collector' who provided a continuity of service, a permanent address, as it were, and an agency which must have become necessary as the finances and business arrangements of the trustees became ever more complex and required ever more sophistication. Not that there could have been much that was sophisticated about the early Deputy Collectors. The first two were father and son — Humphrey and William Moseley — who served consecutively for the almost unbelievably long period of 91 years, from 1729 to 1820. But the Moseleys were not lawyers or any other kind of professional men. They were ironmongers, with a shop in Stourbridge High Street, and their accounts to the governors regularly included items for postage and travel on the governors' confidential business, side by side with other items for such things as nails, 'hold-fasts', and other hardware. It was a strange system, but it seems to have worked, under the Moseleys and their successor John Perry, also an ironmonger, until 1842. At that stage a touch of sophistication crept in, and the next Deputy Collector, now known by the title of Secretary, was more of a professional man than a tradesman, being a Land Surveyor named Walter Witton Shutt, doubtless related to one of the governors of the time, William Shutt. Then there was a period during which the governors made sure that one of their own number was a solicitor, with the legal experience necessary to manage the school's legal business, of which there was a good deal to be done in the middle years of the nineteenth century. There were four of these unoffical legal advisers in succession* — Henry Roberts, William Hunt, Rowland Price and John Harward. Then in 1857 at long last the system changed again and the governors appointed their first Clerk to the Governors in the modern sense of the term, a solicitor who was not himself a governor but who served the governors as a paid official. This man was E. H. Freer, a partner in the law firm of Freer and Perry, with offices in Stourbridge High Street over what is now Cranage's Royal Turf Café.

At this stage in the enquiry along comes another discovery. I say 'comes' rather than 'came' because the sequence is logical and necessary rather than historical and factual. The discovery was made in the archive repository of Harward and Evers' offices in Stourbridge High Street. These offices were situated at that time almost opposite to the offices of Freer and Perry's successors (referred to in the last paragraph). The offices themselves were tucked away behind the High Street facade, and occupied what was said to have been the stable-block of 'Mr. Harward's town house'. This splendid echo from more spacious days found an answering chord once in my hearing which is worth putting on record. There were in Stourbridge High Street in the 1950's not a few old family businesses still surviving from the days of personal service, delivery to the customer's door, white aprons, brass and mahogany. One of these was the gentleman's outfitters shop of George Gardiner, at that time on the same side of the street as Harward and Evers offices and very close to them, opposite to the cinema. Old Mr. Gardiner was indeed very old, a provincial-town tradesman in the best English tradition and of a breed now unhappily almost extinct. He was talking to me once in one of those conversations which were an inseparable part of business done between gentlemen customers and the tradesmen whom they respected and admired. He told me that in his young days his father's shop had been on the other side of the High Street, on the site of the cinema, and about opposite to Harward and Evers' present offices. Of course in those days, he told me, the Evers offices were still functioning as Mr. Harward's town house, and he himself could remember very well how on occasion Mr. Harward would hold an evening party, whereupon he, the young George Gardiner, used to ask his father's permission, for a treat, to slip across the High Street to the Harward front door and there to listen to 'the band of music' discoursing its pleasant

*But see page 152 below

melodies within; and there he would stay awhile and watch the ladies and gentlemen drive up in their carriages and alight, to be ushered inside for the evening's entertainment. So near did that past world come to me from old Mr. Gardiner's boyhood recollections, that I was encouraged to believe that we could bring back to life even older themes and memories of times even further sunk 'in the dark backward and abysm of time'.

And so it proved. For the time had come when the hunt was on for the Grammar School records in the Harward and Evers archives, and I had joined the hunt. The legal records were not kept in the offices themselves, that is to say in the Harward stable-block at the back, an ancient and Dickensian pile of gently crumbling buildings through whose portals one walked direct from the 1950's into almost any past century one cared to imagine. Instead, one turned one's steps to the building with the elegant though much decayed Georgian facade fronting onto the High Street, above the central flight of steps which led up from the pavement to the three or four stories of gracefully proportioned brickwork, symmetrically pierced by the balanced rows of Georgian sash windows. This building I was always given to understand had once been the magistrates' courthouse, and it certainly looked the part, though of its history I never knew anything. Courthouse or whatever else it had been in the past, it now contained the accumulated records of an old and long-established provincial English law practice. The accumulation was immense: when the firm moved out, the records were sent to the county record office at Worcester, and the number of pantechnicons which they were said to have filled almost defied belief. I say 'almost', because after the experience of searching through them, one could believe anything; and after one or two forays up the rickety staircases of the old courthouse into even only one room of the archive store, one believed that one could find anything. The rooms were small and numerous, and seemed to be even smaller than they really were; for they had been lined with wooden staging and shelves, built in rectangular 'nests', as it were, to hold multitudinous deed-boxes of the same type as the two which had been mistakenly hailed in 1951 as the Black Box. In places the staging had collapsed from age and the weight of the law, or rather of its records. Some boxes lay topsy-turvy and broken open, their contents strewn across the narrow alley-ways which wound between the staging and the central fixtures which housed other boxes. There were also books and papers everywhere. On the top of one box on one occasion, I remember, lay a leather-bound volume which proved to be the log of one of His Majesty's ships from the Napoleonic period. Across the aisle on a drunken piece of staging lay the minute-book of an eighteenth-century canal company. That is what it was like, and it went on through room after room. In one room at the top some unprincipled and obsessive stamp-collector had been misguidedly turned loose with permission to take what he could find — and the floor was covered about a foot deep with torn and discarded envelopes, devoid of stamps, and also, unhappily, by their contents.

So anything, one felt, could turn up - provided, that is, the searcher would persist, and could survive the all-pervading clouds of choking dust which rose and swirled around with every box or book or paper that was disturbed — and provided also that one had a little luck.

The luck was there when we turned up E.H. Freer's daybook, recording his services to the governors as their clerk for the grammar school. It will be remembered that he was the first clerk to the governors in the modern sense, appointed in 1857, and that he was a partner in the law firm of Freer and Perry, in the offices on the other side of the High Street, almost opposite to the place where we found the daybook.

Later research into the history of the school's clerks to the governors showed that E. H. Freer was clerk until 1874; and the firm of Freer and Perry and their successors retained the clerkship until 1913. The firm was successively Freer and Perry, Perry, Perry and Travis, Travis, Travis and Sheldon, and finally Sheldon. The clerks in succession were E. H. Freer, George Perry, who died on 2nd April 1891, William Travis, who was in office in 1898, and finally Sheldon (first name unknown), who came to a tragic end when he shot himself in a London taxicab on 22nd August 1913. These last particulars were communicated to me by Mr. H. E. Palfrey (of whom I shall have much more to say later) and I accepted them on his authority.

It was after Sheldon's death that the clerkship was removed by the governors and transferred to the firm of Harward and Evers. At that time also the mass of school archives must have been carried bodily across the High Street from one office to the other. That was undoubtedly the path which Freer's daybook had followed, and it was not far from half a century later that it came to light and told us, if not in so many words, how the original Black Box became 'Mrs. Rupert Deakin's blanket-box'.

The day-book was a tall (perhaps folio height) volume, but only about six inches wide. It was a typical piece of Victorian office stationery, originally well-made and substantial; and it proved to be complete and tolerably legible for the period from 1857 to 1877. Of its binding nothing at all remained, and the mass of its leaves had been mangled (it is the only word) by some vandal's hand which had ripped it across into pieces and cast it to join the rubbish on the floor. Fortunately it proved possible to rescue it, put it together, have it bound, and restore it to a usable and indeed quite handsome volume. Several of its early entries tell us what we wanted to know.

1857
Dec. 22   Mr E. H. Freer appointed Secretary in the place of Mr. W. W. Shutt.
Dec. 23   Attending at Mr. Shutt's office ...
1858
Jan. 2   Journey to Evesham and Worcester with Mr. Shutt who introduced me to many of the tenants ...
Feb. 24   Journey to Birm'm to search through Mr. Price's papers in order to procure such as related to the Grammar School.
Mar. 9   Wrote to Mr. Shutt again, urging him to settle.
May 27   Saw Mr Price, asked him about the keys, when he said that they were kept in a cash box in his office ... and he said he could not tell to what the said keys belonged to.
June 9   Attending at Grammar School bank to open the locks of the chest and taking away the deeds in order to inspect same. Deeds in a very dirty and confused state.

It is clear from E. H. Freer's book, that it was high time the governors changed their system — and their clerk. Incidentally, the Mr. Price he speaks of must have been the Rowland Price who was the third of the four unofficial lawyer-governors, to whom we referred earlier. This man was locally notable in his time — one of the makers of modern Stourbridge. In the school records he appears first when he signs a property lease only as a witness (probably a lawyer's clerk) in the year 1845. But in 1847 a similar lease is witnessed by James Girdlestone, clerk to Messrs. Price and Harward, Solicitors for the governors: Rowland Price himself signs as a governor, and later on his partner John Harward also joined the governing body. Their law firm, Price and Harward, was predecessor to the Harward and Evers of our own day; so in a way the clerkship to the governors was returning to its old home when it went across the High Street from Sheldon to Harward and Evers in 1913.

E. H. Freer's daybook makes it clear that he had no little difficulty in recovering keys and papers belonging to the school, not only from Price but from another firm of solicitors, 'Messrs Collis and Co.' or 'Collis, Bernard and King', predecessors of yet another of the present-day Stourbridge law firms. How they came to have the school papers remains a mystery, unless we assume that the school's affairs had been so haphazardly managed that its records and property could reside with any of the lawyers in the town.

However that may be, it is evident that E. H. Freer did track down the school papers and did find and open the ancient muniment chest. It is to be remembered also that he had come onto the scene at a time when the old system of chests under lock and key, cash in hand and deeds and evidences all "in the box" and ready to hand when required — all this was giving way to the new system of credit finance, — the cheque book and the joint-stock bank with its branches and its clearing system. And as the old system died, the 'chest with three locks' became as old-fashioned as the sock under the mattress. In these circumstances the muniment chest was clearly redundant; and one can only assume that in the fullness of time the firm of Freer and Perry, or one of its successors (since we are not sure of the date) having taken possession of the school chest from the bank, eventually realised that it was redundant, and then either found it to be a nuisance in their offices, or else perhaps scrupulously decided that it must go back to where it strictly belonged, that is to the school. This may well have happened after 1885, and the headmaster living in the school house from that year was Rupert Deakin. When the great black oak chest came down the High Street and was delivered to the headmaster's house, it is difficult not to believe that the Deakins put their heads together and decided that muniment chests might well be redundant, but blanket-boxes were as useful and important as they had ever been.

That was the story which we deduced from reading E. H. Freer's daybook, and nothing that has emerged amongst the plethora of further discoveries in the archives has suggested that it is in any way seriously astray from what actually took place.

So the Black Box went away to the restorers, and came back fitted with one lock that worked, and with its ironwork refurbished, looking now very impressive and well deserving of an honoured place in the school library. It was a visible and persisting reminder that the school was rooted in the past, and that records and legacies of that past existed still, ready perhaps to yield themselves to the hand of the dedicated searcher.

That was even more strikingly true of the next discovery, though this was of a very different kind. It came from the top of the cupboards in the masters' common room, and the dust that lay thick upon it suggested that there it had lain, forgotten and ignored, for a great many years. It was a portrait, painted in oils on a wooden panel in the Tudor style, of a youth garbed in Tudor dress. He was dressed in black — which was perhaps just as well, since the background to his figure was almost equally blackened by the effects of smoke and dust and heat and time. According to the Latin inscription on either side of the figure, again typical of the Tudor portrait style, he was none other than the young king, Edward the Sixth himself, the founder of the school.

He was found in 1958, and after a temporary clean-up was hung over the fireplace in the headmaster's study. There in the month of November of that year my Prize-day speaker at once remarked on him with interest and admiration "That's a very fine picture. Tell me about it." At that stage there was very little to tell — nothing, in fact, except the story of how he had been found on the top of the cupboards. But here again, as with the Black Box, once the questions had been asked, no active and intelligent mind could bear to leave them unanswered. So once again the search was on, and once again the Harward and Evers archives yielded the necessary evidence. It was yet again one of the results of the school's extraordinary continuity in the same place, of the fact that it had stayed on the same site since the year 1430 — it was one of the results of this that yet again the archives gave us the answers that we were looking for, and gave them what is more, in extraordinary detail. In the case of the portrait there were various pieces of evidence which dovetailed together to tell the whole story. They were not even found all at once, but turned up piecemeal in a quite astonishing way. It was almost as if, whatever the difficulties, we were fated to complete the story. It was possible for me to tell that story in detail in an article for the school magazine in November of 1959.

If we reproduce that article now, it will serve to show the remarkable good fortune by which so much of the evidence from the past has survived, to be brought by dedicated persistence in the search back to the light of day. Here it is.

PORTRAIT OF THE FOUNDER

... The portrait used to hang in the masters' common room. Its age, the identity of the artist, its provenance, and the circumstances in which it came into the possession of the school, were apparently unknown. Its quality as a work of art does not appear to have been highly regarded, and its historical importance seems to have been overlooked, perhaps because it was somewhat obscured by the grime of years: and it was no doubt this which stifled general curiosity about the questions suggested above.

The first two questions, when was it painted and by whom, were the first to be answered, when in January of this year it was sent for an opinion to the Birmingham City Art Gallery. The Keeper of the Department of Art there, Mr. John Woodward, had no hesitation in declaring, "It is undoubtedly from the Studio of the artist Guillim Streets, sometimes known as Scrots. He was Court Painter to Edward VI and it is only in recent years that his work has become disentangled." This being so, the artist's own inscription painted on the background of the portrait — EDWADUS SEXTUS AETATIS SUE XVI — dates it precisely to the sixteenth and last year of the young king's life, between his birthday on 12th October 1552 and his death on 6th July 1553.

As far as I have been able to consult them, the catalogues of the portraits of Edward VI do not mention this one in an identifiable form. The article on Guillim Streets in the Dictionary of National Biography lists seven portraits of the king which survive from his brush, and this list again does not include the Stourbridge portrait. It may therefore be supposed that this picture has been lost to sight for a very long time, and we may well feel some satisfaction that we have helped to rescue it from oblivion, as well as some pride in its possession.

How it came to be the property of the school remained a mystery for a little longer, and the question was answered in two stages, as follows.

First, in the course of a general search for old records of the school in the archives of the firm of Harward and Evers, Mr. J. Corns of that firm turned up a small paper-wrapped packet, tied with string and marked with the words 'Stourbidge Free Grammar School. Papers relating to portrait of the founder King Edward VI presented to the school.' This packet contained two pieces of manuscript, both written in ink on folded letter-paper, but in different hands. They read as follows:

LYE VICARAGE
STOURBRIDGE

(1) PORTRAIT OF KING EDWARD VI

In possession of Rev. G. D. Boyle, Vicar of Kidderminster.
This picture is known to have hung in the vestry of Kidderminster Church for generations.
Sir. W. Moxall, Keeper of the National Galley, pronounced it to be by Clowdesley, a pupil of Holbein.
It is to be disposed of for benefit of the Church Restoration Fund at Kidderminster.
It is now at Colnaghi's in London — they have cleaned it, re-framed it and covered it with glass.
If it were not that it has been much touched up in past time it would be worth a large sum — as it is, Colnaghi's value it at £25 or £30.
Mr Boyle is willing to sell it for the Stourbridge School at £20 — and any communication should be made to him.

(2) COPY OF A LETTER DATED 31/5/78 i.e. 1878

I have at last found out that the picture of King Edward the 6th now at Stourbridge was given to the vicar of Kidderminster by a Lord Foley along with the old altarpiece of the stoning of St. Stephen.
Archdeacon Onslow, one of my predecessors, believed that they both were bought when Canons, the Duke of Chandos' place near London, was dismantled. The church at Witley contains in its interior nearly all the fittings of the private chapel at Canons. More than this I have been unable to discover.
Y.t.
G. D. Boyle.

Following this fortunate discovery came an even greater piece of luck, again as the result of a general search for school records. Amongst a mass of papers dating from the time of the Rev. W. J. J. Welch, Headmaster here from 1858 to 1885, was a letter which he wrote to the then Clerk to the Governors, E. H. Freer, the first part of which is relevant to our search. It reads as follows:

Stourbridge
September 21, 1875.

Dear Sir,
    Mr. Thomas of the Kidderminster and Stourbridge Banking Co., and Mr. T. F. Bland, of High Street, have been appointed a Deputation to wait on the Governors for the purpose of presenting to them a portait of King Edward the Sixth — purchased by subscription for this purpose. They propose to go to your office at 11.30 this morning.
                   Yours truly,
                   W. J. J. Welch.

These three documents are self-explanatory and require no comment, except that it may be pointed out that without the letter from Mr. Welch the date of Mr. Boyle's letter in 1878 would certainly have side tracked the search for corroborative evidence of a transaction which took place in 1875. Moreover the evidence of the Kidderminster Churchwardens' books for the period (for which we are indebted to Mr. A. J. Perrett, late of King Charles School), while conclusive as to the sale of the picture, is not conclusive as to the precise date. That date, however, is now confirmed by a paragraph from the *Kidderminster Times* of 25 September 1875, from which the following is taken:

STOURBRIDGE
PRESENTATION TO KING EDWARD'S SCHOOL

    Some short time back a suggestion was thrown out by the Rev. Dr. Robertson that it would be desirable to purchase a portrait of Edward VI, founder of the school, and of Dr. Johnson, who was one of its pupils. Subscriptions were received by Mr. Thomas, of the Stourbridge and Kidderminster Banking Company, and the requisite amount having been obtained the portrait of the young king has been purchased and presented to the governors. The likeness is believed to be a faithful one, and is supposed to have been painted by a pupil of Holbein taken when Edward was in his 16th year, and therefore but a short time before his death. It will be placed in the Grammar School.

The Reverend Dr. Robertson was doubtless the Rev. David Robertson, M.A., Vicar of Lye at the time and one of the twelve school governors, whose chairman was Colonel T. W. Fletcher. It was no doubt the Rev. Robertson who wrote the unsigned note from Lye vicarage which we have quoted above.

An interesting footnote to our story is provided by an entry in the Governors' Rent and Account Book for the years 1850 to 1909, a folio volume which has also come to light in recent months. Here in the accounts for the year 1876, in the credit column, appears the item:

Welch, Revd. W. J. J. . . . balance of portrait fund . . . 6s.0d.

From this it appears that the money subscribed for the purchase of the portrait actually amounted to £20/6/0d. I have unfortunately not yet been able to find Mr. Welch's account of his stewardship as treasurer of the fund.

As for the earlier history of the portrait, we have seen the then Vicar of Kidderminster's statement that he had found out that it came to his church as a gift from a Lord Foley — no doubt the second lord, who was patron of the living and who died in 1766.

In that case it remained to check Archdeacon Onslow's belief that Lord Foley bought the portrait at the sale of Canons, that magnificent house near Edgware, which 'the princely Chandos' built at the cost of a fortune, and which was totally dismantled and put under the hammer by his heirs. The sale, or rather sales, lasted from 1747 to 1753, and the main picture sale took place on May 6-8, 1747. Catalogues of the sales survive, but none of the authorities whom I have been able to consult have found in them any trace of our portrait or of its sale. Nor, apparently, is it included in the inventory of Canons taken in 1715, nor in that of 1725, which is included in the Stowe Collection in the Huntington Library at San Marino, California.

It may be that further search will bring something to light. For the moment we are at a stop in our backward search through time, at a point about 200 years in the past, roughly half-way between now and the moment when Guillim Streets set his brushes, probably for the last time, to present to the world the likeness of his royal patron and our royal founder.

R. L. CHAMBERS

At that stage, then, we had recovered the Black Box — the original muniment chest of the original foundation — and the portait of the royal founder of the Tudor Grammar School, together with the complete — or all-but complete — documentation of its acquisition by the school. It is perhaps not surprising that by this time the lure of the ancient records became ever more insistent, and that the search was rewarded by ever more discoveries. Even the one missing item in the story of the portait eventually came to light. In the course of the year 1959 a great mass of documents issued from the Hardward and Evers repository, and amongst these was a notebook, kept by the Rev. W. J. J. Welch, setting out his account as treasurer of the subscription fund set up to buy the royal portrait. In this book he listed the names of 29 subscribers, who provided a total of £20/10/6d. Of this sum four shillings and sixpence was spent with Robert Broomhall, printer, for the supply of forty appeal circulars, twenty pounds went to Kidderminster for the portrait, leaving the balance of six shillings. This sum appeared, as we have seen, in the credit column of the governors' income and expenditure account for the year 1876. That was the last piece in the puzzle.

It is to be remembered that all this time the original hoard of Black Box papers was under treatment by the historians. Eight years had passed since they were first found, and half-way through that period, in July 1955, Mr. Burley had returned a third-stage report to the National Register of Archives, comprising a calendar of six foolscap pages for the Black Box contents. Now, however, after the stimulus of the two discoveries in the school itself (the Black Box and the royal portrait) there was an incentive to work on the documents of the original Black Box collection, and once again I found that one thing led to another. Amongst the Black Box papers there were, I learnt, a considerable number of deeds recording the leasing of school properties at Evesham or Worcester to various tenants at various times. It occurred to me that it would be an interesting exercise to study some or all of these leases, to see whether any picture or pattern would emerge to throw light on the nature of the school's ancient properties, the value of the endowment at different times, the methods of management of the properties and so on. So I set to work — actually on the evening of Christmas Day 1959, with the collection of 83 leases in front of me, their dates ranging from 1546 to 1760. I had no clearly defined programme or purpose when I started, but I very soon found one thrust upon me. I gathered very soon that one lease is generally very much like another; they follow a similar pattern, and by moving from clause to clause and looking for the identifiable proper names occurring at the readily recognisable intervals, it was possible to move rapidly from one lease to the next. It also soon became clear that some of the leases contained a requirement that the rent should be paid at the schoolhouse in Stourbridge; and by another of those lucky chances that I was getting used to, one of the very first leases that I looked at included at this point a further clause identifying the schoolhouse as the place 'wherein so-and-so, schoolmaster, now dwelleth'. I turned hastily to the same point in other leases in the hope of finding the names of other headmasters. I was soon disappointed to discover that there was no consistency as between leases in this matter of giving the headmaster's name. Some gave it, others did not. However, this was the immediate origin of my book about the headmasters of the school from 1552 to 1688. It simply occurred to me that here, amongst the 83 leases of its first two hundred years, lay the best chance of naming those men who had been my earliest predecessors in office. Once named, I was willing to take a chance on being able to fit an identity to each name — or at any rate to some of them. So in fact it turned out. The leases did not give every name — or rather they did not cover the whole period up to 1688 without a gap. But, true to the luck which we had experienced so far, they fell not far short, and it became possible to build a very solid framework to one aspect of the school's history in its first two hundred years of life. The choice of the date 1688, of course, was not arbitrary: it was the date of the first entry in the two folio volumes of the governors' minute-books. They covered the years from 1688 to 1849, so for those years there were no problems: from 1849 to the present day I was fairly confident that the answers could readily be found. The only real problems in this field lay with the first two centuries, and it became clear that what is true of climbing mountains is true also of solving historical problems. As long as the questions present themselves, you cannot bring yourself to leave them without an answer.

The history of the headmasters was finished on 17 March 1960, at which point we had moved well into what I have called 'the great age of discovery' in the field of the school archives. There was a great deal still to come, as we shall see: but the disentangling of the early headmasters sent me first back rather than forward, to repair an omission rather than to break fresh ground. That omission was the failure to make a serious study of Mr. Burley's pamphlet of 1948.

He had named that pamphlet 'The History of King Edward's School Stourbridge', but he would have been the first to recognise that it was really at that stage simply not possible to write a history of the school. Not enough was known. What he had done was to bring together all the information then available about the origin and development of the school, and to write, in the Nash tradition, materials for a history rather than the history itself, and to present them as more or less disconnected items of information. Much of that information, I discovered, was owed to the enthusiasm, backed by the financial resources, of a man who had made it his life's passion and pleasure to collect material for the history of Worcestershire in general and Stourbridge in particular. That man was H. E. Palfrey, a businessman in Stourbridge, a prominent man in the public and municipal life of the town, sometime mayor of Stourbridge and sometime Chairman of the governors of King Edward's School, of which he was an old boy. This last position he had relinquished only shortly before I came to the school in 1951, after which he continued to serve as vice-chairman to his friend and colleague, H. P. Jones. H. E. Palfrey spent his time and much of his substance on the accumulation of historical materials. He was happy in the time when he lived, since in his day you could still afford to employ historical searchers without the risk of rapidly ensuing bankruptcy. You could bid for, and even buy, historical materials — documents, manuscripts and printed books. All these things he did in the pursuit of his hobby, and the result was an astonishing private collection of massive proportions. His house in Pedmore was positively lined with books, the shelves in most cases double-banked. He collected anything about Worcestershire, anything about Stourbridge, and — most important for our purposes — anything about its grammar school. He had composed several historical pamphlets which he had printed at his own expense; but he always himself insisted, and he should have known, that he was not himself a scholar, but strictly a collector. It was indeed a collector's passion that drove him. but he provided material for the exercise of scholarship, and he provided it in abundance.

When Mr. Burley wrote his history of the school, he opened with a tribute to the efforts in the field of research of two people — the late J. E. Boyt (Headmaster of the school from 1905 to 1934) and Alderman H. E. Palfrey, the Chairman of the Governors. Of J. E. Boyt we shall speak later. For the moment let us say of H. E. Palfrey that of the information which was presented in Mr. Burley's history a very great deal must have been the fruits of Mr. Palfrey's work, or rather of the work of his professional searchers.

Perhaps the most important material thus accumulated was that which related to the suppression of the original so-called chantry chapel and the establishment of the Tudor grammar school. Here Mr. Palfrey's searcher had been instructed to find and copy everything from the archives of the Public Record Office that related to the school. As a professional he knew where to start, and he provided transcripts of all the relevant official documents concerning the dissolution. The first one of these recorded the origin and purpose of the Stourbridge chapel, its income and the properties from which that income was derived, the names of its founders, an outline of its constitution and so on. The second document named the existing incumbent and made it clear that he was required as one of his chief duties to keep a school in Stourbridge and to teach the poor men's children of the parish freely — i.e. without charge. He was also to aid and assist the parson of Oldswinford, because of the widespread area of the parish. There was a third document which added the information that the chantry priest had always since the foundation taught a grammar school, taking no fees. Attached to this last was the 'continuation warrant', by which, in accordance with Edward VI's act, the Commissioners gave a certificate under their authority for the school to be continued. This was of crucial importance, for this reason: if the continuation warrant had been put into effect the original income from the chantry chapel's landed property would have passed to the Crown, and it would have been replaced by a similar amount as an annual grant from the Augmentation Office. In that case the school would inevitably and rapidly have been extinguished, by the inexorable progress of monetary inflation. Only the income from landed property was immune from the effects of that process. However, there now followed from Mr. Palfrey's searcher a transcript of the grant from the Crown of a new endowment for the foundation of a grammar school, with details of its properties, the names of the eight first governors, and the constitution of the new school — in essentials the new foundation charter, dated 17 June 1552. The great mystery was, and remains, why the school had been given a continuation warrant by the commissioners, and yet in spite of that had attracted a new endowment and a new constitution, which it would certainly not have needed if the continuation warrant had been put into effect. It becomes clear, in fact, if you study the documents, that King Edward's School Stourbridge owed its very birth in 1552 to an extraordinary piece of good fortune.

Mr Burley had clearly had Mr. Palfrey's transcripts under his eye, but for some reason he entirely ignored the matter of the continuation warrant. He must presumably have overlooked it, since there can be no question of its importance in the history of the school's foundation. He was, of course, clearly at the time most concerned to establish the continuity of the school, and indeed its existence *as a school*, in the days of the chantry-chapel between 1430 and 1552.

Of this continuity, and of the functioning of the priest as a school master and the chapel as a school there can be, in face of the statements in the dissolution documents, no possibility of doubt. What is doubtful, however, apart from the vexed question of the continuation warrant, is the true nature and purpose of the original chapel foundation. As far as I have been able to discover, there is no reference whatever in the early documents to any endowment for the purposes of ensuring prayers for the souls of the founders, or of their kin, or indeed of anyone at all. The chapel was actually used 'for thease of the parochiners there' — i.e. it was a chapel of ease to Oldswinford parish church, the need for this being explained in the phrase, 'the parishe being very large and brode'. The priest's duty as a schoolmaster, to teach a grammar school and to charge no fees, bulks larger than anything else in the early documents; and otherwise his duty is 'to ayde and assyste the curate there'. The great authority on chantries, A. F. Leach, drew a clear distinction between a chantry on the one hand and a service with stipendiary priest on the other. He held it as proved that 'a service' of a particular saint was an endowment not so much for the benefit of a particular person's soul as for the maintenance of services subsidiary or additional to the main services of the church. This exactly fits the description of the Stourbridge chapel given in the official documents, starting with the preamble, 'The service of the trynytie in the chapel of Stourbridge within the parish of Ouldswynford'. Leach also stated that there was a technical difference between the two types of foundation, in that a chantry priest was, like a rector or vicar, his own governing body, being a corporation created under a licence in mortmain, while a stipendiary priest drew his stipend from lands placed in the hands of trustees who were the governors of the goods and possessions of the foundation, and sometimes of the priest himself, over whom they were given a power of dismissal. This also exactly fits the Stourbridge case, for here the priest was 'removable at the will of the parochiners there'. (Chantry Certificate, cited above as document (1))

It is clear from this that the Stourbridge chapel was, if we apply the terms strictly, a service and not a chantry. In fact, however, the two categories were constantly confused even as early as the Dissolution, and indeed the very next sentence after the preamble quoted above starts with the words, "The said chaunterie was founded by Phillipp Hareby and Johan his wife ...." So no-one should blame anyone for calling the chapel a chantry, so long as they do not think of it as primarily conducted, or intended to be conducted, for the purpose of saying prayers for the souls of Philip and Joan Hareby, or of anyone else. That it certainly was not.

In actual fact Philip and Joan Hareby never existed — or if they did, they were not the founders of the chapel in Stourbridge.

This is an extraordinary story. When I first came to the school, I was duly introduced, as it were, to the figures on the very impressive stained-glass windows in the west end of the assembly hall. Here was Edward VI, here was George V, and here also, of course, were the founders, Philip and Joan Hareby. Nobody knew who they were or where they had come from: but Mr Palfrey's searcher had found and transcribed the chantry certificate of 1546, which clearly stated 'The said chaunterie was founded by Phillipp Hareby and Johan his wife, by their ded dated the Sunday next before thassencion of our Lord 8 Henry VI'. This date means 21 May 1430.

So, not unnaturally, we were thought to have our pre-Tudor origins in the Hareby chantry. I do not know the date when Mr. Palfrey's searcher came up with this evidence, but it was most likely before 1930, when the assembly hall was built; it could well have been before 1923, the year when the then headmaster, J. E. Boyt, contributed some articles on the early history of the school to the newly inaugurated Stourbridge Edwardian. In one of these he quoted the text of the 1548 chantry certificate, which he is most unlikely to have seen without also seeing its predecessor of 1546, containing the name of Hareby.

However that may be, the Harebys were certainly well-established pillars of the foundation long before I came on the scene in 1951, let alone in 1960, when the great age of discovery in the field of the school archives was just about at its height. In June 1952 a few original-minded members of the sixth form founded, with permission, a new society in the school, dedicated, if I am right, to the pursuit of tasteful living. They sought and obtained permission to wear straw boaters and to carry umbrellas: and the name which they chose for themselves was the Hareby Society, — which seemed at the time to be a very good idea. No one knew who the Harebys were, but everyone knew that they were the founders of the chantry.

I found myself eagerly pursuing the Harebys in the following circumstances. It will be remembered that the study of the leases, leading to the book on the early headmasters, started at the end of 1959 and was finished in March, 1960. One of the results of working on the leases was that I noticed at quite an early stage, that several of the leases had identical seals attached to them: most of the seals were fragmented or broken, but in some cases there was enough left to show that these seals might be struck from the same matrix. This was exciting, because it suggested the possiblity that here were examples of the governors' own seal. This was because all the leases were originally executed in duplicate, one to be signed and sealed by each party to the transaction and handed over to the other party. But expired leases apparently reverted to the party which had signed them. So clearly the leases with identical seals must be the governors' copies, signed by them and sealed with their seal. So indeed it proved to be, and there we had before us the original seal of the foundation — or at least, not the seal itself but several wax impressions of the seal, and, what is more, a sufficient number of them in a complete enough and reasonably clear-cut form to allow them to be studied in detail.

This was the start of a long chase. Expert photography, magnification and close examination, reference to those authorities who knew about seals, — all these were applied, until at last, after many false starts, wrong assumptions and disappointments, eventually two words of the Latin legend round the outer edge of the seal yielded themselves to the investigation. They were totally unexpected and at first inexplicable — CIVITAT' LINCOLN, or CITY OF LINCOLN! What on earth had the city of Lincoln to do with the chapel at Stourbridge?

This led to a lengthy correspondence with the Lincolnshire archivist, and the facts which emerged brought us eventually to a conclusion. First, the seal was undoubtedly the Seal of the Office of the Staple of the City of Lincoln. The Staple was, of course, the Wool Staple, or state-controlled monopoly of the overseas woollen trade, granted at different times to different towns which were centres of the trade. Second, the Staple belonged to the city of

Lincoln in the years up to 1369: in that year the Lincoln Staple went out of existence. Third, in the year 1430 the Harebys founded the Stourbridge chapel. Fourth, there were several places called Hareby in Lincolnshire, and the surname was clearly derived from one of them. The conclusion was that after the demise of the Lincoln Staple, its seal became surplus to requirement, was kept in the hands of one of its last officials, passed to his descendants as private property, and one of those descendants came to Stourbridge (perhaps in the way of trade, on the track of the famous Herefordshire fleeces) and when he founded a chapel in the town of his adoption, he gave to his trustees a very handsome and ready-made seal which doubtless saved everyone a great deal of trouble and expense!

This reconstruction was faultless; and it led to a lengthy search in the Lincolnshire archives to find any family named Hareby who could possibly be traced to a connection with the Lincoln Staple. Nothing, however, emerged. But the reasoning behind the theory was impeccable, and it seemed a certainty that the Harebys came originally from Lincolnshire.

The search for them might still have been going on. but after about a year of fruitless endeavour, it came to an abrupt end. This was due to yet another great discovery in the Harward and Evers archives. In this case we had the most remarkable surivival of all that had so far emerged from the hazards of the centuries of oblivion. It consisted of two documents, quite brief manuscript deeds, of similar style and format. To our astonishment they proved to be the two deeds which established the original foundation — not of the school in 1552, but, unbelievably, of the chapel in 1430. One of them was dated the Sunday before the Ascension and the other the Sunday after the Ascension — that is to say May 21st and May 28th — 8 Henry VI, or 1430. The first was a deed of gift from the two donors, transferring to 22 named trustees a piece of land in Stourbridge on which a new chapel was already built: the second was a legal quitclaim of the same piece of land, made by the heir of the two donors in favour of the same 22 trustees. The documents were in very good condition and entirely legible. But to complete the bombshell effect of this remarkable discovery, the names of the two donors were not Philip and Joan Hareby, but Philip and Joan Hayley!

There can be no doubt about this. The text of the two deeds is clear, and the name of the principals is certainly Hayley and not Hareby. As for the Harebys, it is to be remembered that our only evidence for their name is in the chantry certificate of 1546. This was 116 years after the foundation of the chapel, and it is to be presumed that someone in the service of the commissioners — possibly a lawyer, possibly a clerk — either misread the name on the documents supplied (or misheard it from a witness) — or possibly the mistake had been made at Stourbridge and the wrong name had been sent in.

So much for the impeccable reasoning behind the perfect theory! Even so, it is only fair to add that when further search was made for deeds referring to anyone named *Hayley* at the relevant time in the fifteenth century, only one such reference was found by the searchers. Imagine our feelings when we saw that it came from Lincolnshire! So the reconstruction which we based on the discovery of the seal remained substantially valid. True that the name of the founders changed; but the story behind the foundation stayed firm.

There is one footnote of interest to the story of the Hayleys. The whole of the area of land on the east side of the lower High Street in Stourbridge, that is to say the land on which the chapel and later the school was built, was know in Elizabethan times as Elcoxe's Close, from the name of its longtime owners, Thomas Elcoxe and his forebears. But earlier manor-court records show that Elcoxe's Close included parcels of land which had formerly been named from previous owners. One such plot was named Hayles' Ground, and although we have no clear evidence to identify its precise whereabouts, it is very tempting to suppose that that name might well be a corruption of an original Hayley's Ground. If we could find the evidence for that, our story would indeed be complete. Even as it is, we can perhaps reasonably claim to have gone most of the way.

This leaves us with only one more main chapter to write in the story of how the school's ancient history came to be brought to the light.

For now, in what we have called the great age of discovery in the field of the school archives, came the single greatest discovery of all. In February 1959 a mass of material belonging to the grammar school emerged from Harward and Evers' offices. A good deal of it was of negligible interest — routine tax returns and pro forma records from the nineteenth century — possible material for some social historian nose-down on a statistical trail of minimal human interest, but in no way really informative about the real life and development of the ancient school. But fortunately that was not all — far from it!

Nash had written in 1782, in the introduction to his remarks about the school; "The following is taken from bishop Lyttelton's MSS, copied, I suppose from the Evidences at Hagley, or from the Evidences belonging to the school." What we now found, tucked away, as it were, in the Victorian waste-paper-basket, was one of those 'Evidences belonging to the school', and it had certainly at one time also belonged to the 'Evidences at Hagley' as well. It was, in fact, an original from amongst bishop Lyttelton's manuscripts. It turned out to be, in its substance and in the volume and importance of the information which was contained in it or could be deduced from it, the single greatest archive amongst all our discoveries; it threw a great flood of light on the whole history of the Tudor grammar school's first fifty years of life.

This discovery was a book, a foolscap octavo volume measuring twelve inches by eight, bound in thin boards with a leather-covered spine and corners. It contained 302 pages, mostly filled with manuscript, though the last four and several in the body of the book were blank. The rest was filled with the record of a lawsuit, heard before the Court of the Council in the Marches of Wales in the year 1595. An inscription on the inside of the front cover records that it was 'Given by Sir Thomas Lyttelton, Bart., to Stourbridge school, anno 1740'. This is followed by an introduction, descriptive of the book's contents, signed by Charles Lyttelton. (This Charles was, of course, the same bishop Lyttelton to whose manuscripts Nash was referring.) Sir Thomas Lyttelton was the bishop's father. So this record had been collected, possibly even put together in the first place, by bishop Lyttelton, had taken its place amongst 'bishop Lyttelton's Manuscripts', and even before his death had been handed on by his father to become 'one of the Evidences belonging to the school'.

It was discovered in February of 1959. In March, after a preliminary reconnaissance which was enough to set the curiosity alight, I set to work to transcribe it from beginning to end. It was written in the old Secretary hand, but fortunately there was enough of it to allow of learning the script as the work went on. The transcription took four months, and was finished in July of 1959. The study of its contents was like Father William's 'muscular strength which it gave to my jaw' in Lewis Carroll's poem — it has lasted the rest of my life!

At this point let us go back for a moment to Mr. Burley's pamphlet of 1948. In this, after lamenting the paucity of surviving records of the school, he went on to quote, as he put it, from Bishop

Lyttelton's MSS. The bishop was, of course, a noted antiquarian and collector of manuscripts, and was elected President of the Society of Antiquaries in 1765. Three years later when he died he bequeathed his manuscripts to that society, and they formed the documentary basis for much of Nash's great History of Worcestershire (1782). Mr. Burley's quotation was in fact taken from Nash's printed work (vol. II, p.210). In his article on Oldswinford Nash said a good deal about the Stourbridge school, and amongst this was the passage which Mr. Burley quoted:

> "One Richard Allchurch was schoolmaster thereof, who being a pettifogger and reputed conjurer, was put in the chancellor's court by Mr. Gilbert Littleton, and being legally convicted of such male* practices, was turned out of the said school, 20 October 1590, by Arthur Purefoy, then chancellor."

Mr. Burley made no comment on this fascinating story, but he clearly must have found it unusually interesting, or he would not have included it in his brief outline. Nothing else whatever was known about Richard Allchurch 'pettifogger and reputed conjurer', and the curious thing was that neither Nash nor anyone after him seems ever to have tried to find out what was really meant by these mysterious words. On one occasion I even heard it suggested, by a very scholarly person, that the word 'conjurer' might be a bad transcription of the word 'non-juror' — in cheerful disregard of the fact that the term 'non-juror' did not appear in our history until long after the time of Richard Allchurch! It occurred to me privately that here was the hoodoo again (see page 1), playing tricks with the sense of logic. All I could do was to maintain a tactful silence.

But the new discovery soon made everything clear. It turned out that the lawsuit which it recorded was a case brought by a Stourbridge mercer, who was a governor of the grammar school, against no fewer than nine defendants — four of his fellow-governors, Gilbert Lyttelton, who was lord of the manor of Oldswinford, Gilbert's brother George, Godfrey Goldsborough, who was Archdeacon of Worcester, and two men whom the plaintiff claimed to have been servants of Gilbert Lyttelton and to have done his nefarious bidding. The plaintiff's name was Richard Madstard, so the case is best known as the Madstard Case, and the book which records it as the Madstard volume.

*Note: Mr. Burley changed this form to the word 'malicious', which unfortunately alters the meaning.

The Madstard Case was concerned partly with Gilbert Lyttelton's manorial rights in Stourbridge, but very considerably also with the affairs of the school. Madstard claimed that Gilbert Lyttelton and the archdeacon had 'intermeddled' with the school and had procured the corrupt appointment of an unsuitable man as headmaster, after the dismissal of the previous master, Richard Alchurche. Out of the complex and repetitive statements of the various parties and of numerous witnesses it is possible to put together a picture of the extraordinary activities of this extraordinary man. Gilbert Lyttelton, for example, justifies his interference in the affairs of the school on the grounds that Alchurche's activities were a public scandal and that Alchurche was "a very dangerous person ... for the said causes to have the instruction and education of children'. Archdeacon Goldsborough specified the charges against Alchurche as being first a man 'suspect in religion', because he took it upon himself to be 'a deviner or teller of things lost', second as the keeper of an alehouse in the schoolmaster's house, and third as being an 'Attorney in their town court, and not any way diligent in the said school''.

We are beginning to see more clearly the meaning of 'a pettifogger and reputed conjurer'. The pettifogger was a small-time lawyer — referred to elsewhere in the case as 'a common maker of instruments' — i.e. legal instruments. As for the conjurer, one of Madstard's questions to witnesses asks: "Did he as you know or think use any erecting of figures, divining, or telling of things lost, or any fortunes or any such like, and was he commonly sought unto for such causes, and did he take any sum of money of her majesty's subjects for the same?"

This becomes clear when we turn to the dictionary and find that 'erecting of figures' means 'casting of horoscopes'. We now see our schoolmaster accused of being a practising astrologer and fortune-teller or magician, as well as a pettifogging lawyer, and thirdly the keeper of an alehouse on the school premises. He was also, we discover as we make our way through almost three hundred closely written pages, a good teacher, a good disciplinarian, a very clever man and a very powerful man in the community of Stourbridge — a man of considerable substance who used his money and his brains to make himself more powerful still. He was, indeed, a rogue of Shakespearean proportions, a strange and fascinating figure whose shadow falls across every corner of the Tudor scene so luridly illuminated by the flickering torchlight from question and answer in the long and devious progress of the Madstard Case.

Richard Alchurche is not the only strange character from the sixteenth century who comes to life for us in the pages of the Madstard Volume. Richard Madstard himself, the plaintiff, emerges as a very strange person — a man of smouldering and vicious temper, obsessive hatreds, hair-trigger responses to any slight or wrong, real or imagined, of foolhardy courage, and of dogged tenacity in the face of any odds when he feels his interest or his amour propre in the slightest degree impugned. The other governors of the school, though seen in far less detail, yet become much more than mere names as we hear them answer questions or make accusations or defend themselves in their own words. They were all substantial citizens, prominent in the small community of Elizabethan Stourbridge. Clearly the governors of the grammar school were important people, and to be elected to that body was a prize to be valued and fought for, a prize given only to the few. Clearly also the governors formed a very closely knit company, linked together by many ties of common interest and personal relationship. Clearly again there was a tendency — indeed, more a practice than a tendency — for sons to succeed fathers, or brothers to follow brothers, on that body of eight; and already we can trace what can be best described as family dynasties, stemming from one or other of the eight original governors of 1552, and in more than one case continuing in uninterrupted succession right up to the year of the Madstard case, 1595. This dynastic process tended to produce a self-perpetuating body, responsible to none but themselves, self-sufficient and self-justified.

All this the Madstard volume brings to light, and with this, not surprisingly, a sorry picture of the management, or rather mismanagement, of the school's finances during those first fifty years — of carelessness at the best, peculation and corruption at the worst, going on for decades in spite of widespread rumour and suspicion throughout the town, and in defiance of all efforts to stamp it out. And behind it all is the long-continuing scandal of the disgraceful headmaster, again and again under threat of dismissal, and again and again apparently immune from attack and avoiding his just deserts, most likely by the exercise of his wits and the judicious use of the profits from his nefarious activities in the yet more nefarious practice of bribing his governors.

One way and another the Madstard volume presents in astonishing detail a picture of the Stourbridge grammar school over roughly the first fifty years of its life. Not only that, but it also sets the school in the contemporary scene of the Tudor town. We see the weekly market, the brawls and knife fights, (sometimes private affairs but sometimes more like 'set pieces' between the Lyttelton henchmen, for instance, and the servants of the Grays of Enville); we see the crude pranks and practical jokes, the grammar school boys misbehaving in church, the quick Tudor tempers with the hand ready to fly to the sword-hilt and the dagger, and in the background all the time the Queen's officers striving to establish the Queen's peace in a society which still felt more at home in a world of Montagues and Capulets than in one of justices and constables.

How It All Came To Light
II

It would not be accurate to call the rest of the story of our discoveries an epilogue, but it is tempting to do so. For the Madstard disovery marked a very definite stage in the unearthing of the school's archives. It was almost as though, having brought us on the flow of the emerging evidence almost precisely and neatly to the year 1600, the historical gremlins — or goblins — of the archive store decided that it was time to take a rest. Of course it was certainly not by any means true that there was nothing left to discover, though it was not to be expected that anything could come to light comparable in volume and importance to the discoveries made so far, and especially to the last one, the Madstard volume. It is to be remembered also that the research and reconstruction demanded by the study of that book went on and on for year after year, indeed for decades, as a continuing preoccupation. The consequence of that is that it is now much less easy, looking back over the later stages of the search, to remember in detail the important moments and the greater discoveries. There were, however, one or two occasions when the pulse quickened, as it were, and the attention concentrated on a particular incident from the past, though the memory cannot now dredge up a picture of the actual moment when the evidence emerged.

One such incident from the past was the appointment in 1705 of John Wentworth as headmaster. In Mr Burley's history this man had had quite a part to play. He was, of course, Samuel Johnson's headmaster, and that in itself booked his place, as it were, in Mr. Burley's pamphlet. One of the Public Record Office documents transcribed by H. E. Palfrey's searcher, and consequently available for study in the early stages, was an isolated contribution from the records of Chancery — quite separate in theme, date and interest from all the coherent group of evidences concerning the dissolution of the chapel and the foundation of the grammar school which we have glanced at and which formed the whole of the remainder of the searcher's contribution. It was almost as if the searcher, having bagged all his birds carrying the evidence of the dissolution from the records of the Augmentation Office, had then taken a random shot and brought down an exotic quarry of another species over another piece of water.

But the chancery document by itself simply did not give enough information to allow of any coherent explanation or understanding of what had happened. Mr. Burley gave the main facts as far as they could be extracted from the document, and then had to be satisfied with conjectural conclusions of a general nature. This was, as it turned out, a great pity, because the story of this incident of the Wentworth appointment, when the detailed evidence did emerge from the archives, was to draw back the curtains on yet another astonishing picture of the past. At this point we had advanced almost exactly a hundred years from the incident of the Madstard case. For we know that the infamous Alchurche returned from exile in Staffordshire to take up his post as headmaster at Stourbridge for a second term of office (but not, we may hope, a second term of his out-of-school activities!) in the year 1602. The incident of John Wentworth's appointment spread itself mainly over the year 1704. The stark and total contrast between the manners and way of life of the Stourbridge men of those two dates will tell us more clearly than a thousand history lessons that in a single century a society can emerge from a state of essential simplicity into one of essential sophistication. Alchurche's governors, like Alchurche himself, lived in a world of magic and of simmering violence — the world of Shakespeare, or, as we have put it, of Montague and Capulet. Wentworth and his governors were political wire-pullers in a world of sophisticated intrigue, manoeuvre and counter-manoeuvre, of eighteenth-century patronage and polish: they lived in the world of Pope. The remarkable thing is that from the records of this one school there have emerged two vivid and astonishingly detailed pictures of these two stages of English society. Madstard's picture we have seen: Wentworth's started with the Palfrey searcher's record of proceedings in Chancery, dated 22 June 1704. This took the form of an application to the chancellor in the name of one Richard Bach of Stourbridge. He was an obscure individual of no real interest or importance, and he eventually proved to be, as we had suspected, no more than a 'front' for someone else. He is asking for power to be taken by the chancellor to place a fit schoolmaster at Stourbridge, for the good of the school and town. He presents a full and lengthy account of how the situation has developed since the death of the last headmaster, and how the eight governors are locked, or rather deadlocked, in disagreement over the choice of his successor. He names all the eight governors and separates them into their two factions, and he also names the candidates currently favoured by each faction.

The recovery of all the records of this incident was once again little short of miraculous. I remember that I was already sufficiently far advanced on the study of this most complex and mysterious incident to have written a quite substantial paper about it, in which, working steadily forward I had proceeded to follow the evidence step by step towards its conclusion: I was nearly there when suddenly, just before the end, the evidence ran out, leaving me to take a leap into the darkness of probability in order to bridge the gap. This I cheerfully did, or was about to do, when in the Spring of 1963 along came another discovery from Harward and Evers, this time a whole dossier of papers, accompanied by a note which explained their origin. This reads: "These writings were in the possession of John Wheeler of Wooton Park, Esq., now deceased, and came into the hands of Clement Kynnersley of Loxley Park, Esq., now deceased, whose father Thomas Kynnersley married Mr. Wheeler's daughter; and so came into the custody of Thomas Sneyd Kynnersley of Loxley, the executor of the said Clement Kynnersley". On the back of this note is a list of the papers included in the dossier, of which our relevant twelve were only one part, and a receipt signed by one William Cope on 12 January 1841, and by William Hunt and G. Grazebrook, two of the school governors, a week later. The John Wheeler mentioned was the leader of one of the two factions of the governors in 1704. Once again one is astonished by the way in which the records found their way back, this time after 137 years, to their old home, and then after another 122 years came to the eyes of the student of today. That student needed all those documents, as well as the chancery record dug out by the Palfrey searcher and the diocesan records from the Worcester Record Office; he needed (and it had already been found in the Harward and Evers archives) the copy of a public petition in the names of no fewer than 109 named inhabitants of Stourbridge, dated 19 July 1704 and addressed to the Lord Keeper of the Great Seal of England; he needed a book, The Life of Bishop Lloyd, by Dr. A. Tindal Hart (London, 1952) and another book, The Diary of Francis Evans, Bishop Lloyd's secretary, published by the Worcestershire Historical Society in 1903 and now scarce; he needed also the admissions records of several Oxford colleges and, last but not least, he needed the two folio governors' minute-books from the original Black Box hoard. All these, and more than these, had to be examined if we were to get to the bottom of the tortuous story of the appointment of John Wentworth. But the documents, the printed books, the transcripts, the letters and papers, the minute-books — whatever the odds against their coming together, come together they did. So we saw, by actually tracing step by step the proceedings of the different parties throughout the progress of one actual case, a living picture of eighteenth-century political patronage as it was actually practised. We saw the manoeuvre and counter-manoeuvre of Whigs and Tories through a detailed record of the proceedings of the Stourbridge governors, as their internal wrangling drew into their orbit the local magnates, the London bigwigs, the bishop, the Chancellor, the Headmaster of Eton, the string-pullers in Whitehall and the Queen's Majesty herself — all in the cause of the choice of a headmaster for a small-town grammar school in Worcestershire at a salary of £45.00 a year!

The simple fact is that, just as without the 'Evidences belonging to the school' no one would have believed what the world of Madstard's Stourbridge was like, so also without the same evidences the world of John Wentworth's governors in the same town would have defied our imagination.

The elucidation of what really happened in the matter of John Wentworth's appointment proved to be a substantial task, and in the end it took several years to complete it satisfactorily. This was partly because of the complex and tortuous machinations of the Stourbridge governors at the time, but partly also because by now the volume of evidence had reached such proportions. Instead of straws in the wind, hints here and indications there, odd and isolated documents bringing with them fragments of the truth and calling for a sustained exercise of the historical imagination, we found ourselves facing complex and detailed records in black and white, deliberately preserved or surviving by mere chance. There was so much of it that the problems of study and interpretation were multiplied. In the Wentworth case one or two of the documents were legal 'briefs' submitted for counsel's opinions: these were annotated in a form of legal shorthand which defied interpretation even after time-consuming submission to the experts. In some cases, again, papers had been preserved in the Wheeler-Kynnersley dossier only for the sake of completeness, and appeared to have become abortive or to have been cancelled and replaced by others without any acknowledgement of the fact. So it could be said that the problems to be solved and the questions to be asked and, if possible, answered, were changing their nature by comparison with those of the early years of research, such as those connected with the seal, or the portrait, or the identities of the early headmasters. The fact was that we were beginning to accumulate what might be called 'clusters' of evidence, massing together and cohering like a colony of bees swarming round their queen, and clinging round one particular incident or time. So it was with Madstard around 1600; so it was now around 1700 with Wentworth.

This clustering process took us back from the Wentworth period itself for several years into the later time of his predecessor as headmaster, one John Browne, and produced another strange story about another strange character. Many essential details of this story in fact lay concealed in the first of the two governors' minute-books, specifically in the annual accounts of the governors' expenditure over the period from 1698 to 1705. But the significance of those details would certainly not have been understood, had it not been for the discovery of two documents which were included amongst the Wheeler-Kynnersley papers — that dossier which had descended from John Wheeler's heir to that heir's grandson, Thomas Sneyd Kynnersley of Loxley Park, who restored the papers to the school in 1841. The two documents in question were written in the hand of John Browne himself, headmaster at Stourbridge from 1692 until his death in 1699. They reveal a sad and sorry situation in the school. They reveal a headmaster who is a man in a rage, first with his usher or assistant, Martin Crane, and secondly with his governors, more especially with one of those governors, whom he is accusing of laying plots to get him sacked from his post. They lead us to the extraordinary fact that one of the two masters' houses on the High Street front — the upper of the two, which was the usher's house and in modern times became the Victorianised dwelling in which the caretaker and his wife served dinners to a small number of boys —

this house had had spent upon its maintenance out of the governors' funds *over a period of seven years* the astonishing sum of five shillings! The results of this in turn led, or compelled, the governors to arrange for the rebuilding of the house for the new usher, Martin Crane. This expense made hay of the school's finances and upset the regular payment of the masters' salaries. This in turn put John Browne into a raging fury of envy, jealousy and all uncharitableness. This led him to write his two diatribes. This led to a situation in which the governors went to the bishop and adopted an entirely new set of Rules and Orders for the regulation of the school. These Rules and Orders were, it would seem, unhappily necessary in dealing with a headmaster such as John Browne, but were nevertheless an insult to any headmaster worth his salt, as must have been plain for all to see. This in turn led to a 'show-down' between the governors and the two masters, and eventually to the so-called 'submission', expressed in writing in the governors' minute-book, of Mr. Browne and Mr. Crane. Then Mr. Browne died. Then the governors decided to rebuild the other school house on the High Street front, the Headmaster's house, which survived until it was demolished to make way for the assembly hall in 1930.

The unravelling of the story of Mr. Browne and Mr. Crane is an object-lesson in the way in which one thing leads to another. It was the two John Browne diatribes which led us to the governors' accounts. It was the accounts which brought out the facts leading up to the rebuilding of the usher's house, and which led us also, via an item which said, 'Pd. for ye Schoole Orders ... £1.00' to take a closer look at the new Rules and Orders of 1702, and so to a rational explanation of much that was very strange in those Rules and Orders. Then the minutes attached to the accounts led us to the written 'submission' of Mr. Browne and Mr. Crane. The whole story hung together and threw a searching light onto a very troubled passage in the life of the school. Yet without the key documents — the complaints of John Browne in the Wheeler-Kynnersley papers — none of this could possibly have been deduced from the facts and figures which were to be found, but only if you knew what to look for, in the official records. It was not until the two papers set light to the train that the sparks crackled through the darkness and the light flared.

There was an added bonus appended to the story of Mr. Browne and Mr. Crane, though it was some years before it made its appearance. It has to be remembered that the most striking fact about the school of the early eighteenth century is its connection with Samuel Johnson. Apart from his own spell as a pupil there, his mother's family had many connections in Stourbridge, and the Johnsonian scholars, especially the Americans, were constantly on the alert for anything, fact or artefact, however small and apparently insignificant, which might be added to the squirrel's hoard of 'Johnsoniana' and put through the process of microscopic investigation in what has been described as the study — or industry — of Dr. Johnson's Waistcoat Buttons! I can well remember a visit to the school many years ago, paid by Dr. J. L. Clifford, a very eminent American Johnsonian. I recall how fascinated he was by, for example, the initials said to have been carved by the young Sam Johnson himself on the wainscot preserved from the old schoolroom. I remember how Dr. Clifford could hardly bear to get up from the eighteenth-century oak master's desk, with its hooded seat, which resided at that time in the same room as the wainscot.

It was in 1978 that another eminent American academic, Professor W. J. Bate of Harvard University, had a book on Samuel Johnson published in England. Two years later I came across a copy of this book and in it I found an illustration entitled 'The School at Stourbridge' which I thought was both mysterious and fascinating. The picture seemed to have been taken from an original watercolour, very amateurish, and it showed two houses side by side fronting onto a street, and behind the houses was a tower with a sort of cupola on its top. The houses were of brick, and built in the style of the early eighteenth century.

That was the start of another long search. Letters went to and fro across the Atlantic, and ultimately a coloured photocopy (and a very good one) of the original picture came to me. This now adorns my study wall. Professor Bate introduced me to Mrs. Mary Hyde, one of the husband-and-wife team who originated the famous Hyde Collection. She was kindness itself — patient and helpful. She wrote: "The original rather amateurish water-colour is in the iconography collection in my library. It was removed with other items from the extra-illustrated Life of Johnson which belonged to A. F. Somerset and which my husband and I purchased in the 1950's." We never succeeded in tracking down the painter of the picture, nor even the A. F. Somerset who had owned it and from whose estate it was bought. But the photocopy of the original made it clear that we were looking at an earlier version of the two houses which had stood on the High Street front of the Stourbridge school as a victorianised pair, until the lower one was demolished for the assembly hall in 1930.

My information had always suggested that the Victorian casing covered an original vernacular exterior of medieval 'Black-and-white', timber-framed with plaster infilling. The newly-discovered water-colour showed that this was quite wrong. The Victorian rebuilding, in fact, could not have been the first in the history of the two houses. Consider this fact in the light of the information from the Governors' minute-book which we turned up for the story of Mr. Browne and Mr. Crane, and you see at once that the earlier rebuilding took place, first for Mr. Crane in 1699-1700, and secondly after Mr. Brownes death, in 1704−6. In both cases we know the builder's name — one John Ellis, and he was paid £43/10/0d in two instalments for the first house, and £103/16/6d in four instalments for the second. There can be no question that this is the truth, and once again the necessary evidence came to us from widely separated sources, each piece fitting in until the puzzle was complete.

In this case, however, one mystery remains which has never been solved. The tower and cupola which lay behind John Ellis's houses are an enigma. They must have been a prominent feature not only of the school but of the town. They appear, indeed, on the perspective view of Stourbridge which appears as an illustration in Nash's famous History of Worcestershire published in 1782. But they could never have been built on the basis of any of the original school buildings — either the chapel or any of its extensions. When the great reconstruction took place and the old school was demolished in 1859-60, the architect left a drawing of those original buildings which is still in the school archives. There is no sign that the tower with its cupola existed then: so we have to accept that it did not. We know that it existed in 1782, and from other sources we know that in 1813 there was a bad fire at the school, in which the tower was involved, so that the bell fell down and was smashed. The governors proceeded to have a new tower built, and engaged the Coalbrookdale Company, makers of the first and famous Iron Bridge, to construct and erect a new cupola. So there was a cupola in 1813, and a second cupola to replace it after 1813. But when the first cupola was built, and when the second cupola was destroyed — so far this remains buried in oblivion. Some day perhaps the luck will turn, and yet again the ancient records will speak. But up to now nothing has emerged.

How It All Came To Light
III

If in the story of our search the period from the Black Box to Madstard was Part I, and from Madstard to the cupola was Part II, what then remained to be found that would give us the substance and subject matter of Part III? The answer must be that this time we really have come to what is essentially an epilogue.

When the water-colour illustration in Professor Bate's book was found, we were already at the year 1980 and I myself was already five years into the period of my retirement from the headmastership which had first introduced me into the world of the Black Box in 1951. I carried into that retirement the very considerable task of going through the Madstard Case, teasing out the tangled threads of its various themes, clearing up its confusions, organising its personalities into plausibly coherent groups with consistent relationships, directing the searchlight of enquiry more widely onto the lives and circumstances of the Madstard principals, and blocking in the background features of the town of Stourbridge and parish of Oldswinford, both geographically, socially, manorially and as the home of a community of individuals. That was only the beginning of the task, the preparation and organisation of the material out of which the edifice was to be built. The edifice itself was the story of the Madstard Case in the form of a book, and the building of that edifice, the writing of that book, was the work of years.

Side by side with the work on Madstard, however, there was another task. I had brought into retirement not only the great accumulation of material which centred round Madstard, but also two trunksful of miscellaneous and haphazardly gathered 'evidences' from the Harward and Evers archives. The task remaining here was to examine the hoard, bring it into some sort of order and list its contents, in however rough a fashion, in order to hand them back to the school in the end as a rationally and coherently, and if possible accurately, annotated collection.

These two tasks constituted what I have described as an epilogue. There were to be no more really startling discoveries: the work was to a great extent one of consolidation.

First, it proved possible to put together a complete collection of the school's successive 'constitutions', starting with the original charter and the manuscript 'Rules and Orders' from Tudor, Stuart, Augustan and Georgian times, progressing to the hand-printed broadsheets of the early and middle years of the nineteenth century, and concluding with all the later official 'Schemes of Management' which successively reformed the school and brought it into the modern world as part and parcel of the state system of education. The collecting, listing, annotating and transcribing (in whole or in abstract) of this mass of material proved to be a labour of some magnitude; but it was well worth the doing, because of the extraordinary fact that in the end the collection appeared to be complete.

Another theme which readily presented itself as the evidence came to light, was that of the part which the governors had played through the centuries as apparently *ex officio* trustees appointed for the management of charitable funds and endowments by a succession of benefactors to the town and people of Stourbridge over the centuries. Had these charities been confined to educational purposes, this would not have been surprising. We know, for instance, that when the Oldswinford Hospital School was established in the seventeenth century, its Foley founder turned for help and for the benefit of their experience to several of the contemporary governors of the Grammar School. We know also that those governors managed the Glover Charity School and the Wheeler Charity School throughout their existence; the complete records of both those schools resided in our archives. Stourbridge, it is to be remembered, was a small place, in which it would have been difficult to find anyone else fitted by experience to look after anything resembling a school, other than those eight "of the more discreet and honest of the inhabitants of the vill of Stourbridge and parish of Oldswinford" who were elected to be governors of the grammar school. But the practice did not stop there. Besides the Glover School records and the Wheeler School records, the archives contained many other original deeds and documents setting out founders' conditions for the establishment of their charities. There is a letter dated 8 July, 1618 offering to extend to the parish of Oldswinford the benefits of the Sebright charity of Wolverley, which was intended partly to provide a dole of bread for the poor of the parish, and only partly for the foundation of the Wolverley free school. From 1640 came a parchment indenture creating a rent-charge out of two acres of land in the Washing-pool Field in Stourbridge, in order to provide an income of thirteen shillings and fourpence a year for the Dallyber-Poole charity to aid the poor of the parish. In 1657 Richard Foley by his will left twenty pounds to the governors of King Edward's School in Stourbridge (and his wife Alice similarly provided ten pounds) to set up a fund for the purpose of lending capital to 'poor beginners' at five per cent interest for one year, the profits to go to the poor of the parish. Oliver's Charity, by an indenture of 18 November, 1723 gave twenty pounds to the governors to invest for poor widows and housekeepers. There were others as well.

It becomes clear, in fact, that the governors dispensed most, if not all, of the charitable funds available for the relief of the poor and needy in the town and parish. This is yet another indication of the prestige which was felt to attach to their office. The phrase 'more discreet and honest of the inhabitants' takes on a more than merely formal meaning when we consider it in this light. In this field of the governors' activities a further matter of interest is the practice which we find was their normal procedure in managing the various trusts, of investing the capital by a purchase of land or property, then leaving the vendor in possession, and then drawing a rent-charge in perpetuity to provide the income of the charity. Time and again the details are set out in the legal indentures which have survived in the school's archives. There is quite a substantial collection of such documents.

Then, parallel with this charitable activity and related to it, comes the interesting episode of the building of St. Thomas's Church in Stourbridge. It was always an odd feature of the town of Stourbridge and parish of Oldswinford, that the parish church in Oldswinford was a mile and more distant from the town, which of course had grown up long after the ancient parish was first formed. Indeed, as we have seen, the building of the Hayley chapel in 1430 was an early attempt to remedy the inconveniece of having the parish church so far away from the main centre of population. In other words, the chapel, and therefore the school, was in origin a chapel of ease for the parish church. So it was curiously appropriate that it was the governors of the Grammar School who were chosen and charged to be the committee of trustees who should supervise the building of the next chapel of ease. The benefactor this time was "John Biggs, late of Stourbridge, clothier", and the benefaction came in the form of a legacy of two hundred pounds. This is recorded in full in the governors' minute-book for the period. Here they duly acknowledged receipt of this sum, together with six pounds interest, in the minutes of a special meeting dated 2 November 1728. Seven months later, at the Trinity audit of 1729, they record in full and precise detail how the two hundred and six pounds has been spent on the actual process of building the chapel; and in December of 1734 they acknowledge the receipt of a further one hundred pounds as contingent legatees of John Biggs's estate.

We had been in a position to know all this, of course, ever since the minute books came to light in the original Black Box hoard. But now, tucked away amongst the miscellaneous accumulation from the Harward and Evers archives there appeared a dossier of six papers relating to the process of the building of the chapel and the purchase of its site — a process which was still going on at the end of 1736. These papers were clearly thought to have belonged to the governors of the Grammar School and to have stayed in their rightful place amongst the school's 'evidences' — and this in spite of the fact that the legal standing of the governors in relation to the church soon came to an end. This is an apt comment upon the power and influence of the governing body in the town of Stourbridge. That power and influence was most effectively demonstrated by the fact that for no less a period than 116 years, from 1742 to 1858, the governors claimed and exercised the right (in spite of strong local opposition and in spite of the fact that the claim had no foundation in law) to appoint the minister of St. Thomas's church. Four such ministers in succession they appointed, and made each one of them also headmaster of the Grammar School, a practice which may have been very convenient for them, but which was probably far from beneficial to either the school or the church. However that may be, certainly the dossier relating to the building of St. Thomas's church formed yet another section of the 'evidences belonging to the school' and illuminated yet another episode in the history of the town.

Perhaps the largest section of the evidences, not surprisingly, concerned the activities of the governors as managers of their own properties, whether the school site, with its buildings and its masters' houses, which was a constant source of expenditure, or the endowment properties, mainly in Evesham and Worcester, which provided the bulk of their income. These two elements generated a very large volume of business and a very considerable mass of business records. It would be tedious to present any detailed picture of these records. We have already come across the collection, or rather the accumulation, of expired leases, which led us to the names of some of the early headmasters and also to the strange story of the origin of the school seal. We have referred to the Tudor account-book of 1573-88, which gave us the evidence for the mismanagement of the school's finances in the Madstard era. Both these sources, and much more, were amongst the original Black Box papers. There also was a great deal from the seventeenth century, very haphazard and unorganised, scraps of letters from tenants and agents at Evesham or Worcester, isolated accounts and estimates of expenditure, bills for building work, lawyer's accounts, and so on and so forth. Now, amongst the later discoveries there came to light further and later records of the same basic type, but also account-books, ledgers, cash-books and the like, and, from a later period still records of stock receipts and investments — a mass of material which had accumulated, and incidentally gathered the dust, over the ages. Some of the records of the endowment properties went back before the foundation-date of the grammar school in 1552 to the time when some of them belonged to earlier religious foundations doomed to be 'liquidated' at the Dissolution. There is material here for a substantial book on this theme alone — property management from the time of the College of Fotheringhay to that of the education service of the Metropolitan District of Dudley. It is not, however, a subject which scintillates with human interest or throws light on strange incidents or characters. Perhaps the most interesting question which it raises, 'en passant' as it were, and which is almost certainly unanswerable, is what on earth could have possessed the governors in Victorian times, presumably men of intelligence and integrity, to sell off their properties in the middle of the city of Worcester (where they were "sitting on a goldmine") in order to buy — what do you think? The answer is Australia Stock, and/or railway shares! This is surely an astonishing and unhappy example of financial eccentricity, if not incompetence, though of course it cannot compare in interest with the far less serious but more culpable and colourful depredations of Madstard's contemporaries. Here, it seems, are sleeping dogs that had better be left to lie.

It will by now be clear to the reader that our story of the unearthing of the school's records is coming very near to its end. If that story were to have an alternative title, or an epigraph that would hit off its essential nature in one word, that word would surely be 'Serendipity'. The dictionary defines serendipity as 'the faculty of making happy chance finds'. But it goes on to admit that the three Princes of Serendip whose discoveries in the oriental fairy tale first gave rise to the word, made those discoveries 'by accidents and *sagacity*'. So perhaps our extraordinary series of happy accidents has been to some degree a due reward for virtue and effort — i.e. for sagacity — rather than simply and solely a case of 'pennies from heaven'. We should like to think so.

But whichever it was, rewards or fairies, there is after all one case more which ought to be mentioned. Recorded in one of several notebooks which I kept over the period when I was examining the contents of the last two trunks from Harward and Evers, I find the following:

> *6 October 1981.* In the large tin trunk, amongst a mass of Victoriana, mostly blue forms and the like — *a brown paper parcel*, tied with string, no endorsements outside — modern make-up by the look of it.
> *Contents.* Records of a chancery action of 1851, brought as a petition under Abuses of Charities, (a) to get the headmaster removed as being incompetent from ill-health, and the usher (aged 69) ditto, from age and infirmity; (b) to reform the school and enlarge the numbers of the governing body.
> A *large* collection: numerous copies of the petition, and affidavits in support: copies of comments upon same: affidavits in opposition: collected breviats of same. Demands to examine leases, minute books, etc. Lawyers' drafts of affidavits, etc. Original and copies of petitioners' notice to abandon the suit and to pay costs. Original and copies of court's dismissal of the petition. List of lawyers' charges — both those of *Rowland Price* (who was both a governor and the governors solicitor!) and those of the London agents.
> A big mass of material, with much of interest about the school, the town, its institutions and inhabitants..................

2 printed copies of 1841 Rules and Orders
  12 miscellaneous large copies of Petition ... etc.
  72 other miscellaneous affidavits etc. etc.

These notes were written almost five years ago, and it seems to me, reading them now, that a whiff of the old Black Box magician's smoke can still be detected, floating in the air. This 1851 case has never been nosed out, traced back and fully investigated: but at least we know now that there it is, resting in the school archives, and ensconced now in the school's archive-room, waiting its turn, perhaps — who knows? — to be taken out, and shaken out, by some lover of the past still to come upon the scene, and destined to form yet another chapter in the long, long story of King Edward's School.

If that comes to pass, perhaps the searcher will find that he has stumbled on a nineteenth-century Madstard, or a Victorian Wentworth. More likely, however hot for certainties he may be, he will find himself choked off (almost literally) with a dusty answer.

So let us leave Rowland Price, as well as his insidious opponent (for there certainly was one) together with all those mid-Victorian worthies and not-so-worthies, to rest undisturbed amongst the faded and crabbed script of those eighty-six documents. Perhaps when we come to that stage of the school's history we may yet take them out and dust them off. Compared with Madstard they belong to only yesterday. But that yesterday is now one hundred and thirty-five years in the past. In 1951, when we first came into contact with the world of the Black Box, there were still men alive, and to be talked to, who had themselves talked to some of those who were alive in the year 1851. Not so now. Whatever we may say of them now, there will be no one to answer back. So there for the moment let us leave them.

Having thus, it may be hoped, cleared the ground for the erection of the rest of the edifice, we can now lay out the history of King Edward's School Stourbridge in broad and main outline, fairly rapidly and with a reasonable hope that the story which we have already told — that of the unearthing of the records on which the history must be built — will provide many points of reference, signposts and clarifications, which will carry us along with some momentum and some sense that we are moving on not altogether unfamiliar ground.

Origins and Mysteries

We already know that the school originated as a chapel of ease for the parish church of Oldswinford. The dissolution documents, as we have seen, make it quite plain that the chapel was established not for the purpose of saying prayers for the souls of the founders or the founders' kin, but in a double role as (a) a chapel of ease for the parish church of Oldswinford, and (b) a grammar school where the sons of the poor men of the parish should be taught grammar (that is to say, of course, Latin) without charge. In other words, the chapel priest of 1430 was to be, in more modern terms, the parish curate and the parish schoolmaster. The chapel, together with the land on which it was built, was entrusted by the foundation deed into the care and possession of twenty-two trustees, all named. The site of the chapel was a plot of land just behind the houses on the east side and near the top of the Lower High Street — or what became the Lower High Street in later times. It was a hundred yards or so below the butter-cross and market-hall, close to the site of the present town clock. When the present school assembly-hall was built in 1930, contemporary sources said that the builders turned up the site of the chapel priest's original altar, very close to the platform at the east end of the assembly-hall. A plaque was placed in the end wall behind the platform to commemorate this fact, if fact it was.

The founders, as we know from their original deed of gift of 1430, were Philip Hayley and his wife Joan. We have concluded that the Hayleys came from Lincoln, and brought with them the redundant seal of the dead-and-gone Office of the Staple of the City of Lincoln, defunct in the year 1369. That seal became the official seal of the trustees of the Hayley foundation and later of the governors of King Edward's School, who went on using it certainly until the 1870's.

The name of Hayley, as we have seen, found an echo amongst the ancient landholders recorded in the Oldswinford manor court rolls. The chapel site was part of a large enclosure which stretched from the Lower High Street eastward to the parallel road coming up the hill from what used to be called The Cliff and going on roughly southward to be the 'back lane' to the Upper High Street, along the line of the present Ring Road. That large enclosure was called in Tudor times Elcoxe's Close, from the name of its holder, and was commonly known, both then and in later times, as The Green Close, Elcoxe's holding was stated to include three parcels of land called severally by the names of their ancient tenants, Parry's Lands, Warner's Lands, and Hayles' Lands. It must be more than a coincidence that the last of these three bore a name so closely similar to that of Philip and Joan Hayley. But, Hayley's Land or not, that piece of ground has remained for five and a half centuries part of the school site.

The names of the twenty-two trustees are listed in the Hayley deed as follows:

William Smith, clerk (i.e. parson)
William Everdon
William Haket of Stourbridge
Richard Flemyng
William Leeche
Stephen Rok
William Perot
William Tommeson
John Styler
Thomas Corff
John Hondy

Thomas Wats
William Reygnalds
John Hull
Henry Smith
Wiliam Haket of Lye, Junior
Ralph Seggesley
Thomas Hull
John Hayley
Richard Styler
Thomas Cardell
William Goppe

There are several points of interest here. It looks as if the first-named trustee, William Smith, being a parson, could well have been the rector of the parish of Oldswinford at the time. It would make sense for the chapel priest's 'boss' to be one of those in charge. On the other hand, the chapel priest himself could not, one would have thought, have been included amongst his own trustees. Then we see signs of the family influences which became so marked a feature of the government of the school in later times. Here are two Smiths, two Hacketts, two Stylers and two Hills. There is also, of course, one Hayley, and he was neither Philip the founder nor his son and heir William, who signed a legal quitclaim to the ownership of the land one week after his parents completed their deed of gift. Perhaps John Hayley was Philip's brother, and the idea was to establish a continuing Hayley interest in the management of the chapel. Certainly the families of Perrot, Thomson and Rock had numerous later representatives among the governors of the school; and, most interesting of all, the last priest of the chapel and first headmaster of the grammar school was named in the 1548 chantry certificate as Nicholas Rocke. He would undoubtedly be a member of the same family as the 1430 trustee Stephen Rok, and as the John Rocke, shoemaker of Stourbridge, who became a school governor in 1602.

But if the Hayleys counted on setting up a family 'dynasty' amongst their trustees, they were to be sadly disappointed. The reason for this involves a point of the medieval English law of land tenure which is quite abstruse to the layman, and the understanding of which we owe to the kindness and patience of Professor Ernest Scamell of London University, who took the trouble to clear it up for us in a letter of 26 August 1963. We had been able to tell him, from the evidence of a later deed of gift, dated 1625, that at some stage in the fifteenth century the property of the Hayley trustees came by the process of law into the sole possession of the last survivor of the original twenty-two. This man proved to be Ralph Sedgeley, and he then by a cruelly unlucky chance died without heirs. The property thereupon became forfeit, as it were, by the legal process known as escheat, to the manor of Bedcote and Stourbridge. In 1625 that manor was bought by Nicholas Sparry of Stourbridge, and he proceeded by the deed of gift just mentioned to hand the chapel property back to the governors of the Grammar School.

Professor Scamell explained that the Hayley's deed of gift of 1430 had established the trustees in possession of the property under the wrong form of co-ownership in English law of the time. There were two relevant such forms, *joint tenancy* and *tenancy in common*. *Joint tenancy* meant that, as any joint tenant died, the surviving joint tenants took the entire property, to the exclusion of any heirs or successors of the dead. This is what happened to the chapel property; and the last surviving joint tenant was Ralph Sedgeley, and he died with no heirs. If the trustees had been *tenants in common*, each one who died would have had his place filled by his heir or successor, and there would have always been twenty-two trustees. In order for the trustees to be *tenants in common*, the words of the deed should have included 'words of severance' — i.e. words indicating a sharing, such as 'equally', 'between', 'amongst' etc. Unfortunately for the Hayley trust there were no such 'words of severance' included, so the co-ownership became a joint tenancy and the rest followed.

We even know the date when the chapel property escheated to the manor. Amongst the Hagley Hall MSS is an Oldswinford bailiff's account for the year 1488-9, which shows that a piece of land formerly in the tenure of Ralph Sedgeley had been without a tenant "through lack of heirs" for a period of 43 years, that is, since 1446. That must be the date of Ralph Sedgeley's death, and from that date until 1625 the school site and its buildings were alienated from the trustees and legally in the possession of the manor of Bedcote.

It must be added, however, that the above explanation of the escheat of the chapel and its site to the manor of Bedcote, like many other matter of law, has not been left undisputed. There is an alternative view, for which we are indebted to a Stourbridge Old Edwardian, Mr. C. R. Unsworth, late of Brasenose College, Oxford and now of the Cardiff Law School. He put the matter to a friend and colleague, Mr. Thomas Watkin, who is both a legal historian and a property lawyer. Mr. Watkin's view is as follows. "Joint Tenancy, so far from being 'wrong', would be the right form of co-ownership to invoke for a medieval charitable use, as it is to-day for the modern trust. The real mystery is why the feoffees failed to appoint replacements, as they could and should have done, for their deceased colleagues as their numbers dwindled." According to this view that would have been the normal way of preventing the defeat of the use by an escheat in the case of a sole surviving joint tenant dying without heir. Mr. Unsworth points out, as a possible explanation for this failure, the apparent fact that all twenty-two feoffees died in the years between 1430 and 1446 — a rate of demise so rapid even under medieval conditions that it suggests some natural calamity such as an epidemic disease, which might have disrupted all normal procedures. We do not know whether this is in fact the answer: what we do know is that the escheat, for whatever reason, did in fact take place.

This bring us to another question which we have tried but failed to answer. If the school site and buildings became legally the property of the manor, did the manor charge the trustees a rent for the use of them? We have not been able to find the evidence which would give us the answer, but fortunately this is of no great significance. Much more important is the undoubted fact that the *endowment properties* of the chapel, which the 1546 chantry certificate tells us had been given by various men at various times "for the maintenance of a priest to minister there", remained in the ownership of the charity. We know this to be true because at the Dissolution they were certainly bought by the two engrossers, William Wynlowe and Richard Felde, as one element in an enormous list of purchases of sequestered properties from the Crown, for which they paid in all the vast sum of £1500.13.7. Wynlowe and Felde then sold them to Richard Jervoise, lord of the manor of Bedcote, in 1550 or thereabouts. We possess in the school archives the annual rental of the Bedcote manor for that year, a document in which ten properties belonging to the manor are described as "late belonginge to our Lady Service in the churche of Ouldswynford and our Lady Chappell in Sturbridge and Bedcott and to the stipendiary prieste there."

This brings us, of course, to another mystery. It had always been assumed that the name of the Hayley chapel was 'the Service of the Trinity'. It was so named, clearly and unequivocally, in the chantry certificate at the dissolution. But we have now found, in the Bedcote manor rental just quoted, an equally clear and precise reference to "our Lady Service in the Churche of Ouldswynford and Lady Chappell in Sturbridge and Bedcott." The two descriptions cannot both be correct, and so far we have found no means of telling which is right. On the one hand the chantry certificate certainly went into gross error in naming the founders as Hareby instead of Hayley; so an error there in the name of the chapel would not be unthinkable. Moreover the Bedcote manorial officers should certainly have known the facts better by far than did the commissioners for the survey of chantries. On the other hand there is, so far as we know, no other breath of a hint that there existed a service or a chantry — whether of our Lady, the Trinity, or whatever — in the church of Oldswinford. So the mystery still remains; and without the help of yet another piece of serendipity, it seems probable that we shall not know the answer.

The First Phase

That must be as it may. Whether the priest ministered to the Service of the Trinity or to "Our Lady Service in Stourbridge", minister he did, and continued to do so until in common with all such establishments the service met its fate at the hands of the king's commissioners at the dissolution. During that period of a century and more we can be confident that Stourbridge had its grammar school, though not so called, and that generations of the sons of Stourbridge — most of them following in their fathers' footsteps and to be followed in their turn by their own sons — wended their way with books and satchels and the Tudor equivalent of an apple and a packet of crisps, to the schoolhouse behind the houses near to the top of the Lower High Street, there to sit under the eye of the priest and imbibe the rudiments of learning. For that was what the chapel was intended for and that was how it served the community of Stourbridge, until Government in its wisdom (as it was to do again in our own times) brought it to an end.

The last priest-schoolmaster was Nicholas Rock, and evidence from the Record Office tells us that in the year *after* the dissolution of the Service he was still being paid his wages. By that time the foundation charter of the king's new grammar school had already been signed. So we can be sure beyond doubt that the first headmaster of the grammar school was also Nicholas Rock. We also know that he had eight governors, one of them an absentee, being Thomas Jervoise, the youthful lord of the manor of Bedcote and Stourbridge, who resided at Herriard in Hampshire and rarely if ever set foot in Stourbridge. We know the names of the original governors and of their successors. We know that some of them set up powerful family connections and successions, which we have referred to as 'dynasties'.

We know also that the school's financial affairs were at a very early stage beginning to be mismanaged. We have spoken of the Tudor account-book, covering the years from 1573 to 1588. It tells us a sorry tale — of carelessness, or of peculation, or of both. Then we know, from the voluminous evidence presented in the record of the Madstard Case of 1595, that there was another abiding scandal in the affairs of the school, that of the activities of its headmaster, the extraordinary Richard Alchurche, pettifogger and reputed conjuror — or in more modern terms professional astrologer, magician and fortune-teller — as well as keeper of an alehouse on the school premises! He was, be it remembered, headmaster for a period of almost twenty years, from 1575 to 1594. He was cousin to the Addenbrookes, one of the 'dynastic' families referred to above, and doubtless owed his appointment to that relationship. The whole town knew of his scandalous behaviour, and there was widespread suspicion that he kept his position by bribing his governors. There were moves to get rid of him. Richard Madstard himself, a mercer in the town in succession to his father Thomas and a governor of the school as Thomas had been before him, gave Alchurche notice to quit almost as soon as he joined the governing body. But nothing seemed to avail against the skill and determination of Alchurche and the entrenched strength of the close-knit corporation of the governors and their 'dynasties'. What is more, so far as appearances went — discipline in school, behaviour of the boys in the town and at church, and so on — Alchurche evidently gave all the signs of being a good headmaster.

So things went on, year after year, until at last the tenure of the scandalous Alchurche was brought to a summary conclusion by the efforts of the equally scandalous Gilbert Lyttelton. He was lord paramount of Stourbridge, by being lord of the manor of Oldswinford; and as the devil can quote scripture, so Gilbert Lyttelton called to his aid the Church, in the person of the bullying archdeacon Godfrey Goldsborough and the chancellor of the diocese, Arthur Purefoy. The fatal chink in Alchurche's armour was that as an astrologer and magician he was "suspect *in religion*", and it was this which brought him down. So in 1593 he was presented in the chancellor's court, and ultimately he "yielded and agreed to departe" — and so in fact in 1594 depart he did.

He was succeeded by Marmaduke Chapman, a young man of 24 or 25 — far too young for the purpose, and almost certainly a kinsman of the archdeacon who got rid of Alchurche, and who browbeat those governors who objected to Chapman. Richard Madstard denounced Chapman's appointment as corrupt, and to the extent that he doubtless owed his post to 'good honest nepotism' corrupt it may well have been. On the other hand, Marmaduke Chapman was certainly a "maister of Arte proceeded in the Universitie of Cambridge" and consequently far better qualified academically than any of his predecessors at Stourbridge had been. Alchurche certainly had arts of which he was master, but certainly also he had no degree: he was a local boy, doubtless brought up in the school. So had been Nicholas Rock, last priest and first headmaster. So had been the only other sixteenth-century headmaster whose name we know — one John Cole, who was in office in 1558, before he moved away to become schoolmaster of Kinver. We know nothing else of him, but in his will he mentioned his "poor kinsfolk in Oldswinford", and that doubtless betrays his origins. It is a matter of commonsense that in those early days the only way to find a schoolmaster was by personal acquaintance or recommendation. The degree requirement was to be a thing of the future, and Marmaduke Chapman's Cambridge M.A. really put him before his time in the matter of qualifications.

That M.A. entirely failed to impress Richard Madstard. He persisted in his accusation that the appointment was corrupt, and he went further by maintaining that Chapman's salary, which Godfrey Goldsborough had insisted should be raised from £11 to £15 a year, was in fact a fiction, and that Chapman was secretly paying the extra four pounds, or more, as a bribe to the governors who had wrongfully elected him. Be that as it may be (and Madstard certainly failed to prove his claim) the salary 'on paper' was indeed fifteen pounds; and when it is remembered that the total income of the foundation still stood, according to the evidence of many witnesses in the Madstard case, at or near the original figure of £17/10/8d a year, it becomes clear that something was wrong somewhere. Besides the headmaster there was the usher to pay and the buildings to maintain; and after Chapman had had his fifteen pounds, there was simply not enough money left for these purposes.

We do not know the explanation, but it certainly looks as if financial irregularities did not cease with the departure of

Alchurche. As the century draws to its end this thought must linger in our minds; and it has to be admitted that an objective observer at the time, if required to forecast the school's future from the story of its first fifty years, would have had little grounds for optimism.

The Seventeenth Century (1)
Peace in Time of Conflict

As things turned out, however, the next century saw a period of uneventful and steady development. The word progress would be inaccurate, since it would imply the concept of an effort to improve, which certainly never dawned on the consciousness of those seventeeth-century Stourbridge men. They simply carried on, content to offer old answers to old questions, never sick of that disease of our own times which sees no good except in change, never hot for innovation — indeed, never hot for anything much at all. And since a school, like a nation, can almost always be counted happy if it has no history, so the Stourbridge Grammar School seems to have gained strength from the sheer uneventfulness of that most eventful century in the history of England.

The nation, it is true, was split asunder by civil war; the armies marched, the battles were won and lost; the Puritans bound their kings in chains and their nobles in bonds of iron. His Sacred Majesty became the Man of Blood, and paid in his own blood for everyone's sins. Cromwell ruled, and for a time there were no more cakes and ale, until the pendulum swung back again and the Stuart Restoration led on to the Glorious Revolution.

As for the school throughout those stirring times, nothing of moment seems to have disturbed its tranquillity — or if it did, the records of the disturbance are entirely lost. We may well pause for a moment at this point to reflect that if the Madstard volume alone — one item only amongst thousands — had eluded our search in the Harward and Evers archives, we might still have been assuming that the Tudor twilight too had been as uneventful for the school as was in these later times the Stuart morning. Or, if we were to look at the thing from the other end, we might believe that conceivably there is still another Madstard volume, waiting to be discovered. In this field, however, we have no choice but to work on what we know; and so astonishingly fertile have been the results of our searches so far, that we may not unreasonably assume that what we have not found either was never there, or is not there now, or will never be found in the future; and if any one of these three propositions is, as it has to be, accepted, then we can safely proceed with our uneventful tale.

There are in the school archives two hints, and only two, of the national upheaval. They come in a royalist document of 1645 and one from the puritan side of 1652. The first was found in the original Black Box collection, and reads as follows:

Black Box number endorsed: (91)

Charles R.

    Whereas humble Suite hath been made vnto vs by Richard Foley Jasper Nubrough and the rest of the Feoffees of the Free Grammar Schoole in the Towne of Stourbridge in Our County of Worcester, That Wee would be pleased to recommend it unto you to assist them, with yor Power to collect and gather the annuall Rents belonging to the sayd schoole; wch the Tennantes have not in any part payd for these two yeares last past; Wee being graciously inclined to favour the Peticoners in this theyr humble Request, Whereby the sayd Schoole may be maintayned, and the two Masters belonging thereunto enabled and encouraged to attend theyr severall Charges : Our Pleasure and Command is that accordingly either of you be ayding and assisting vnto the sayd Feoffees or such Persons as they shall appoint, when you shall bee desyred by them, for the speedy and effectuall collecting of theyr sayd Rents and the Arrerages thereof. For Wch this shall bee yor Warrant. Given at our Court at Beaudley this 18th of June 1645.

                  By his Ma(jes)t(ies) Command
                      George Digbye.

To Our trusty and Well-beloved
Our high Sheriffe of Our County
Of Worcester and to Our Governor
of Our City of Worcester or either
of them for the tyme beinge.

Sheriff of ye County of Worcester & Gouernor of ye City of Worcester.

Endorsement: His Ma(jes)ties Order for ye
　　　　　　　 Schoole of Stourbridge
　　　　　　　 For collecting Arreares.

This requires no comment, but it is a useful reminder to us that, uneventful as the school's affairs seem to have been in the seventeenth century, nevertheless the civil war brought its problems. It is in a strange sort of way reassuring to learn that even amidst the drums and tramplings of contending armies those who tried to take advantage so as to evade their due debts were rapped over the knuckles and called to order.

The puritan document reads as follows:

> To the chiefe Magistrates
> of ye Corporacon of
> Sturbridge
> in ye County of

Worcester.
franck.

Endorsement on the back fold as follows:—

a lr. to renew our
Charter

Gentlemen,
　　The Committee for Corporations and Renewing of Charters haveing taken into their Consideration an order of Parliament of the fourteenth of Septembr 1652 touching the alteration and renewing of the sevrll and Respective Charters of this Nation And upon a serious debate had the ... (*damage to the paper at this point*) ... (Judging it most agreable with and suitable unto the Governmt. of a Comon wealth that they bee held from and under the authority of ye same) Comanded mee to signify unto you their pleasure therein viz that (in pursuance of ye said order of Parliamnt ...) you faile not to bring or Cause to be brought unto the said Comittee upon the fifth day of Aprill next at two of the Clock in ye afternoon (sitting in ye Queens Cort in Westmr) the originall Charters pattents or other instrumts by which you hold

or exercise any privilege This being all I have in Comand I Remaine
Gent.
Yor. friend and Servt.

xxxxxxxxxx(*Illegible*)

Queenes Court
Westminster
Jan 20th 1652

This time our intrusion onto the national stage is not quite so straightforward. For why should this document be addressed to the authorities of the town and not to the governors of the grammar school? It may possibly be that it has in fact nothing whatever to do with the school. But it was found in the school archives and endorsed with the phrase "Letter to renew our charter" So far as we know, the only charter to be found in relation to Stourbridge is the charter by which Edward VI founded the grammar school. Perhaps the most likely explanation is that when the letter arrived and was delivered to the chief magistrates of Stourbridge, those gentlemen, knowing nothing of any charter save that of the school, and being in any case most probably themselves either identified with the governors of that school or very closely associated with them, decided that its only proper destination lay at the school; so to the school it went. Certainly it was in the school's archives that it found its resting-place.

In general terms the seventeenth-century evidences are a haphazard accumulation, many of them from the original Black Box hoard and almost all of them concerned with the school's income and expenditure and its endowment properties — lands and tenements in Evesham and Worcester and the tithes of Martley and Suckley. We learn that the properties were in a rough sort of way 'managed' by a series of senior tenants in each of the two main centres. These men collected and remitted the rents due, less such as the other tenants were unable or unwilling to pay. Their notes are totally informal and colloquially expressed (the agents frequently addressed their correspondents as 'cousin'), often not clear, uncertain in sequence and sometimes in date, incomplete and often quite obscure. Even so they give a lively impression of the school's business and financial affairs actually in process, and in combination with the annual Collectors' Accounts, which survive in a haphazard sequence at irregular intervals, they make the general complexion of the school's finances reasonably clear. Things were much healthier than in Madstard's time.

When the history of the early headmasters was put together in 1960 it was possible to show that the wages, as they were called, of the masters, both head and usher, were steadily increasing throughout the whole of the century. Richard Alchurche had had eleven pounds a year, and, as we have seen, this was increased to fifteen pounds for Marmaduke Chapman. He went off, to a living in Gloucestershire in the year 1601, and was succeeded in office by none other than the previously ejected rogue and rascal — magician, petty lawyer and alehouse-keeper — Richard Alchurche!

This, surely, is the point at which we most long for a new discovery. For we cannot but believe that only something very much out of the ordinary could have brought Richard Alchurche back. It is true that all three of the men chiefly responsible for his expulsion in 1594 had departed from the scene in 1598 and 1599. Arthur Purefoy ceased to be chancellor in 1598, and in the same year Godfrey Goldsbrough became bishop of Gloucester. In 1599 Gilbert Lyttelton died, and was buried at Halesowen. To that extent the way may have been cleared for Alchurche to come back. Moreover Richard Madstard had ceased to be a governor, while three of the governors who survived were three of those whom Madstard had attacked, and who must have belonged to the Alchurche faction on the governing body if any such ever existed. Elcoxe, Perrott and Roger Sparry — all, be it noted, 'dynastic' figures in the affairs of the school, must surely have had a hand in the Alchurche restoration. Even so one wonders how on earth they, or anyone else, managed to do it. But for once our luck has failed us, and the archives at this fascinating point are voiceless.

Alchurche died in 1610, very likely still in office. The parish register accorded him the rare distinction of an entry in capital letters, an evident indication that he was a person of special status and importance in the parish. We do not know the details of his salary, nor that of his successor, Edward Davenport, a university graduate as Chapman had been. But in 1617 William Panting, later to be ejected, possibly for his royalist sympathies, from St. Michael's Coventry, was paid £32 for two years, as is shown in the account of John Sparry. So the salary is creeping up. Panting's successor, Thomas Owen, served from 1619 to 1633, and in those fourteen years his salary rose by stages from £20 to £30 a year — almost three times the amount paid to Richard Alchurche less than half a century before.

Following Thomas Owen came Ambrose Sparry (of whom we must say more later). He received £35 a year and his usher £15. That usher was James Dalton, a local man and a boy at the school in his time, certainly a figure of great importance to the seventeenth-century school. He too will call for something more than a brief note.

Ambrose Sparry served until 1648, when he went off to be 'Minister and Register' at Wolverhampton. He was succeeded by Joseph Baker, another puritan divine and another member — and beneficiary — of one of the dynastic families of the body of governors. Baker did not last long in office, and we have no details of his salary, nor of that of his several successors in office — Jonathan Grew B.A. (1651-54), Robert Dale (1656-62), John Kent, M.A. (1662-66), Ambrose Sparry, M.A., (for a second term, 1666-75), and Samuel Mountfort, M.A. (1675-82). We can be sure, however, that the process of inflation went on, and it is no surprise to learn that by the time of Joseph Withers, M.A. (1682-91) the salary had reached the figure of £45 a year, precisely three times as much as was paid at the beginning of the century.

This implies, of course, that the endowment income, the rents and fines from the tenants of properties in Evesham and Worcester, must have suffered a somewhat similar increment. The evidence has not previously been put together and analysed, but a cursory inspection of the haphazardly collected accounts for the period in the Black Box hoard readily bears out our expectations. Here are some of the figures:

Date	Collector	Income	Salaries (H.M. and Usher)
1619	John Rocke	£27.16.0	£20 and £10
1624	Richard Hottofte	£40.4.10	£24 and £10
1626	?	£66.10.4	£26.13.4 and £12
1627	John Rocke	£51.10.0	£26.13.4 and £12
1629	Thomas Smyth	£45.18.5	£26.13.4 and £12
1633	John Baker	£54.3.8	£30 and £15
1634	George Winshurst	£55.4.3	£30 and £15
1635	Nicholas Sparry	£67.14.7	£35 and £15
1636	?	£52.6.7	£28 and £13.6.8
1641	John Baker	£57.18.0	£30 and £13

In the last account, that of 1641, we learn that the total rentroll, including rents in arrears, had now reached the figure of £74.2.9. There are also entries recording considerable legal expenses, and it becomes clear that the governors were involved in lengthy and complex disputes at law concerning the rents due for the 'pensions and portions' of tithes in Martley and Suckley, which were part of the original Edwardian endowment and which provided a good proportion of the foundation income. So when we speak of the uneventfulness of the school's affairs in this period, we must remember that we are speaking comparatively.

These, then, were the preoccupations of the seventeenth-century governors — income and expenditure, tenants good and bad, management of the properties, headmasters and ushers to be appointed at fairly frequent intervals, vacancies on the governing body to be filled by election. Of strange events, such as those of the Tudor twilight, and outlandish characters such as Alchurche and Madstard, there are no records, and we are prepared to believe that none such made their appearance. The age of scandal in the school's affairs had come to a lengthy pause.

It would, however, be naive and mistaken to suppose that the black picture of dishonesty and exploitation which we discerned in the pages of the Tudor account-book had been totally transformed, as if by the magic curtain in a pantomine, to a scene of pristine innocence and pure honesty, played out by characters who were 'whiter than white'. The history of the early headmasters, when it was brought to light by the study of the leases in 1960, showed this very clearly. We have seen already, it is true, that financially things were much healthier than in Madstard's time. Peculation and bribery seem to have become a thing of the past. But there are more ways than one of making the most out of a pot of gold such as the grammar school endowment undoubtedly was. The growing sophistication of English life and society is well illustrated here.

In the first place, the continued existence of family 'dynasties' amongst the governors clearly indicates that a place on this powerful and close corporation was still much sought after and highly prized. Prestige no doubt had much to do with this; but there was also power, and there was inevitably profit. Direct and illegal profit was evidently a thing of the past, but patronage is a different matter. Let us consider the families of Sparry and Baker.

As for the Sparrys, it would be difficult to exaggerate their importance in the affairs of Stourbridge and its school at this time. When the history of the early headmasters was being put together, more than 70 documents were counted, dating from 1593 to 1654, in which the name of Sparry appeared in connection with the government of the school. The Sparrys were originally of Clent, with branches in the surrounding villages and at King's Norton. It proved to be difficult to discover how and when they first came to Stourbridge, but after much research for the purposes of the Madstard Case it emerged that the first Stourbridge Sparry was Roger, who established himself as a mercer in the town in the 1570's and become a governor of the school in 1592. Thereafter the Sparry connection was of very great importance. We now quote from The Madstard Case, page 60 as follows:

> "Roger Sparry was a governor from 1592 until his death in 1601. His son John followed from 1602 until he died in 1643. Moreover at some time between 1628 and 1633 he was joined on the governing body by his own son Nicholas Sparry, who continued in office until he in turn died in 1655. That gives us 63 years of continuous Sparry governorship. But that is not all. After an interval of only about ten years another John Sparry was elected, and this name, possibly representing two men in succession, stayed on the list of governors for almost another half-century, until the death of 'Mr. John Sparry' was recorded in the governors' minute-book on 16th December 1713. That is an impressive record. But to gauge the real power and importance of the Sparry influence on the school, we have to recall that from 1633 to 1648 and again from 1666 to 1675 the headmaster was Ambrose Sparry. He was first elected by a body of eight which included his father John and his brother Nicholas, his sister Dorothy's husband Nicholas Addenbrooke, and also John Baker, who in his 1640 account refers to 'my cousin Nicholas Sparry'. It only just missed including also John Rock, who presented the accounts in 1619 and 1627, and who speaks of money he had received 'of my uncle John Sparry'. . . . We often use the word 'network' loosely and with little reference to its original meaning; but it would be hard to think of a better metaphor than 'the Sparry network' to describe the situation just outlined."

We now remember also that it was Nicholas Sparry who bought the manor of Bedcote and Stourbridge from the Jervoises in 1625 and then proceeded to restore to the governors of the grammar school as a free gift the site of the school house which had escheated to the manor by a series of accidents in 1446. His deed of gift, a fine document in Latin still preserved in the school archives, is dated 10 April, 1626; its value to us is enhanced by the fact that it cites in detail in its text the original Hayley foundation deed of the chapel, dated 1430. The later discovery of this foundation deed in the original we have already described.

So the benefits of the Sparry connection with the school went both ways. Nicholas made a valuable gift to the foundation in 1626. In 1633 Nicholas's brother Ambrose was elected headmaster. What is more, he was appointed at the age of 20, while he was still an undergraduate! He was baptised at Oldswinford on 28 February 1612/13, matriculated at Clare College, Cambridge at Easter of 1631, and became B.A. in 1633/4, not until more than half a year *after* his appointment as headmaster. It was therefore necessary for the governors to pay a substitute to do the headmaster's work until Ambrose Sparry was in a position to take it on for himself. But he did not fail to benefit financially: during the three successive quarters following the death of the last headmaster the substitute, a Mr. Malpass, received, first, five pounds out of the seven pounds ten shillings which was the full quarter's salary, then five pounds again, then three pounds. Ambrose Sparry received the remainder. What is more, as soon as he took up office continuously in person, his salary went up. For his brother Nicholas was Collector for that year, and the first item under disbursements in his account reads:

> To my brother Ambrose ... ... 35.0.0.

That, then, is why we said that, while direct and illegal profit was a thing of the past as a perquisite of the governors, patronage was a different matter. It was evidently no small thing to have at one's disposal the appointment of headmaster of this small-town grammar school. How big a thing it was to become in another half-century we have already indicated in our references to the Wentworth appointment of 1705-6. But here as early as 1633 was the practice in essence already established.

It would be a mistake, however, to see this as an example of dishonesty or scandal of anything like Madstard proportions. We have pointed out already, and it is worth repeating with emphasis, that in those days there was no advertising, no instant communication, no sitting by the telephone and calling up one's friends in high places. If you needed a good headmaster, what better way to find one than by personal acquaintance or recommendation? Ambrose Sparry was almost certainly a former pupil of the school. He was beyond question well-known to those who appointed him. He was of graduate qualification and of the soundest possible family back ground. What is more, he turned out to be 'a godlie and orthodox divine', and a man of some prominence in the religious controversies of those times. Everything we know of him suggests that he was a decent and moderate man, and Calamy in his memorial of non-conformist ministers speaks of him as 'a sober, prudent, moderate, humble, learned, judicious, godly man'. It is true that Calamy was an avowed protagonist of the puritans and so not unbiassed. But it is equally evident beyond doubt that here at any rate was no Alchurche, nor even a Marmaduke Chapman: and if he owed his appointment at Stourbridge to patronage, at any rate he seems to have justified it in due time.

Very much the same can be said of Joseph Baker. The story of the Baker family was given at some length in the *History of the Early Headmasters*, and very fully much later in *The Madstard Case* (pp. 71 *seq*). They must, however, be treated, though more briefly, here.

The first Baker to become a governor of the school was Nicholas, elected in 1586/7 and a governor until his death in 1603. He had a brother named John who was a butcher, and who acted as an attorney for the governors in their purchase of a piece of land in the Green Close shortly before 1600. So the Bakers were clearly at that time 'on the network' of the grammar school. After Nicholas's death the next Baker to become a governor came along not until 1633. He was John Baker, eldest son of John the butcher and thus a nephew of Nicholas the first governor. He was also, as we have seen, a cousin of Nicholas Sparry. He remained in office until 1667, and in 1647 he was joined by his own next brother, Gregory. Meantime the Bakers of the senior line, the family of Nicholas the first governor, suffered many vicissitudes: the first three sons — John, Joseph and Nicholas — all died young, leaving a second John to be head of the family. This John moved from Stourbridge, first to Prestwood and then to London, where he made his way in trade. It was his son Joseph who was elected to be headmaster in succession to Ambrose Sparry in 1648 or 1649. We now take up the story from *The History of the Early Headmasters*, as follows:

"... John Baker and his cousin Nicholas Sparry were both governors when Ambrose Sparry left the school in 1648. and we remember that Ambrose Sparry was a good Puritan divine. It should therefore be no surprise to us to find a Sparry followed by a Baker, and one good puritan by another.

"Like Ambrose Sparry in family influence and religious

complexion, Joseph Baker was also like him in being very young when he was appointed. 'Joseph the sonne of John Baker' was baptised on 11 March, 1626/7. This makes him 21 at the time when he became headmaster .... He was admitted pensioner at Emmanuel College, Cambridge on 28 October 1644, son of John Baker of Prestwood in Staffordshire. He took his B.A. degree in 1647/8 and his M.A. in 1651 .... He was ejected from the living of St. Andrew's Worcester in 1662, and we conclude that he was a puritan, which is what we should have expected .... He died quite young, on 25 March 1668; his monumental inscription in Oldswinford Church gives his age at death as 44. The wording is quoted by Nash (Vol. II, p.212-3) and shows that he was a person of some substance and note in the locality.

"As to his character, we have the evidence of Calamy in his *Account of the Ejected Ministers*, where Joseph Baker is described as 'a learned man, of blameless life, one who preached constantly ... one of extraordinary prudence, calmness, patience, gravity and soundness of judgement. Neither for Prelacy, Presbytery, nor Independency, as formed into parties, but for that which was found in all parties, and for concord upon catholic terms. The parish of St. Andrews Worcester had but £6 a year maintenance, of which he took none, but gave it to a woman to teach poor children to read, living upon his own and some small augmentation granted by the Parliament ...''

Moderation, and what we can only call general decency, seem to have been characteristic of the succession of puritan headmasters who ruled the Stourbridge school at this period.

"Joseph Baker, besides being headmaster of the school for a short spell, was also its benefactor ... By an indenture dated 18 April 1692, which is still extant in the archives of the school, two men, Nicholas Baker and John Butler, for the purpose of carrying out the directions contained in the will of Joseph Baker dated 17 February 1667/8, granted to the governors of the Stourbridge school a yearly rent charge of three pounds, payable out of three messuages in the Shambles at Worcester. The income was to be applied to the maintenance of a scholar at one of the universities. This endowment, known as Baker's Exhibition, was still in being in 1863, when we find a full statement of its provisions appended to the Statutes and Orders of the school printed in that year, at which date the income of the Exhibition was about eight pounds. The choice of exhibitioner was vested in the heirs alternately of John Baker and John Swinfen, and only in default of such heirs did the election revert to the school governors. These two men were the father and father-in-law of Joseph Baker, and had been the original trustees of the Exhibition. The funds to supply it had come originally from Joseph Baker's 'interest in the river of Avon, for which he paid £50.' Twenty-five years later Nicholas Baker and John Butler transferred to the governors the rent charge into which the funds had been converted, and this was still maintaining the Exhibition in the nineteenth century. These details were given in the great *Inquiry into Charities* of 1832, which even supplied the names of the owners at that time of the properties in the Shambles — a Miss Nichols and a Thomas Pollard — who were paying the rent charge. We read in the same document that long periods of time have sometimes elapsed when there were no university scholars to claim the Exhibition. Nor is this surprising, because since about 1813 the school had been almost deserted, and at the time of the Inquiry there were four boys in the upper, and four in the lower school! In 1837, however, there was a claimant, a Master Frederick Fisher, who was tactless enough to claim not only the income from the Exhibition but also the accumulated arrears, amounting at the time to £56.11.8d. The governors gave him the Exhibtion, but not the arrears, which were invested in the funds and the interest applied to increase the income of the Exhibition.

"The Exhibition was finally extinguished by the new Scheme of Government of the school of 1876. Paragraph 61 of this states: 'The Foundation heretofore called Baker's Exhibition shall be and the same is hereby consolidated with the general funds of this endowment."

So Joseph Baker, like Ambrose Sparry, doubtless owed his appointment to family influence. He was equally a puritan, and equally also to all appearances a scholarly and conscientious man; and, last but not least, his headmastership, brief though it was, proved equally to be profitable to the school, as Ambrose Sparry's had been.

There is nothing exciting about these seventeenth-century headmasters and their governors. They came and did their stint and went upon their way, most of them leaving little but a name and perhaps an entry in Calamy's *Memorial*, or perhaps, in the case of the governors, a laboriously compiled and miraculously preserved 'Collector's Annual Account' in the Harward and Evers archives.

We do not know with certainty enough about them to prove as fact our impression that "their ways were ways of gentleness and all their paths were peace", but that is what it looks like at this distance in time. Unless and until some record of a scandal or a quarrel or a moral collapse of some kind come to light — and we have no reason to suppose that it will — we can be content to speak of the seventeenth century in the school's history as a period of quiet and of calm.

One great contibutor to that calm and quiet and to the steady development that went with it was undoubtedly James Dalton. He was neither a governor nor a headmaster, but an usher. He served under seven successive Headmasters for a period of 43 years, from 1626 to his death in 1669, evidently acting as a trusted and influential servant of the school throughout the turbulent middle decades of the century. He was indeed a figure like the vicar of Bray, he started under Charles I and finished under Charles II, and went through civil war, Commonwealth and Restoration in undisturbed possession of his office. It is to be remembered as important that the usher taught all the junior boys and brought them on until they were of an age and accomplishment to go up to the headmaster. It is also certain that almost every man who rose to be a governor had been in his time a boy at the school. With this in mind we can begin to gauge the importance of James Dalton in the school hierarchy. What is more, there is interesting evidence to support our belief that he was a respected and important pillar of the establishment.

He was, it is almost needless to say, a local man, baptised as James the son of Thomas Dalton on 25 September 1605. He was no doubt educated at the school, and in his 21st year he was appointed to be its usher. He appears as such first in John Rock's account for the year 1626-7, in which he was paid twelve pounds "for his whole year". He evidently had no degree, and his subscription is not to be found in the diocesan records at Worcester, though this is presumably only because it has been lost, since 35 years later in 1661 at the Restoration he was guaranteed by the school governors "to have long since had a licence for teaching schoole, which as he saith is now lost".

Four years after his appointment, on 21 January 1629/30 he married Susanna Winshurst, and so became son-in-law to George and brother-in-law to William Winshurst. Both of these men were governors of the school in their time, George until 1647, then William until 1675. The Winshursts were a well-known family of ironmasters, and associates of the Foleys; one of them was established by Robert Foley of Stourbridge as his responsible London agent. James Dalton's three children were born in the parish in 1630, 1633 and 1640. His burial is recorded on 23 August 1669.

Effectively his whole life was bound up in the school, and it becomes clear that he was a trusted servant and as an usher something extraordinary. We have several leases dating from 1638 to 1664 in which he signed as a witness. That was not unusual; but on one occasion he himself presented to the governors two lengthy documents which show that he had been entrusted with the management and supervision of considerable building work at the school, including the erection of a kitchen, at a cost of £21.13.10d. This was a considerable sum of money, and he was paid in no less than four instalments over a space of three years for what he had evidently expended out of his own pocket. This was quite evidently outside the normal run of an usher's duties and activities, and it shows also that James Dalton was a man of some substance, far removed from the starveling schoolmaster of tradition. He was also the only usher in the history of the school whose name appears in the records as having a direct relationship with the governors. What is more, these references open up an interesting sidelight upon his quality and character as a schoolmaster.

In the whole vast array of the school archives we find practically no reference at all to the scholastic matters which were the real business of the school and the cause of its being. Teaching and learning, the work and tools of the classroom, even the books without which the school could not have functioned at all, were conspicuous only by their absence in the records. Yet in relation to James Dalton — and in this matter again he is unique — there are no fewer than four instances in the accounts of references to actual books! In one of his own two accounts of 1658, mentioned above, there is an item "for covering a Dictionary with leather", another "for the carryage of a book from Worcester" and a third "Payd my brother Jeston for a Dictionary". Thirty-one years before this, in James Dalton's very first year as usher, two items in John Rock's account read:

For a Coupers dixonary for the schole   11/6d
For an Erasmus addages at large for the schole   5/6d

and these two items immediately follow the entry:—

To Mr. Dalton for his whole year   12/0/0d

In 1633 we find:—

pd for a dixonary and the carriadge   13/8d

and in 1634:—

pd for binding and carriadge of 2 dixonary to and
from Worcester   8/6d
pd James Dalton for mending of books, writing
etc.   6/0d

These are only small indications, but it is hard to resist the conclusion that, coming as they do so closely together after long volumes of records that go on year after year without any mention of books at all, they give us more to think about than a mere coincidence.

The story of the Hickman Library bears out this conclusion to a remarkable extent.

It was long well-known that King Edward's School Stourbridge was the proud possessor of a considerable library. The fact even found its way into the pages of Nash's great history. There he tells us, "King Edward VI founded the school in Stourbridge .... The library was built, and many books given, by Henry Hickman of London, about the year 1665." We shall find that the key words here are "Henry Hickman *of London.*"

The Hickmans were a prominent family of Stourbridge clothiers, who had much to do with the history of the town and school in the seventeenth and eighteenth centuries. It was a Hickman who owned the Green Close and its house, next but one to the school, in 1685, and it was to a Miss Hickman, living in that house, that the young Samuel Johnson, probably while he was a pupil at the school in 1725, addressed some of his earliest verses — 'To Miss Hickman (Stella) playing on the Spinet.' The Hickmans were a prolific family, numerous in and around Stourbridge at this time. Because of Samuel Johnson's verses they later became the object of great interest to the Johnsonian scholars; and in due course the great Johnsonian genealogist Aleyn Leyell Reade, in his monumental book *The Reades of Blackwood Hill and Dr. Johnson's Ancestry*, published an equally monumental pedigree of the Hickman family. He also identified the 'Henry Hickman *of London*' who presented the library to the school. This Henry he took to be the Reverend

Henry Hickman, second son of Richard Hickman of Stourbridge, yeoman (who was buried at Oldswinford 16 January 1656/7) and nephew and namesake of that Richard's younger brother, also Henry Hickman. Of this latter Henry Hickman Reade had nothing to say, beyond the note that he was alive in 1654. But Henry the nephew, perhaps because he was the most notable member of the family at this period and almost a national figure (who found his way later into the pages of the Dictionary of National Biography) received from Reade what we may perhaps call 'the full treatment'. He was a religious controversialist of some note, a graduate of St. Catharine's, Cambridge and a fellow of Magdalen Hall, Oxford, where he was also public orator of the university. He flourished in Oxford as a puritan preacher at St. Aldate's, and as an intruding minister under the Commonwealth at Brackley in Northamptonshire from 1650 to 1659. The Restoration sent him into exile in Holland, where he was admitted to the University of Leyden in 1663, became English pastor in 1675, and was minister of the English Church there until his death in 1692. Grazebrook in his *Heraldry of Worcestershire* knew about him and recalls that on 21 August 1660 he dined with Samuel Pepys. Calamy in his *Nonconformist Memorial* says of him, "He was a celebrated preacher in Oxford, a smart disputant, and a man of excellent general learning. After he was ejected he lived for some time privately in Worcestershire, preaching only now and then".

This, then, according to Reade, was the 'Henry Hickman *of London*' who gave the school its library; nor is it surprising that Mr. George Burley in his 1948 history of the school was content to repeat the ascription. Unfortunately, however, Reade's massive apparatus of scholarship had for once got its conclusion entirely wrong. The real 'Henry Hickman *of London*' turned out to be the Reverend Henry's uncle and namesake. Of him Reade had had practically nothing to say, and we can only conclude that he had considered him to be insignificant. Strangely enough, in his other great Johnsonian work, *Johnsonian Gleanings,* Reade gives abstracts of Chancery proceeding of 1666, which concern *Henry Hickman, late citizen and salter of London,* his widow Alice and his nephew Henry 'at the University'. If only Reade had pursued this line, the whole thing would have become clear.

This is where James Dalton comes back into the story, and where he makes his greatest contribution to the history of the school. For there is another Chancery record, dating from 1667, which escaped

Reade's net and which tells the whole story.

Henry Hickman the elder, formerly of Stourbridge but more recently citizen and salter of London ('Henry Hickman *of London*') and his wife Alice had no children. So he took up his brother Richard's son Henry, his own namesake and godson, paid for his education at Cambridge, and eventually made a will in which he left him no less a sum than £1000. To this his wife Alice raised the strongest objections, whereupon in June 1665, six months or so before he died and while on a visit to Stourbridge, he signed a penal bond, in association with a deed of gift, whereby he bound his executors, within three months after his death, either to pay over to his nephew Henry the legacy of £1000, or failing this to pay him as a penalty the sum of £2000. Alice Hickman, already indignant about the original bequest, is now appealing to Chancery to frustrate the ingenious legal device which was clearly intended to protect her husband's benevolent intentions towards his nephew.

The story which emerges is vivid and circumstantial, and one of its important characters will prove to be none other than our usher, James Dalton. The tale has already been told in a paper on *The Ushers of King Edward's School Stourbridge,* published in 1979, from which the following account has been derived.

Alice Hickman was trying to prove that her husband was either not of sound mind, or was unduly influenced, or both, at the time when he signed the bond during his visit to Stourbridge in 1665. Some of the depositions were taken at the house of one Judith Cole at Stourbridge on 15 April 1667, before John Baker, Nicholas Addenbrooke and Thomas Twittey, gent.

Samuel Hunt of Stourbridge, gent., later to become a governor of the school, as John Baker and Nicholas Addenbrooke were already governors, deposed in these terms:

"The said Henry Hickman the elder about the month of May in the yeare of our Lord 1665 came together with his wife to Stourbridge and resided there until the beginning of December followinge: during which time this witness was often in his company, as also the said Henry Hickman was often times at his house: and he stated that the said Hickman was of good and sound memory and understanding, for he had seen him give entertainment to his friends in hansome and civill manner; he had heard him say grace before and give thanks after meals very deliberately and discreately, also he knowth that during his stay there he negotiated in his affaires and gave bills of exchange for moneys and other matters in order to his trade."

Samuel Hunt was followed by Edward Hickman, Clothier of Stourbridge, age 41. He was younger brother of the Reverend Henry Hickman and thus another nephew of Henry Hickman of London. This Edward had married Dorothy the daughter of Nicholas Addenbrooke, one of the commissioners in the present case, and granddaughter of John Sparry, who had been a governor of the school for almost forty years in his time. Edward Hickman spoke as follows:

"... he did see the bond sealed and delivered at the house of Emma Wheeler in Stourbridge by Henry Hickman deceased, to the use of the defendant Henry Hickman, nephew and godson of the said Henry deceased, haveing no yssue of his own body and saying that he had a more peculiar respect for him than for the rest of his kindred, whoe therefore must not expect that he should do for them as for the said defendant, and words of like import. And further he saith that he was called by the said Henry Hickman deceased, being then in company with him anglinge for fish, the said Henry being skillful therein, to be a witness to the sealing of the said bond.

He was in like manner a witness to the sealing and delivering of the writing purporting a deed of gift, nowe shewed unto him, to which he subscribed his name as a witness, which was so sealed by Henry Hickman deceased at the house of Benjamin Newbrugh in Sturbridge and delivered to the use of the defendant Henry Hickman, who was then farre absent from these parts."

We then move on to the evidence of Nicholas Addenbrooke himself, one of the commissioners and Edward Hickman's father-in-law, aged 64.

"... That the deceased Henry Hickman came to Stourbridge about May 1665 and there continued about five or six months, and that this witness was divers times in his company and had much discourse with him whilst he was at Sturbridge aforesaid, whoe did discourse very sensibly and often gave good advice to divers that were in his company, and made mention to this witness of many things touching many persons, that were done of long time before by them, when they were schollers together at the schoole at Sturbridge ... both in learning and other actions."

So we have found here sure evidence of the identity of two Old Boys of the school, and confirmation, if any were needed, that all the men we are speaking of were in their time almost certainly educated there.

The next witnesses of interest are Emma Wheeler of Stourbridge, widow aged 50, and Elizabeth Polvoe, spinster of Stourbridge, aged 28. These two are mother and daughter, so that Widow Wheeler had outlived not only her husband of that name (which was certainly well-known in Stourbridge at that time) but also a first husband with a much more exotic name and origin — from Ireland, as appears from the evidence. Emma Wheeler was probably an innkeeper, and she states that it was at her house that Henry Hickman was staying when he signed the penal bond. She adds that at that time "he was of as good understanding as any other person to her apprehension, and discoursed very rationally with her touching divers things that had happened long before, and touching her husband; and put her in mind of a meeting he had with her said husband eight and twenty years before, and of several circumstances that had passed between him and her said husband at the said meeting; and caused her to carry some beare to some persons that he had left fishing not farre offe, and afterwards took order to pay for the same of his own account." Her daughter fills in the details a little: "She was present when Mr. Hickman did in the house of Emma Wheeler her mother seale the Bond .... At which time the said Mr. Hickman was of good understanding, discoursing with her said mother concerning divers antient passages, and of the said Mr. Hickman's meeting with Gload Polvoe, her father, eight and twenty-years before at the time of his said Gload's coming out of Ireland — mentioning the particular tavern in London".

Our next witness is John Tristram of Belbroughton, gent. aged 41. He too had connections with the town and the school. His son later became one of James Dalton's successors as usher of the school. His wife was Margaret Hickman, younger sister of the Reverend Henry, elder sister of Edward, and niece of Henry Hickman deceased. John Tristram was one of two or three Tristrams who followed neither the church (where generation after generation of them occupied the rectory of Belbroughton) nor the industry of the locality (like his brother William who was later a governor of the school), but the profession of medicine. Of the Tristram doctors he was by far the most eminent, being described by Grazebrook as "a noted physician, who had the advowson of

Belbroughton". It is as a physician that he presents himself here, and this is what he says:

> "Henry Hickman the elder did frequently consult with him, being a practitioner in physic, concerning a disease then often upon him, which he judged to be a disury. He did sometimes hear the said Henry Hickman discourse, never irrationally or without orderly and competent discourse. This witness coming to visit the said Henry some very short time after the sealing of the guifte in question, and inquiring of him how his wife then did, the said Henry answered that she did not well. This witness then asking what was the matter, the said Henry replied in Latin words ... mente magis quam in corpore aegrotat- ... adding that she was dogged, because he had given his nephew one thousand pounds. But he would let her alone till her stomach did come down; and if it did not, he would give the defendant a thousand pounds more, or words to that effect."

The good old English phraseology brings the scene to life, as did the picture of Henry Hickman and his nephew angling. And when we go on to the next witness we find more of the same kind. This witness is Elizabeth Newbrough, spinster of Stourbridge, aged 20. This is what she says:

> "Henry Hickman now deceased and his wife sojourning in this witness's father's house, parte of the yeare 1665, there happened some difference betweene the said Mr. Hickman and his wife, concerning some guifte made by the said Mr. Hickman to or for the use of his nephew, who, coming into the country some time after, and to the house to visit the said Mr. Hickman and his wife, the said Alice then expressed great distaste towards him, saying she was the worse for him and that she thought he had enough already, her husband having bred him att universitie, or to the effect. And this witness did then understand that she refused to lye with her husband because of that business, but said she would never lye with him again untill he would undoe what he had done in that business, or to that effect."

However, it is the last witness of all whom we have been waiting for, and who brings us right back to our theme and justifies our interest in the affairs of the Hickmans. We set out to show who really gave the Stourbridge school its library in the seventeeth century, and we were led to that question by the interest in "books for the schole" shown by the usher James Dalton. Now here at last he makes his personal appearance. He comes as the last witness on behalf of Henry Hickman the younger (who was certainly an old pupil of his at the school), but it soon comes to light that he himself had played a most active and important part, both in the matter of the penal bond and the deed of gift, and also in the business of the provision of the library. This is how he appears.

> James Dalton of Stourbridge, aged 61. In answer to the question "Did you see the bond or writing now shewed unto you bearing date the four and twentieth day of june 1665?" he replies that not only was he present at the sealing of the bond, but he was a witness to that sealing; and not only was he a witness, but *in fact he himself drew up the bond.* He adds that Henry Hickman the elder stated that he wanted to provide for his nephew "as he had bred the said nephew at the universitie and said he had nothing else to live upon".

We begin to see that the brain behind the device of the penal bond must have been that of James Dalton, and that he was very much at the heart of the whole affair and at the centre of the group of people concerned. Our belief is confirmed by James Dalton's later testimony, when witnesses were called on Alice Hickman's behalf. Here he appears again and states that he personally drew up both the deed of gift and the penal bond; he adds that he discussed the deed of gift with Henry Hickman, but not the penal bond, which he drew up on his own initiative; but the deceased read it before he agreed to it and signed it. Had we not know that James Dalton was usher at the school we should have been hard put to it not to identify him as a lawyer; and we should certainly have had no doubt of his influence and of its importance. In this part of his evidence James Dalton goes on to say that he was also witness to the deed of gift ... "which bond and deed of guifte Henry Hickman the elder left in the hands and custody of this witness, to be delivered to Henry Hickman his nephew when he should come into the country". This puts his position in the case beyond doubt, but it is his further evidence which is most to our present purpose:

> "On Sabbath day when the weather was seasonable Henry

Hickman the elder frequented the Church (although about a mile out of the towne), and on weeke days spent his time in visiting friends and sometimes in visiting the schoole, the place of his education; which wantinge a library, he the said Henry Hickman the elder freely gave a large sum of money for building of such a fabricke. And was very earnest and importunate to have a skillful workman to set upon and finish the same speedily; which was accordingly either altogether or almost finished during his abode at Sturbridge. And also promised to bestowe on the said library a booke of good value''.

This statement clears up two questions. We now know first the true identity of the benefactor who gave the library, and secondly the physical nature of the library. It has sometimes been supposed that the Hickman library was no more than a collection of books: it is now clear that it was in fact 'a fabricke' of some kind — very likely an extension to the existing schoolroom. If this suggestion is correct, we have an explanation of the projecting piece of building, smaller in elevation than the main structure, which appears on the drawing of the pre-1860 schoolroom preserved in the school archives.

There is one last word to add about James Dalton and the Hickman library. In the light of all the evidence from Alice Hickman's chancery action it looks very much as if the moving spirit behind the provision of a library for the school was James Dalton himself. Ushers in those early centuries tended to be unimportant and anonymous. Anonymous in relation to much that he did and certainly in relation to the library James Dalton remained: unimportant is the last adjective that could truthfully be applied to him.

The Seventeenth Century (II)
Conflict in Time of Peace

James Dalton died in 1669, four years after the establishment of the Hickman library and less than a decade after the Restoration of the monarchy. We have several times drawn attention to the fact that his long service to the school coincided with the most turbulent period in English history, and to the paradox that throughout that period the school seems to have enjoyed a spell of uneventfulness and peace. But it will be remembered from our story of the unearthing of the school's records that the dawn of the eighteenth century, only thirty years or so in the future, was to cast its first light upon a scene of conflict in the management of the school. What is more, there were to be three recognisable incidents, three chapters in that story of strife, covering the better part of a decade — from 1697 to 1705 — and they must have rocked the school to its foundations.

It is tempting to look for the reasons why this should have happened. The preceding decades of tranquillity we have ascribed to the qualities and characters of the men who guided the school through that period — the Sparrys, the Bakers, the Daltons and others of their kind, whose general decency seems to have lent a quality of stability and calm to the steady process of the school's activities. By contrast we remember the lurid record of the period of the Tudor twilight, shot through with the dramatic spotlight falling on the strange scenes played out by Alchurche, Madstard and the rest. Surely, then, the reasons we were looking for are reasons of chance, the chance deployment of contrasting characters, the chance which threw up at one time an Alchurche and a Madstard, at another time a Sparry or a Baker or a Dalton.

Who then were the characters who were to bring back conflict to the scene after almost a century of peace? This time there is no easy answer. We shall find that we have no violent sword-and-dagger man, no powerful and ubiquitous magician and astrologer waiting in the wings to leap upon the stage and dominate the scene. Instead we have what seem to be much smaller men, certainly men whose images stand up in much paler colours, if they stand up at all. In place of the bizarre and gigantesque Alchurche there is the pathetic John Browne, a man in a rage, but a little man, in whatever temper — and the enigmatic Wentworth, Samuel Johnson's headmaster ("an able man, but an idle man, and to me very severe") — enigmatic because he hovers always on the edge of our picture and never seems to achieve a solid personality at all. He shares with Richard Alchurche the distinction that they are the only two headmasters in the school's history who got themselves dismissed from their office: but apart from that they might have been men from different races or creatures from different worlds. As for the governors, we knew Madstard well, his smouldering temper, raging self-esteem, rancorous ungovernable spite — Starkmad by nature as well as by name! There was certainly no one like him in this second period of conflict: and for this, as for the absence of a second Richard Alchurche, the explanation is simple and straightforward and can be found in the one word 'sophistication' or in other words, as we have put if before, we have moved from the world of Shakespeare into the world of Pope.

Nevertheless, there is one name amongst the roll-call of seventeenth-century governors round which the dust and heat of conflict seems somehow to swirl and cling. That name is Foley.

This greatest family of Midland ironmasters sprang into power and prominence almost overnight in the period we are describing. Nash's pedigree of the family (Vol II, pp 464-5) makes the founder of its fortunes to be Richard Foley of Stourbridge, "who raised a large fortune by being concerned in the iron manufactories at that place". He died in 1657 at an advanced age. But on page 467 under the same article Nash goes on to quote Richard Baxter, who ascribes the foundation of the Foley fortune to Richard's son Thomas, of whom he writes, "... Mr. Thomas Foley, who *from almost nothing* did get about 50001. a year or more by iron works".

The uncertainty is insignificant to us. Thomas Foley (1617-1676) certainly had enormous wealth, and he used much of it for good works. He was the founder in 1670 of the Oldswinford Hospital

School, which still flourishes in Stourbridge on the basis of his munificent endowment. He bought the landed estate of Witley Court and left behind him three equally prosperous sons — Thomas, also of Witley; Paul, who bought Stoke Edith in Herefordshire, went into Parliament as a Tory and became Speaker of the House of Commons; and Philip, of Prestwood in Staffordshire (once, it will be remembered, the seat of Gilbert Lyttelton).

Meanwhile the Stourbridge Foleys, descending from Richard's fourth son, Robert Foley of Stourbridge, seem to have steered a somewhat separate course, in both business and politics, from that of their cousins, whom it is convenient for us to distinguish as the 'great' Foleys.

There were three generations in succession of Foley governors of the Stourbridge Grammar School. Richard Foley, the originator, was the first, serving from 1637 until his death in 1657. His son, Robert Foley of Stourbridge, acted from 1657 until he died in 1676. Robert's son, also Robert of Stourbridge, lasted from 1676 until he died at the age of 51 in 1702. That gives us 65 unbroken years of Foleys on the governing body: it is, indeed, safe to say that wherever there was power and influence to be found in these parts, there also were the Foleys. Moreover, they found the grammar school connection useful for their good works. Old Richard Foley was responsible for rescuing from oblivion and municipal neglect or malpractice the old Dudley Grammar School foundation, and he is said to have turned for advice and help in this matter to his colleagues amongst the Stourbridge governors in 1637. When Thomas founded the Oldswinford Hospital in 1670 he was not a governor at Stourbridge: but his cousin Robert of the Stourbridge Foleys was; and Thomas's list of original trustees for the Hospital included besides his own sons (Thomas, Paul and Philip) Robert Foley himself, Henry Glover, Nicholas Addenbrooke, Joshua Newbrough, William Winshurst and Ambrose Sparry — all closely associated with the Stourbridge school. Most of their names have cropped up in our previous pages.

With this introduction of the Foleys behind us, it is time for us to revert to our main narrative and to tell the story of the three incidents to which we referred above. All have been recorded in previous papers, and they can receive no more than summary treatment here, if the volume of this work is to be kept within reasonable bounds.

The first incident is still a somewhat mysterious affair, for which no complete explanation has been found. It is officially recorded in the first of the governor's minute-books (which were found in the original Black Box collection), written under the year 1697. In December of that year Robert Foley entered in the minute-book a statement that he himself was the only member of the governing body duly qualified for that office by virtue of having taken the oaths of Allegiance and Supremacy and having 'signed the Association'. He therefore declared that the other five governors (there were two vacancies at the time) were disqualified and that he himself remained the only governor in office. He then proceeded to nominate Edward Dyson, attorney at law, as a governor duly elected by himself. The two newly established governors then together elected a third — one Thomas Batchelor, glasscutter, of Amblecote. Finally these three 'governors' nominated, in order to bring their number up to the statutory eight, the original five whom Robert Foley had declared to be disqualified — Humphrey Jeston, John Wheeler, Edward Milward, William Tristram and Richard Hickman!

That is the essential outline of what can best be described as 'the Foley trick'. That it was a trick, with no real basis in law, becomes clear in the next and following entries in the minute-book. First, the five displaced and reinstated governors declare formally that they have counsel's opinion clearly establishing that the requirements to take the oaths of Allegiance and Supremacy and to sign the Association have no validity or relevance to their positions as governors of the school. This statement is followed by the written and signed resignations of the two 'intruded' governors., Dyson and Batchelor — and we find ourselves back to where we were before the abortive Foley trick was attempted.

On the face of it this was a fairly sophisticated attempt at a legal 'highjack' of the government of the grammar school. It 'fell down' because it was not sophisticated enough. The reasons behind it are, as we have said, still by no means clear: but some considerable clarification has emerged. The Wheeler-Kynnersley papers, referred to on a previous page, contained a dossier devoted to this incident of the Foley trick. It will be remembered that John Wheeler, who evidently took the grammar school papers with him when he retired into Staffordshire, was a principal figure in the incident of 1704-6 concerning the appointment of John Wentworth. He was also one of the five governors displaced by Robert Foley in 1697. His dossier of papers contains a collection of solicitor's cases for counsel on the validity of Robert Foley's action. The answers from counsel are many and various, for this area of the law was clearly something of a minefield of uncertainties and pitfalls. But the dossier also contains, fortunately for our search, clear evidence that the real object of Robert Foley's attack was not the other governors but the headmaster, John Browne; Foley was asking counsel's opinion whether the headmaster too could be considered as legally disqualified and so be turned out of office. John Browne's legal advisers put the case to their own counsel in their own terms, and that too is to be found in the Wheeler dossier. It makes the situation unequivocally clear and includes the following telling sentence:

> "One of the Governors of ye School conceiving some displeasure at ye sayd John Browne, tho he knows not any cause for it, threatens to turne him out and pretends yt he has forfeited his Right to ye Place because he did not subscribe ye Association before ye 1st August 96 in pursuance of the Act made 7/8 Wm the 3rd for ye better security of his Maties Royall Person and Governmt, altho he did subscribe ye voluntary Association in aprill before, wh was ye same in substance wth ye Association in ye Act".

This makes Foley's immediate purpose clear enough, though not the reason behind it, and it renders his strange proceedings a little less peculiar. For if he was after the headmaster and not the five governors, we can be less astonished that he and his assoicates re-elected them. It begins to appear that he perhaps needed only two extra votes to get his way over the headmaster, and that his complex manoeuvres were directed towards that end.

At all events we see here the first shots fired in campaigns which were to last off and on for the next eight years, running well on into the next century. Robert Foley did not live to see the last engagement in those campaigns, for he died in 1702; so also soon afterwards did John Browne. So the third incident, that of the election of John Wentworth, will take its place, as it properly should by its date, not in this section of our story but in the next chapter, devoted to the eighteenth century. Robert Foley did, however, play his part in the second and better documented incident, the attack on John Browne, in the two or three years around 1700. It will be best to let the story of this close our view of the school in the seventeenth century.

The Kynnersley papers include two lengthy effusions from the pen of John Browne himself. They can only be described as diatribes, couched in the bitterest and most plaintive of terms, emotional to the point of incoherence at times, blustering and blundering beyond the limits of decency, if not of literacy — astonishing outbursts from any man's pen, and from that of an academic man and a presumed 'gentleman' quite incredible. The earlier of the two is headed by a preamble in these terms:

> "Reasons why the Schoolmr should tarry no longer for his wages, but the Usher should now tarry without his wages as long as the Master has done ... "

John Browne then proceeds to make an uncontrolled attack upon his usher Martin Crane in the most unbridled terms — starting from the bald accusation (which in our day would certainly be actionable under the law of libel) that the usher had got himself appointed by the use of false testimonials, was notoriously incapable of doing his work, was idle as well as incompetent and dishonest, and so on and so on and so on. The real onus of the headmaster's complaint, however, seems to rest on the fact that the governors have rebuilt the usher's house and so run out of the funds necessary to pay the headmaster's salary promptly and in full. That this had really happened is proved by an examination of the governors' minute-book: undoubtedly John Browne had been shabbily treated by his governors. But whether he deserved to be so treated is a matter for consideration. Certainly his first document of complaint does more to damn him than any evidence from any other source could have done. It brands him as vulgar, petty, spiteful, ignorant, lacking in self-control — a pathetic figure, but one for whom it is quite impossible to feel any warmth or sympathy. We remember now our strong impression that the succession of puritan headmasters who had filled the post through the middle decades of the century had been essentially decent men, certainly dignified and scholarly men, of a mental and moral substance which commanded respect and admiration. Moreover they came from diverse and distant origins, evidently drawn to Stourbridge as to a place of good repute, and clearly committed to the enhancing of that repute as far as it lay in them to do. The contrast presented by John Browne was extreme. He was, it is true, a university man, entered at Pembroke College, Oxford in 1667, but he was also a local boy, the son of John, of Kidderminster, and of no note at all throughout his life. He was curate of the tiny hamlet of Mitton when ordained priest, and was teaching also at Hampton Lovett. Later for no less than seventeen years he was schoolmaster at Wolverley and curate of St. Kenelm's. He was already 42 when he came to Stourbridge, and with his background and quality of experience he could be counted exceedingly fortunate to have been appointed at all.

One can only wonder whether it was this general shoddiness of quality in John Browne which roused Robert Foley's temper and incited him to make his attacks. We know of nothing else at all, and we shall have to be content to accept something of the kind.

At all events we must turn to John Browne's second diatribe. This time the heading reads:

"A true Account of the ways and means by which the Free-school of Stourbridge was brought to its present reducement".

We pause to notice the wording, and we realise that the 'reducement' of the school must have been obvious — even notorious — for its headmaster to refer to it in this way: we are bound to think that if he himself was anything like what we have suggested he was, then we are not surprised to hear of the 'reducement'. So we read on.

The substance of the document is an accusation that John Browne and his school are the victims of *"A Complication of Lyes made by a faction in conspiracie to disgrace and spoil the school"*. He refers to complaints by parents (of excessive punishments, neglect of duty and other things), to public criticism of the bad behaviour and bad language of the boys, to the fact that the governors had left the school without an usher for a year, and had then appointed a bad one, and discouraged the headmaster by favouring the usher. He refers very emphatically to a remark made by the late bishop Stillingfleet, *"The difference between Mr. Foley and the Schoolmaster was what ye Ld. Bp. Stillingfleet said would effectually and unavoidably spoil the school"*. He traces the other evils of which he speaks clearly back to the effects of this 'difference'. Finally, he calls it *"barbarous oppression and injustice to conspire the ruin of a schoolmaster by an insidious alteration of the school statutes, fraudulently imposed on a holy Bishop and five honest governors, on pretence of reforming and raising the school"*.

It is a sorry tale, and if it were true it would brand Robert Foley as the blackest character in the school's history since the days of

Richard Alchurche. But in fact a careful examination of the new statutes of 1702,* to which John Browne took so much exception, demonstrates clearly that John Browne himself was the serpent in this Eden, and that it was his failings, both of character and of practice, which rendered the new statutes unavoidably necessary. The purpose of their changes was certainly to make it much more difficult in the future for a bad headmaster to bring the school into disorder and disrepute by reason of his failings and malpractices.

The new statutes were thus, it is safe to say, clearly intended as a radical cure for the school's ills: as statutes they were clearly not ideal, but that was no doubt because they were created to deal with a far from ideal situation. Whether they succeeded we cannot tell. The governors were doing their best to 'nail down' the unsatisfactory John Browne and to put a stop to the disastrous bickering between him and his usher. Both men were constrained to sign in due form, at the end of the governors' minute-book, a document required by the new statutes in the shape of an 'oath of allegiance and submission'. This they did on 7 December 1702. By that time Robert Foley was dead, and that may have helped things to settle down. But there was to be very little time for anyone to assess how far the problem had been solved. For in little more than another year John Browne himself was dead, and his hated usher was left to hold the fort (though not, be it noted, to teach the upper school) during the protracted battle which the governors fought out amongst themselves over the choice of his successor.

---

*The case for this has been made out in detail in the paper entitled '*Mr. Browne and Mr. Crane, 1699-1704.* and the reader is referred to this.

The Early Eighteenth Century: Thomas Wentworth

Robert Foley died in the latter half of the year 1702. John Browne died in January 1704. We have suggested that it was their enmity ('difference' was the word which Browne himself said was used by bishop Stillingfleet) which set the school by the ears at the end of the seventeenth century. That must be essentially true, but it cannot be the whole story, because the faction and strife went on after they had both departed from the scene.

The complex and lengthy story of the appointment of John Browne's successor has been told in the paper entitled *The Appointment of John Wentworth 1704-5*, and once again the reader is referred to this. It will be remembered also that we described how the unearthing of that story (much of the evidence coming from the Wheeler-Kynnersley papers) opened up an astonishing picture of political intrigue and the working of patronage in England at the time. It will not be advisable, and it would certainly be unsuitable, to tell the whole story again in detail here. But we must try to add a sensible and relevant commentary.

The two main conclusions to be drawn from the evidence of the archives about this incident were (1) that the issue lay between four of the eight governors who were Whigs and four who were Tories, (2) that the Foley family took a central part in the dispute, that the two opposing factions were led by a Foley on the one side and a Foley agent on the other, the two branches of the family being in opposition, and that the Stourbridge Foleys represented the Whigs, while the 'great' Foleys were Tories.

If we look at the composition of the school's governing body for the relevant period, we shall find much to our purpose. In 1697, when Robert Foley attempted what we have called 'the Foley trick', there were only six governors — Foley himself (from 1696), Humphrey Jeston, a Stourbridge clothier (from 1661), John Wheeler, agent and representative of the 'great' Foleys, later to reside at Wollaston Hall, a newcomer to the parish and a stranger (from 1691), Edward Milward, of the ancient and dominant family who owned most of Wollescote and who had been governors of the grammar school for generations (from 1683), William Tristram, steelmaker, the first of the Belbroughton Tristrams to settle in Stourbridge and to go into the local industry, and Edward Hickman, another Stourbridge clothier, of the family which owned the Green Close and lived next but one below the school. Of these six we know that Foley himself, Jeston and Milward were Whigs, while Wheeler and Tristram were Tories. Hickman's allegiance is not known.

In December 1699 the governors moved to fill up the two vacancies. One of these was due to the death of Samuel Hunt. He was a close associate of the 'great' Foleys, and so must have been a Tory. But he was replaced by Francis Clare, a prominent member of a prominent local family and a Justice of the Peace. Clare was certainly active in the Whig interest, and his signature was the first of 109 at the foot of a public petition addressed to the Lord Chancellor in favour of the Whig candidate for the headmastership. The other vacancy was caused by the removal from Oldswinford parish *several years previously* of John Sparry. Of his family and their importance in the history of the school we have already had much to say. Here the point of interest is that not only had the governors not attempted to replace John Sparry, as they were bound by the charter to do, but they now proceeded to "nominate, elect, reinstate and confirm" him as a governor. So we find them once again playing fast and loose with the rules of their proper procedures in a way that is strongly reminiscent of the activities of their Tudor predecessors — and no one seems to have complained. When it came to the political tug-of-war, Sparry turned out to be a Whig. So there is no discernible political pattern so far in the governors' elections.

Shortly afterwards Francis Clare asked the governors to release him from his post because of his years and infirmities. He was promptly replaced by the new rector of Oldswinford, William Hallifax. He was an appointee of the 'great' Foleys, and rapidly became the leader, or joint leader with Wheeler, of the Tory faction.

At the same time William Tristram resigned, just as Clare had done, on the grounds of age and infirmity, and was replaced by his son, William Tristram junior, also a steelmaker and also a Tory. That was late in 1700. Two years later Robert Foley died and Richard Hickman resigned because of age and infirmity (the third such resignation in three years!). These two were replaced by Richard Baker, a mercer who lived next to the school and who was a Tory, and by Thomas Oliver, another Whig. There was now no Foley on the governing body, but waiting in the wings, as it were, and to be elected in 1708 as successor to the Tory John Wheeler, deceased, was Robert Foley's son, North Foley, who certainly played the leading part, even before he became a governor, in the Whig faction throughout the battle over Wentworth's appointment.

The important thing about all these changes is their lack of any kind of political pattern. Whig replaces Tory and vice-versa with apparent ease, so that the eventual outcome — an evenly balanced pair of fours out of eight, which could be considered as the most costly element, from the school's point of view, in the whole series of events — seems to have been due merely to the chance outcome of a series of accidents. If either faction had managed to tot up its numbers to five, there would have been no deadlock, no conflict, probably no 'incident' at all, certainly no complex and lengthy dossier of records.

The purpose of going over these perhaps rather tedious pages of details is to show that however sophisticated, comparatively speaking, life had become in the century since Madstard, and however complex the system of political wire-pulling, intrigue, manoeuvre and counter-manoeuvre, in the world of patronage and polish which had come about in the course of history, nevertheless there was still much that was rough and ready, almost naive and rustic, in the game as it was played by the men of Stourbridge in the year 1704. One wonders, indeed, just how seriously they took their politics, if they could cheerfully replace Tory with Whig and vice-versa amongst their number of eight. Evidently they either did not foresee the importance of their respective political allegiances and those of the newcomers to their company of eight, or else they did not take them seriously. When it came to the point, of course, they showed themselves adamantly intransigent to the point of unreason. But they seem to have arrived at their impasse without deliberation and as if by chance. Probably the truth of the matter is that they were governors, townsmen, old boys of the school, friends and acquaintances first — and politicians last. The Foleys, who had stepped into the great world and still had a foot in it, brought the politics of that world back to Stourbridge and fostered the trouble which sprang from their introduction. In other words it was the Foleys who were, in the strictest sense of the term, the troublemakers. The others were ordinary men who simply liked having their own way and who objected very strongly indeed to getting the worse of an argument.

In the end it would be difficult to say who, if anyone, did get the worse of the argument over the appointment of the headmaster. That argument terminated with the unanimous vote of the governors to appoint John Wentworth. He had started as the Tory candidate favoured by the faction led by John Wheeler and Dr. William Hallifax. But he was later dropped by them; and when after some time he reappeared on the scene (in a letter written to John Wheeler by the Tories' legal adviser Edward Dyson) he was there reported as stating that "Mr. Foley and his party" — i.e. the Whigs — "had assured him of being elected, if you and the Dr. will concur therein." How he effected this strange conjuring-trick remains a mystery, but effect it somehow he did — so it is perhaps not surprising that in the end all eight governors voted to appoint him. He had managed to make it impossible to say that either party had won, or lost!

After his appointment, in February of 1705, the school went quietly and uneventfully along its way for no fewer than 27 years, throughout the period of Wentworth's term of office. Then on 4th September 1732 he was suddenly dismissed by his governors for gross neglect of his duties. He appears to have sent the boys home for the Whitsuntide holidays, and then simply to have abandoned his post, removed himself to a distance of seventy-five miles from Stourbridge, and simply stayed away. His dismissal was confirmed at a governors' meeting of 2nd October 1732, and although he was able, by taking his stand upon the wording of the school's charter, to defy the dismissal to the extent that he remained 'on the books' and drew at least part of his salary until his death early in 1741, nevertheless his tenure of office as active headmaster was in fact terminated by his dismissal.

So Wentworth left the school in conflict, as he had come to it in conflict. The strange thing is that throughout the 27 years between those two conflicts there appears to have been undisturbed peace; after further study however, one is tempted to say that it was a period of somnolence. The early part of the eighteenth century was in any case typically a period of stagnation in the church, the universities and the academic world generally. The characteristic Church of England parson or scholar was indolent in his spiritual and professional life, perfunctory in his devotions and devoted mainly to his own comfort. Perhaps this was what the young but perspicacious Samuel Johnson meant when he said that Wentworth was "an able man but an idle man ..." Perhaps that also was the reason why the school had more than a quarter of a century under Wentworth of placid calm. It was not just Wentworth who was indolent. He was only typical of the whole educational world of his time. The spiritual leaders and educators were merely 'going through the motions.' So too, not surprisingly, were the lay trustees who were charged with the guidance and management of the pious founders' endowments, their funds, their properties and their purposes. It is a fair assumption that if Wentworth was capable (as he certainly showed himself to be) of doing what he did at Whitsuntide of 1732, then he was never from the beginning a devoted worker, a gifted administrator or a keen and inspiring teacher. And it would be surprising if his governors even noticed his lack of enthusiasm as anything to be remarked upon, let alone criticised, since the indications are that they shared it to the full.

The clearest and most immediate evidence for this lack of commitment (neglect would be too strong a term) on the part of the eighteenth-century governors is to be found in the records of their attendance at governors' meetings, written out in the contemporary minute-book which we still possess and which tells the whole story. We have already referred to the career as a governor of John Sparry. He was already a governor of long standing in the year 1697, but the minute-book shows that at that time he had not attended a governors' meeting since at any rate 1688 (which is the date when the minute-book begins) — and this for the extraordinary reason that he had indubitably departed from the parish with his family and gone to live elsewhere. He was thus disqualified under the terms of the charter from serving, and ought to have been replaced at once. Instead, the governors kept him on the books, as it were, for over ten years, and then, we have seen, in 1699 re-elected him, after stoutly resisting Robert Foley's attempt to have him replaced. Even more remarkable is the story of John Wheeler. This was not the John Wheeler who served for more than twenty years until 1708 and was the leader of the Tory faction in 1704-5, but a third representative of that family name, elected in December 1726 in succession to a Richard Wheeler, elected in 1719. We do not know the relationships between these men, or even whether they were of the same family, though that seems probable. The remarkable thing about the second John Wheeler however, is the astonishing fact that throughout the whole seven years of his governorship, from December 1726 to December 1733, he never attended a single governors' meeting! Moreover, in May of 1733 we learn that the annual audit was rendered abortive because John Wheeler, officially deputed by his colleagues to serve as 'collector' for the year, had neither acted as such nor deputed anyone else to do the work in his stead. In the following December he was finally declared to have ceased to be a governor by reason of his having "removed from the town of Stourbridge and parish of Oldswinford with his family".

These two examples by themselves throw a cold and unflattering light on the devotion of the governors during that period to the duties and responsibilities of their office and on their attention to the rules of their procedures. Furthermore the minute-book discloses that the normal practice was to hold only one formal meeting in the course of the year, on Trinity Monday, when they passed the audit of the 'collector's account' showing the income and expenditure for the year, and dealt with other matters concerning the management of the school's properties. Matters concerning the management of the school itself were either not discussed or not thought important enough for the discussion and decisions to be recorded. Extra meetings did take place, but occasionally, for the purpose of appointing a master or usher, or to fill vacancies on the governing body: and that was all. These extra meetings were not very frequent. In the period from October 1700 to July 1710 there were fifteen governors' meetings *in all*. Somewhat later in the century there was a very important extra meeting — on Saturday, 2nd November 1728. The chosen day of the week on that occasion was not merely unusual, it was unique. Six governors attended, and that was more than at any previous meeting since 1st June 1724. The last time all eight governors had attended a meeting was on 20th February 1705 — and that was the red-letter day on which the great crisis of 1704-5 was resolved and John Wentworth was elected headmaster! Edward Milward missed seven meetings in succession after May 1714, covering a period of no less than five years. Thomas Hunt attended one meeting only between 12th February 1722, when he was elected, and 11th September 1727, when he was replaced. John Jeston served for nine years, from February 1719 to September 1728; during that time he attended nine meetings and missed ten.

So if we had to write a report on the performance of these eighteenth-century worthies as governors, we should be bound to sum it up in some such phrase as "Honest but idle", or "Could take more interest", or "Does not really seem to try". Clearly they were not 'on the job', as Madstard, for example, had been. Clearly again, of course, they were not 'on the make', in the manner of Elcoxe or Perrott or Thomson. Times, indeed, had changed. On the other hand there was evidently no change in the local importance and prestige of the office of governor of the grammar school. They were still 'the people who mattered' in the community, as they had been in Madstard's time and ever since.

These, then were the governors, and this was the school, at the time when it opened its doors to admit the boy who was to become immeasurably the most illustrious of its pupils. He, of course, was Samuel Johnson, and no history of the school could conceivably pass over his advent in silence. Not, of course, that his importance was in any way recognised at the time. How could it be? Nor is his name ever even mentioned in any of the whole vast array of records in the school archives. As far as those records are concerned, Samuel Johnson might never have existed. It is from the other end, from the Johnsonian scholars and their associates, hot on the trail of what we have called 'Dr. Johnson's waistcoat buttons', that we pick up crumbs of information to illuminate the school's history, rather than the reverse. That is probably why we know a good deal about these early eighteenth-century governors. It was in a paper presented to the Johnson Society of Lichfield in 1969 that Samuel Johnson's family connections with the Stourbridge Grammar School were followed out. That paper forms the basis of our next paragraphs thought it happens, no doubt by the force of serendipity, that two other prime sources of information have presented themselves to our enquiries in the course of the years. One of these is the dossier discovered in the school archives concerning the foundation of St. Thomas's church in Stourbridge; the other is owed entirely to the work and devotion of Peter Prattinton (1776-1841), a Bewdley grocer who was also an inspired and indefatigable antiquarian and collector of Worcestershire 'evidences'. One of those evidences was the day-book of a Stourbridge attorney, Thomas Milward (1670-1724). This man was the son of Edward Milward, whom we have recently met as a governor of the school. Thomas undoubtedly acted as legal adviser to the Whig faction on the governing body of the school during the battle over the appointment of a headmaster. Both the foundation of St. Thomas's and Thomas Milward's Day-book have been fully treated in two separate studies by the present author, and these also will be drawn upon for our purposes.*

Samuel Johnson came to Stourbridge or more precisely to Pedmore, in the autumn of 1725, at the age of 16, stayed until Whitsuntide of 1726, entered King Edward's school immediately after that, and stayed there until about the end of October in the same year. In fact, he ended his schooldays there. He came originally on a family visit, and stayed with his cousin, the Reverend Cornelius Ford. The two cousins evidently got on well together, and Cornelius must have felt some responsibility when Samuel's headmaster at Lichfield refused to have him back in the school there when he presented himself after his lengthy absence. So the Ford family influence was put to work and the young Johnson was admitted as a 'stranger' under John Wentworth at Stourbridge. He was already, of course, enormously learned for his age, and the tradition has it that Wentworth used him as a sort of supernumerary usher. There is no evidence for this, but it would not be out of keeping with Wentworth's known character for indolence. Johnson, as we have seen, recognised the headmaster's ability as a scholar, was aware of his idleness, and evidently did not get on with him. In after years he accepted that he himself and his situation were responsible for this. Boswell put it as follows:

> "Mr. Wentworth (he told me) was a very able man, but an idle man, and to me very severe; but I cannot blame him much. I was then a big boy; he saw I did not reverence him, and that he should get no honour by me. I had brought enough with me to carry me through; and all I should get at his school would be ascribed to my own labour, or to my former master. Yet he taught me a great deal.

He thus discriminated to Dr. Percy, the bishop of Dromore, his progress at his two grammar schools ... 'At one, I learned much in the school but little from the master; in the other, I learnt much from the master, but little in the school'."

---

*St. Thomas's Church, Stourbridge: the Story of its Foundation, 1979: Thomas Milward's Day-book, 1976. (Both published by the Dudley Teachers' Centre.)

Samuel Johnson's connection with Stourbridge is essentially a connection with Fords and Hickmans. His mother's brother was a Stourbridge physician, Dr. Joseph Ford (1662-1720) who had been a governor of the school from 1710 until his death five years before Samuel's visit. Joseph's younger brother Nathaniel Ford (1676-1729) was a mercer and clothier, also of Stourbridge and still alive. In 1690 Joseph Ford had married Jane, the recent widow of Gregory Hickman (1651-1690). This man also was a clothier of Stourbridge, a wealthy and prominent citizen, who lived in and owned the Green Close House, a large residence with much ground, next but one below the school on the High Street. Jane Hickman, now Jane Ford, after fifteen years of marriage already had three daughters — Mary, Jane and Honor — and one son, Gregory Hickman II (so defined here only to distinguish him from his father). The son was born in 1688, and so was a man of 37 at the time of his cousin Samuel Johnson's visit. Gregory Hickman II had succeeded to the Green Close House when he came of age in 1709, and became a governor of the grammar school in 1713. But in 1721 he lost his governorship when he went off with his family and became a merchant in the city of Chester. He returned to Stourbridge in or about 1724, and was to be re-elected a governor in 1733, by which time he would be living at Wollaston Hall. Gregory Hickman II was brought up, of course, at Green Close where his mother Jane Ford produced five children by her second marriage: of these Ann (b.1692), Cornelius (1694) and Phoebe (1696) — all Ford — survived when their cousin Samuel Johnson came to the town in 1725. So he had three full cousins (Fords) and four cousins by marriage (Hickmans), all but one living locally. The two Ford girls were unmarried; Cornelius lived at Pedmore and had just taken deacon's orders after holding a fellowship at Cambridge. Mary Hickman was married to an Acton of Halesowen, Honor to Daniel Scott, another Stourbridge clothier who was a governor of the grammar school since 1721 and who lived in a Hickman house below the Green Close on the High Street. It is always Daniel Scott who is said by the Johnsonians to have been the governor whose influence decided that Samuel should be admitted to the school. Jane Hickman had complicated the relationship by marrying her stepfather Joseph Ford's younger brother Nathaniel, above mentioned, and so became Samuel Johnson's Aunt Jane.

We now pass to Cornelius Ford, with whom Johnson stayed during the first half of his visit to Stourbridge. Boswell describes him as "*the Rev. Mr. Ford, a man in whom both talents and good dispositions were disgraced by licentiousness!*" He was certainly well known for this quality and is said to have been the original of the drunken parson in Hogarth's satirical picture, A Modern Midnight Conversation. He was a considerable scholar and wit, later a profligate and parson, who married for money, was prosecuted for fraud, imprisoned for debt, and died in a London pot-house, to which his unquiet ghost shortly afterwards returned. He was born in 1694, presumably at the Green Close, where he was brought up with his half-brother Gregory and his half-sisters. In 1725 he was a man of 31, recently married to an heiress of 40 and living at Pedmore. He had gone away to school at Mansfield, to Cambridge in 1710, where he graduated B.A. in 1713 and M.A. in 1720, and held a fellowship from 1720 to 1724. He had recently taken deacon's orders and was soon to use his wife's money to purchase the advowson of South Luffenham rectory in Rutland, before presenting himself to the living in 1727. It may seem a harsh judgement to say that he was a typical establishment parson of his time, but one is tempted to do so.

It has been argued by devout Johnsonians, in view of his latter end, which was utterly disreputable, that his drunken profligacy disgraced only his later years, and that his cousin Samuel, who clearly liked him, found in him a responsible, elegant, scholarly, respectable and sober man, well befitting the quiet and genteel circle of provincial society in which he moved and into which he introduced his clever but ungainly cousin. This impression, however, is in reality a long way from the truth.

The truth is that Gregory Hickman's circle in Stourbridge was a dissipated set of drinkers and gamblers. The evidence, which is irrefutable, is to be found in Thomas Milward's day-book. For Thomas Milward was himself most certainly a gambler, and he recorded his losses (and occasional gains) as faithfully and regularly as he recorded his outlay on household expenses. His gambling companions included Dr. Joseph Ford, Gregory Hickman, John Henzey, John Jeston, William Tristram and North Foley — every one of them at one time a governor of the grammar school — as well as Cornelius Ford, reverend by title but hardly, so it would seem, by habit of life.

Prattinton says of Thomas Milward's gambling: "On a very hasty sketch he appears to have lost, in 1699 – £62.15.0d; 1700 – £51.16.0d; 1701 – £177.14.0d; 1702 – £102.1.0d; 1703, a year of abstinence, – £3.0.0d; and 1704 – £132.19.0d. He also lost three watches; he sold his black mare to a Capt. Bradley for 34 gross of glass buttons (Can he have been sober at the time?) He bought three pairs of dice in London for Mr. Daniel Clarke, his great friend, and host of the Talbot in Stourbridge. He ran the Stourbridge horse-races and bought the plate for the prizes, also in London, on several occasions. His gambling games included hazard (i.e. dice), cards and hustle-in-the-hat, a form of pitch-and-toss. One day in 1704 he "lost at Hazard at the Talbot with Mr. Chas. Lyttelton and *Mr. John Henzey* — 49 guineas; he forgave me four: again — £21." On one day in 1699 he "lost at cards with Mr. Wm. and Mr. Roger Waldron and *Wm Tristram* — £10.0.0d", and again "Lost at Hustle-in-the-hat to Mr. Waldron — £5.0.0d".

These were not insignificant amounts in those days, and these gamesters were by no means 'penny-punters'. In the second of the two surviving pieces of the day-book, covering the years 1715-20 and therefore much nearer to Samuel Johnson's visit to his cousin, the gambling element is if anything more prominent. He lost money in 1719 "at the cocking" and again "at the horse-race". He provided a bull for a man named Thomas Blount, to be baited "on Monday and Tuesday next at Kinfare Wake".

The picture is all of a piece — gaming, horse-racing, cock-fighting, bull-baiting. These were the pursuits of an English provincial gentleman of the time of George I. As for Thomas Milward's dealings with the particular circle of Gregory Hickman, here is an incomplete but illuminating summary.

1715	Jan 1st.	Lost at *Mr. Hickman's* — Mr. Arthur Dean, Mr. *John Wheeler* and J. *Henzey* at Hazard ...	£17.0.0d
	Jan 23	Spent with Thomas Littleton Esq, and Will Plowman Esq, Mr. W. Foley, *John Henzey* and *Gregory Hickman* at the Talbot at cards and Hazard ...	£5.7.6d
	Mar 3rd	Lost at the Talbot at Hazard with *Mr. Gregory Hickman* ...	£16.12.6d
1717	Nov 18	Gave to *Mr. North Foley's* man when I drank punch and supped there and *Mr Gregory Hickman* struck me and I returned ...	£0.1.0d
1718	Sept 17	Repaid *Mr. Gregory Hickman* what he gave me for 5 pictures when in his cups the 15th evening ...	£0.5.0d
1719	May 25	Won of *Mr. Gregory Hickman* and *Dr. Ford* at Hazard at the Talbot, though very much concerned with wine and punch. Mr. Hum.	

> Butcher being present and sober said the Dice
> were changed and several unfair things
> offered, which he prevented. Scarcely sober
> when I began to play, yet by strange luck won
> ... £25.14.0d

By any reckoning this was a dissipated social set, and the Hickmans, Dr. Ford and the Foleys were all in it. Cornelius Ford appears only once in the day-book, but the story seems perhaps to betray a streak of depravity in him at the age of 23 which required very little training in London to develop into that of the central figure in Hogarth's Midnight Modern Conversation. He may have gone to Mansfield for his Classics, but his dissipation he surely learned at home in Stourbridge. One wonders what Samuel Johnson really thought of him.

> 1717 Nov 21 Paid to Mr. Foley as a wager with Mr.
> Cornelius Ford, viz. that I was not a winner,
> nor had so much money as I brought in, viz
> 5/- and £4 borrowed of Mrs. Clarke: upon
> search it appeared I had only £3.11.1 but Mr.
> Ford was very busy and not only obliged me
> to strip naked, on pretence of his more exact
> search, but unless I would yield the wager lost
> — which was fairly won — he swore he
> would rip every stitch of my coat, wasitcoat
> and breeches; and he did begin to rip them
> and forced me to sit naked for a long time,
> and afterwards took my Coat, Waistcoat and
> Breeches with him. So Mr. Foley is to pay me
> 10/-. £0.5.0d.

So much for Mr. Cornelius Ford's youthful respectability! As for Thomas Milward, apart from wondering how on earth he managed to get home to Wollescote that night, we can now leave him to enjoy the relaxations of his private life, at the Talbot or at Green Close or wherever his grammar school cronies foregathered. In public he — and they — doubtless retained the image of eminent respectability which was proper to the governors of the school. That image made it the most natural thing in the world for anyone who aimed to be a benefactor to the town and parish in any way to follow the example of many who had travelled the same path in years gone by, and to name the governors of King Edward's School as the trustees of his benefaction.

So it was when six of the governors assembled at the school for their important meeting on Saturday 2nd November 1728. On that occasion they had been brought together to be informed of a benefaction which was to have a great effect upon the history of the school for the next hundred and fifty years. They were being asked to accept formally a legacy of £200 (together with interest of six pounds added) under the will of one John Biggs, yet another of the Stourbridge clothiers, for the purpose of erecting a chapel, to be built in the town of Stourbridge for divine service according to the usage of the established Church. The money was clearly not enough in itself for its stated purpose, and it devolved upon the governors to set up a separate body of trustees (including some of their own number) to receive subscriptions from a public appeal.

All this they did, and in the fulness of time the chapel (later to become St. Thomas's church) was built, upon land bought for the purpose, and the first minister took office in 1736.

This minister was none other than the Rev. Walter Hickman. He was born the son of Richard Hickman, clothier of Stourbridge. This Richard was nephew of Gregory I of the Green Close, and so cousin to Gregory Hickman II. Richard Hickman died young in 1710, leaving a widow Dorothy, who was a Moseley of Enville, together with an infant son Walter, born in 1709. Gregory Hickman II proceeded in all haste to marry his cousin Richard's widow (in the year 1711) and took on the two-year-old Walter as his stepson.

We now see why Gregory Hickman II (who we remember ceased to be a governor of the grammar school while he was at Chester from 1721 to 1724) now came back into the fold and was re-elected, to fill the vacancy caused by the departure of John Wheeler, in 1733. There could be no doubt that the governors would be in a very strong position to influence events when it came to the choice of a minister for the new chapel. Walter Hickman, now in his mid-twenties and a graduate of Christ Church, Oxford, was a very suitable candidate (who better?) for the incumbency of the new chapel.

So it turned out; and it is difficult not to conclude that that first appointment of a protege of the grammar-school coterie must have had a powerful effect upon the later history of St. Thomas's and its connection with the grammar school. The next four ministers in succession, though not Walter Hickman himself, were all headmasters of the school as well as ministers of the chapel. From the early 1740's until 1858 the two offices were always held by the same man. It is perhaps more than a coincidence that it was during that period also that the fortunes — and value — of the school reached their lowest ebb. But when the church was founded, all that, of course, was still in the future.

The establishment of St. Thomas's brought a good deal of conflict with it. There was contention almost from the beginning.

We know from the governor's minute-book that the governors were united at first in forwarding the progress of the new chapel. In November of 1728 they accepted the legacy from the estate of John Biggs, paid over by one of their own numbers, Joseph Best, who was the executor of John Biggs' estate. They deputed another of their number, Thomas Saunders, to oversee the spending of the original £206 on the building-work. Seven months later they endorsed his account of how the money had been spent, and recorded the details in the minutes of their proceedings as governors. In December 1731 they formally accepted an additional sum of £100 from the Biggs estate for the furtherance of the building of the chapel, and in December of 1734 they once again endorsed Thomas Saunders' account of how he had fulfilled this second part of his stewardship. In this last minute we read for the first time the signature of Gregory Hickman, re-elected the previous year after an absence of twelve years from the governing body, which we have noted. Here also we see it recorded that the Rev. George Wigan, rector of Oldswinford, in whose parish the new chapel was being built, had not only joined the other governors in welcoming and supporting the project, but had actually lent cash for the purpose, and was now being reimbursed for his loan to the extent of £57.7.4d out of the total £100 which was being accounted for.

It was around this stage that the contention arose. For when it came to the point of settling the constitution of the new church, there were two opposing factions among the interested parties. The rector, George Wigan, following his patron, Thomas Lord Foley, and in close concert with Gregory Hickman, wanted the new chapel to be constituted as the church of a new parish. Foley and Wigan insisted that the chapel could be used only by consent of themselves and the bishop. Gregory Hickman was suspected of wanting the rector and his patron to put his own stepson Walter Hickman into possession of the new chapel, and of following their lead for that reason. The opposition was led by Thomas Milward, one of the trustees but not a governor of the school, though his brother Edward had been elected in 1728 and the Milwards were one of the chief 'dynastic' families in the history of the school. Thomas was a solicitor, as his father had been (see page 93-4) and as legal adviser to John Biggs he was the originator of the idea that Biggs should leave his money to provide a chapel in Stourbridge.

Walter Hickman seems to have taken possession of the new church in 1736 regardless of the opposition of the Milward faction, and stayed there until his early death in 1742. He subsisted on an income of about £80 a year, which he derived from pew-rents, and neither the rector nor the patron gave anything at all. The public of Stourbridge apparently accepted this arrangement under the impression that the minister was in truth a curate, whom the rector had the right to nominate. The next step, indeed, was a public petition actually asking Lord Foley to have the chapel made into a parish church by act of parliament; this the Foley party proceeded to do, or rather to try to do; and the three principals brought the bill into parliament. It made out a very good case for Stourbridge's need of a church *in the town*, independent of Oldswinford. It asked for the creation of a new parish, the presentation to be in the hands of Lord Foley, the parish to be exempt from tithes, and its income to be derived from a glebe, which was to be created by the enclosure of parts of Stourbridge Common.

Thomas Milward's party took the strongest exception to all this. Their case was as follows:

> The Church belonged to the inhabitants, who had subscribed £2000 to provide it. The rector was now claiming it *without any right* as a chapel of ease, claiming also to appoint the minister, but refusing to help to support the living, and proposing into the bargain to rob the inhabitants of part of their common land for the purpose. The rector was also bamboozling the public into believing that they could not use the chapel without the consent of the rector and the patron. Moreover, now that the first minister Walter Hickman, had died, the pew-rents had ceased with him, and Wigan had proceeded to argue that as the trustees would not allow him to put in his own nominee, and as the public would not subscribe for an income, he and Lord Foley would now exercise their right to stop the chapel's being used, and would shut it up. The public were so alarmed by this threat that they had offered to put in a curate and pay him themselves. But the rector had refused to agree even to this, got up the petition for the bill, and without giving any proper notice of any public meeting to consider it had induced some people to sign it in the

mistaken belief that unless they agreed the chapel would be shut. A further objection raised by Thomas Milward was that the proposed enclosure of common land would seriously damage the raising of sheep which was essential to the local manufacture of fine narrow cloths and would be disastrous to the principal clothiers of Stourbridge, as well as to many of the poor.

That was the main drift of Thomas Milward's case. Gregory Hickman, in spite of Walter's death, persisted in his support of the bill, and in April 1742 he was hopeful that its promotion would be successful. But in fact the bill was defeated. Thomas Milward wrote the following comment:

"Thos. Lord Foley grasping at this Chappel brought a bill into the house of Commons by the treachery of the Rector Geo. Wigan and Greg. Hickman to make this a parochial Church and settle the nomination in Lord Foley and to take part of the Common to endow it. I then offered Lord Foley, if he would endow it, and let the inhabitants of the Town sit in the Chappel without paying for their seats, or be eased in their payments, and if the Rector and Lord Foley would allow the Easter dues arising in the Township towards the maintenance of the Minister, that I would consent to the bill. Which Lord Foley and the Rector refusing, I opposed the bill, and by a Committee of the whole house the bill by a second reading was thrown out, after Lord Foley had paid the fees of the house."

For much of the detail concerning St. Thomas's, especially in the matter of its consitution and the moves and counter-moves of the two opposing parties who were concerned, I am indebted to Miss Sylvia Edward's excellent history of that church (in the original version of 1952, Mark and Moody). The issues, legal and constitutional, which were raised by the creation of the church in the town of Stourbridge, are difficult and troublesome, and it is not easy at first to see what the two parties were aiming at and why. Perhaps the best starting-point is to remind ourselves that an Anglican church and its living constituted a piece of property, which could change hands by sale or gift like a piece of land, and which had a monetary value. Originally most English parish churches were provided by the baron of the manor, and such a foundation became an adjunct to the manor. Hence the attachment in so many cases of the advowson, or right of presentation of an incumbent to the living, to the manor, considered as a piece of property (whose value included and was enhanced by that attachment). Such original parishes usually included amongst their provisions an allotment of land within the manor to provide a basic endowment. This was known as the glebe. The inhabitants of the parish were then liable under the law to make up 'the living' by the payment of tithes.

The problem of the new chapel at Stourbridge was that it had no clearly-established owner, or patron, and was set up within the territorial limits of an existing parish, that of Oldswinford (By an accident of history the town and centre of population had grown up inconveniently far from the original parish church, which must have been established at Oldswinford long before Stourbridge town came into being.) In such a situation normally (as at Stourbridge itself in 1430, when the Chapel of the Trinity, later the grammar school, was founded) the new chapel was considered to be a 'chapel of ease' to the parish church, and its priest was a curate under the authority of the rector of the parish. In such a case, however, it was to be expected that the chapel of ease *would be provided by, and therefore the property of, the patron of the parish*. But this new chapel was in fact provided by a public subscription promoted by a body of trustees in augmentation of a private person's legacy. This was why Thomas Milward accused the patron of 'grasping after' the chapel by seeking to establish it as the church of a new parish, carved out of Oldswinford: for the patron wanted the chapel to be *in his gift*, i.e. *his property*, and yet he refused to provide land for a glebe out of his own demesne, and thrust that burden onto the backs of the inhabitants, who were to bear it by the loss of part of their common. Foley wanted things all his own way, and if one reduces his motive to the simplest, we are bound to put it down as essentially greed. That also was why Milward spoke of the rector's 'treachery' in supporting the patron's wishes. For Wigan was backing him up in order to grind his own axe by currying favour with Lord Foley. On the face of it his support of the bill to create a new parish out of the body of his own Oldswinford looked like noble self-sacrifice, but in reality the motives were far different. The new parish was to cost Foley nothing and to add to his property; it was to cost Wigan nothing (for there was to be no allocation of tithes, which would in consequence remain with Oldswinford) and it would add to his prospects by giving him an extra claim on the gratitude of his patron. As for the opposition, it is hardly surprising that the prospect of handing over the fruits of two thousand pounds of good money into the hands of Lord Foley did not appeal to the inhabitants of Stourbridge. This was why they acquiesced in the idea that the new chapel was a chapel of ease and its incumbent a curate under Oldswinford. The truth is that they did not know what to do for the best, because there was no easy precedent in law for what they wanted. So what they did was to resist what they knew they did *not* want. In the outcome the legal status of St. Thomas's remained obscure and uncertain for a very long time; its ministers were commonly described in the clerical directories as 'Perpetual Curates', which they almost certainly were not, — and it was not to be until the 1860's that St. Thomas's finally emerged as a parish church; and that development does not belong to the history of King Edward's School.

This is a sorry tale of cupidity, duplicity and self-interest. It is told here because, though not essentially a part of the history of the school, it yet closely concerns the men who were guiding the school's fortunes, and does much to characterise the ethos and the atmosphere in which they operated. It is also to be remembered as important that for a very long time the headmastership of the school and the incumbency of the chapel were treated as a combined appointment, held in common by four successive occupants of those offices. The position becomes clear if we set it out as follows:

Minister of the Chapel	*Headmaster of the School*
1736–42 Rev. Walter Hickman	1741–45 John Hancox
1742–82 Rev. Charles Harris	1745–82 Charles Harris
1782–1808 Rev. John Pattinson	1782–1808 John Pattinson
1808–33 Rev. Joseph Taylor	1808–33 Joseph Taylor
1833–58 Rev. Giffard Wells	1833–58 Giffard Wells

It will be seen that the combination of the two offices did not in fact begin until 1745; the reason for this has not yet come to light; nor is it known how the situation of the joint appointment developed in the first place, and why and how it was allowed to continue as it did. No explanation is recorded in the governors minutes, nor in any other of the surviving school archives. Miss Edwards in her history of the church records that there was trouble over this issue in 1782, but why it should have occurred then is not apparent. In that year died the Rev. Charles Harris, after a long and peaceful term of office. After his death the Rev. Robert Foley, who was rector of Oldswinford and also a governor of the school, in concert with other governors proceeded to advertise the vacancy of both posts to be at the disposal of the governors. Thomas Milward, remarkably enough, was still alive, and as the sole surviving trustee of the church he resisted the governors' attempt, expressing his surprise to see that they "had reserved the Chappell for the schoolmaster *without the least Colour or Shadow of right*". He called a public meeting which unanimously supported his opposition to the rector and the governors. The rector then once again threatened to shut the church. At that point Thomas Milward for some unknown reason changed course and nominated the rector's choice — the Rev. John Pattinson. The townspeople, however, reacted violently (which was hardly surprising) and there were unseemly scenes in the town. Eventually Thomas Milward nominated new trustees, and established that it was their right to manage the church. Even so, Pattinson continued as Minister, and Headmaster, for twenty-five years. His successor, the Rev. Joseph Taylor, followed him — it seems peacefully — in both offices, and was also vicar of Snitterfield in Warwickshire. The peace then continued until 1833, when he died. His death, however, was the signal for a renewal of trouble, with more unseemly scenes — what Miss Edwards describes as "an outburst of the most outrageous behaviour among the inhabitants, in connection with the election of a new minister". She describes the proceedings as being like a parliamentary election; two of the candidates were Giffard Wells, already headmaster of the grammar school, and his usher, the Rev. J. M. Kirby, whom he publicly accused of lying and dishonesty in his candidature. Giffard Wells, as we have gathered, was elected, and once again peace reigned, so far as the church was concerned.

This matter of St. Thomas's Church has been pursued and brought far ahead of the course of our main narrative, partly because it seemed more sensible to treat it as a theme in itself, and to deal with it all at once, but partly also because it will now be easier for the reader to bear in mind the important fact that until more than half way through the nineteenth century the school was to be always in the hands of a headmaster who always had another job. It cannot but be true that this reduced the efficiency of the men concerned. It must have had no good effect upon either the church or the school. The men concerned may have been amiable, even estimable, characters: they were certainly well thought of in their time, and were suitably eulogised in public expressions of appreciation when they departed. But they cannot in the nature of things have done either of their two jobs as well as if they had had only one of them to do.

Doubtless the four headmasters concerned varied in character and efficiency as much as any other four at any other time in the long history of the school. Doubtless no observer at any given time during the "St. Thomas's Period" would have recognised that the school was passing through such a period, or even have let it cross his mind that this was a stage in the school's history which had had a recognisable beginning and would have a recognisable end. But in fact it was so. Never before this period had the school been like this: never after this period would it be like it again.

We shall therefore deal with what we have called "the St. Thomas's period" as a chapter in itself. But we must first go back and remind ourselves of the last incident which we recorded in the main line of our narrative, the dismissal of John Wentworth in 1732 (see page 90). This leaves us with a period of thirteen years to cover before the first appointment of a headmaster who was also the minister of the new church. It is a period about which we know little, except that the school collectors' accounts, surviving in the governors' minute-book, show us that the financial confusion and stringency caused by Wentworth's dismissal lasted on, not only until his death in 1741, but until after the death of his successor in 1745.

The exact terms of Wentworth's dismissal are as follows:

"Whereas John Wentworth Batchelor of Laws Headmaster of ... etc ... without leave of the Governors of the said school or the major part of them did at the boys' Breaking up at Whitsuntide last allow and appoint the whole space of time from Thursday the 25th day of May until Monday the 26th day of June for such vacation or Breaking up, when by the orders of the said school the time ought to be from Wednesday before Whitsunday which was the 24th day of May until Monday after Trinity Sunday which was the 5th June, which unlawful vacation included Twenty extraordinary days, and the said John Wentworth after the 26th day of June attended the service of the school until the 29th day of June only, and hath ever since that time without any leave given by the governors or Notice by him given absented himself and hath abdicated and declined his duty and care of the school, and by the best accounts we can inform ourselves he is and hath been during the greatest part of the said Absence at seventy five miles distance from the school, and the said John Wentworth hath severall times before been very negligent in his duty and care of the said school, we therefore, in regard to our duty and trust reposed in us doe declare such absence a wilful and negligent abdication and desertion of his duty and that he shall not have any further power or authority in the said school, or receive any further salary from henceforth or during time of such neglect. Witness our hands this 4th day of September anno Dni 1732.

Willm. Vernon, Edw. Milward, Joseph Best, John Bradley, Thomas Saunders.

The next entry, equally informative, is much shorter:

"Whereas John Wentworth late Master of ... etc ... returned upon the 21st day of September last, and we, being purposely assembled upon notice to ourselves and our brethren given, have read the entry in this book made upon the 4th day of September last, relating to his absence, which occasioned such entry, to him; and when personally asked he refused to give any reason for his absence, we therefore confirm the said former order, witness our hands this second day of October 1732.

Geo. Wigan, Willm Vernon, Jon Bradley, Edw. Milward, Jos Best, Thos. Saunders.

So, if the governors had had their way, Wentworth was 'off the books' from mid-1732. At the time his salary was £45 a year. In fact, however, the situation was never cleared up in the minutes, but we see in the accounts that payments to Wentworth go on in spite of his dissmissal. In June 1732 he is recorded as having been paid £45 in two equal instalments, being his last year's official salary; that should have been the end. But in the same account there is a significant item:

Pd. for Case to Mr. Talbott of Soll.r General upon severall things relating to School to be advis'd.	3/3/0d
To drawing of Case and fair Coppy	13/4d

So the governors suspected already that they had a case on their hands; and so they had!

In the year 1733-4 the ushers (Baylies, succeeded by Perry) were paid at the usual rate of £20. But Mr. Wentworth had £14/0/0d, followed by £21/0/0d!

On 2nd June 1735 comes the first reference to a Mr. Hancox, with no explanation offered at all:

 Pd. Mr. Hancox — 1 yr. sallary —   £30/0/0d

In the same account Mr. Wentworth is paid — "as per Receipt" — first £30/17/0d and then £15/0/0d. We have to conclude from guesswork that Mr. Hancox was the man appointed to do Wentworth's work: in other words he was the new headmaster. He was a local man, and in Fosters *Alumni Oxonienses* he is described as:

 HANCOX John, s. of John, of Hartlebury, co. Worcester, pleb. *Merton College*. Mtc. 23 June 1726, aged 18; B.A. 1730

So he was a local boy, a conveniently available graduate, aged about 26 and therefore thirty years younger than John Wentworth. During the next four years he is paid at the same rate of £30 a year, while Wentworth's payments settle down at £15. In other words Wentworth was still drawing a third of the money allotted for the head's salary, while the unfortunate Hancox was doing all the work for two thirds of the pay.

Then in March of 1741 comes a minute which clears away any doubts we may have had:

 "We elect Mr. John Hancox of Stourbridge our Head Schoolmaster in the roome and instead of Mr. John Wentworth lately deceased, upon the express condition that the salary to be paid to him be but forty pounds a year till the debts of the school are discharged."

Unfortunate Hancox indeed! For the next following accounts actually show items for "Mr. Wentworth's Annuity" — still continuing; while Mr. Hancox's salary varies unaccountably from £30 to £34/7/6 to £43, until in Thomas Saunders' account of 21 May 1744 it appears in the mysterious form:

 Pd. Mr. Hancox sallry.   £39/0/0d
 Due to him at Lady Day 1744   £13/0/0d

Whether the thirteen pounds due to him at Lady Day 1744 was ever paid, and what his official salary was, is wrapped in mystery. This did not, however, trouble him much longer; for the very next entry records:

"June 10, 1745. We the Governors of ... etc ... the majority of us meeting do elect nominate and appoint the Revd. Mr. Charles Harris of Stourbridge our Head Schoolmaster in the room and instead of the Revd. Mr. John Hancox deceased, upon this express condition, that the salary to be paid to him be but forty pounds a year till all the debts of the school are discharged."

On Trinity Monday of 1746 the accounts showed £15 cash paid to Mrs. Hancox, so her husband was evidently not paid up to date when he died. Another item shows "To Mr. Harris in full to Lady Day ... £30/0/0d." This implies three quarters of a year's salary from the date of his appointment in the previous June, and shows that the promised rate of £40 a year was being duly paid. So it continued until 1748-9, when for the first time his salary reached the 'correct' figure of £45. It had taken almost seventeen years from the time of Wentworth's dismissal for the school's finances to be got back onto a proper footing.

If we cast our mind back over the whole stretch of time, from the moment of Wentworth's appointment in 1705, after the great patronage battle, until this point when the first headmaster of the St. Thomas's period may be said to have settled in, we are struck by the fact that it is "all of a piece". These years, roughly the first half of the eighteenth century, present us with a picture, or rather a picture-gallery of typical eighteenth-century portraits. It happens by a series of accidents that we are enabled to become quite familiar with Stourbridge society and those principal figures who moved in it, and whose activities centred round the demure brick-fronted grammar-school houses near the top of the lower High Street, together with the few hundred yards of provincial townscape stretching down past the Green Close and Daniel Scott's house as far perhaps as the bridge, and in the other direction up past the market cross, still then surviving, at least to the welcoming High Street portals of the Talbot Inn. We have met the Talbot's host, "honest Daniel Clarke", who commissioned Thomas Milward to bring him new dice from London: we know that Mrs. Mary Clarke was the chief owner of the piece of land fronting onto the Ryemarket, once part of the grounds of an ancient residence called Cuckow Oak House, which the school governors, or some of them, in their capacity as publicly elected trustees, purchased for the new chapel and on which they built St. Thomas's Church. So the Ryemarket also would be within the orbit of their regular comings and goings — and then perhaps back they went to the Talbot, through the alleyways at its rear, there to get out the dice and the cards and the coins in order to while away the hours in congenial if not inexpensive company, while the black mare was fed and rubbed down in the stables (at any rate until Captain Bradley had taken her away in return for his load of glass buttons!). This was the grammar-school coterie and it is their portraits which stay in our minds and provide us with our impressions of the school during their time. It is a curious effect of the changed nature of our evidence that we have shifted our attention from the school itself, its headmasters and its ushers, its buildings and its properties, and the activities which centred upon these, and instead of this we are drawn by Thomas Milward and the Johnsonians and the story of St. Thomas's church into the pages, as it were, of a new chapter of Defoe's *Tour through the Whole Land of Great Britain*, or even of another Fielding novel.

The overriding impression which stays with us of the school itself during that half-century of its life is one of uneventfulness, and, to be truthful, of stagnation. The key figure must be Wentworth; for he ruled the school for twenty-seven years, and though he remains a shadow and a sitter-in-the-corner, and never really shows his face, yet we gather the inescapable impression of one who was "an able man, but an idle man", of whom his greatest pupil said, "He saw I did not reverence him, and that he should get no honour by me ... Yet he taught me a great deal" So Wentworth's character emerges — "Able, but idle". He came to a school which was at first so short of money after building him his new brick house that he was never paid a full salary until 1709-10. He was "severall times before very negligent in his duty and care of the said school", so that even the neglectful and essentially worldly Stourbridge governors were constrained to take note of it. He was one of only two headmasters in the history of the school (the other was the bizarre Richard Alchurche) to be dismissed from office. He went on for years after his dismissal extracting a portion of his salary from a presumably reluctant body of governors, who could certainly ill afford it. At that stage he exemplified the dilemma which faced the authorities of many endowed schools to an increasing extent as this and the succeeding century went on, and which was to be clearly set out in a remarkable document (to which we shall again refer) in the 1860's. For that document, the Taunton Commission's Report on the Endowed Schools, speaks as follows:

"Cases occur in which the trustees have in effect to make the choice between three alternatives: whether they shall allow an incompetent or negligent master to ruin the school by treating it as a sinecure, or shall risk a suit in the Court of Chancery by dismissing him, or, in fact, buy him out with a pension. The last is often the cheapest and best course."

According to the Stourbridge school's charter the governors had power to appoint a master and under-master *as often as the place of either of them should be vacant*. Wentworth, we believe, was clever enough to argue that they did not have the power to *make* his place vacant. Hence the continuation of his £15 a year until he died. Hence the items for "Mr. Wentworth's Annuity" even after that.

We can safely say that if any one man left his mark upon the Stourbridge school in the first half of the eighteenth century, that man's name was Wentworth. It is only a pity — and a great misfortune — that we do not really know him.

The St. Thomas's Period and the Dead Hand

It is a curious feature of the history of King Edward's School Stourbridge that its panorama of the past becomes less vivid and colourful as we approach closer and closer towards our own times. There is one quite simple and obvious reason for this; the astonishing array of evidences surviving from the school's earlier times is simply not matched by anything that has come to us from the last two hundred years. But it may well be also that the school has not possessed — or been possessed by — any characters remotely as memorable as those who strutted and fretted their hour upon its stage in Madstard's day; or even as those 'godly and orthodox divines' who conducted their controversies with acrimonious piety through the long winter of the Commonwealth; or as the elderly and infirm citizen and salter of London who angled for fish with his old school-fellows and listened to the advice of his old schoolmaster and stumped up the cash for the building of the school's library; or as the sociable gentlemen at the Talbot with their full-bottomed wigs and their sack and dice and their loans to and from 'honest Dan Clarke'; or even as the spitfire but pathetic John Browne, like some character in rusty black from Gil Blas or Joseph Andrews, straying onto our scene to utter his one big speech, on the edge, as it were, of his unknown grave; or even finally, as John Wentworth, that Alchurche of the Age of Reason, who held the stage and kept the play together for almost half a century, who taught the great Samuel Johnson a great deal, and who taught the gentlemen at the Talbot that they could not dismiss him lightly — and whom we do not really know. It cannot be only that distance lends enchantment to the view, or that there were giants in the earth in those days. We have to accept the simple truth that the days of high drama in the history of the school came to an end eventually, and that what followed derives a much greater proportion of its interest from the fact of its being a chapter in the history of English education than from any larger-than-life quality in the men who continued to play out the tale.

This last description — a chapter in the history of English education — is particularly apt to characterise what we have called the St. Thomas's Period, from 1745 to 1858: for our reference to 'the Dead Hand' is intended to remind us that King Edward's School, in common with the whole body of English endowed grammar schools, was entering upon a period in which the pious hand of its founder was to grasp it so tight by the throat as, in effect, to throttle the life out of it. This is the dead hand to which our phrase refers.

The medieval and Tudor grammar schools were designed for the conditions of the medieval and Tudor world. They were intended to take the cleverer children of the poor, and indeed also of the not-so-poor, and in an essentially classless society to turn them into the personnel who would man the Church and the clerisy and the civil administration of the realm. That is what they did, and what the teaching and learning of Latin grammar enabled them to do. But when a mercantile and then a manufacturing society emerged from the womb of time to destroy the old way of life, the grammar schools, tied by their old statutes to their old curriculum, stayed stuck in their old grooves and awoke to find themselves an unwanted survival in an alien world.

The greatest acceleration of this process took place, of course, during what we have learned to call the Industrial Revolution; and the St. Thomas's period at Stourbridge certainly overlapped the development of that process. So we shall find that we are not so much telling the story of four headmasters in succession or of their ushers or their governors, or indeed of any personalities recognisable as such in the afterlight from two centuries later. We shall be witnessing a process. It was a process of decline, followed by reform, followed by revival. Its history will be found in official documents, in enquiries and reports and recommendations. Individuals, it is true, played their parts, and of many of them we know the names, at any rate, and personal particulars but of what they were really like we have no clear idea.

The four headmasters of the St. Thomas's period were successively Charles Harris, John Pattinson, Joseph Taylor and Giffard Wells. Foster's *Alumni Oxonienses* tells us that Charles Harris, like his predecessor Hancox was a local man, described by Foster as Charles, son of John, of Bell Broughton, co. Worcester, gent., Worcester College, matriculated 31 March 1726, aged 16; B.A. 6 Feb, 1729/30, M.A. 1732. This makes him 35 years old at the time of his appointment in 1745, when he had already been minister of the new chapel for three years. He continued in possession of both offices until the year 1782, when he died at the age of 72. Miss Edwards tells us that even five years before his death, in 1777, he was very old and infirm, and that in that year Thomas Milward, the only survivor of the original trustees of the church, sought counsel's opinion about his right to nominate the minister, with the idea of bringing an action against Mr. Harris. She does not explain this mysterious suggestion, but the implication, we think, may be that Charles Harris was too old and infirm to do his work as minister. If that was so, one can well imagine that he was *a fortiori* incompetent in his capacity as headmaster. But be that as it may, he continued in office for another five years, until he died. His death notice in *Berrow's Worcester Journal* describes him as "a person of a humane and benevolent disposition, and possessed of those virtues which constitute and adorn the character of the divine". One can only hope that the boys 'reverenced' him, to use Samuel Johnson's word, accordingly. It is important to remember that his period of office at the school, which appears to have been uniformly uneventful, took its course in the years before the effects of the Industrial Revolution began to exert their profoundest influence upon the grammar schools. So perhaps the Rev. Charles Harris was happy in the hour of his departure.

He was helped in his labours by only three ushers — first by the Rev. Mr. John Brookes of 'Katherine Hall' in Cambridge, who had become usher on 6 June 1737, then later for four years from 1759 to 1763 by John Gaunt of Corpus Christi College, Cambridge, and finally, for almost the last twenty years of his service, from Michaelmas of 1763 to 1782, by an usher who was, unusually at this period, another local man, and therefore most probably an Old Boy of the school. He is not recorded in any of the university lists, and was evidently not a graduate. His appointment is recorded in the governors' minute-book as follows:

Whereas John Gaunt has given us notice to leave the Grammar School of Stourbridge, therefore we whose names are subscribed being the major part of the Governors of the possessions Revenues and Goods of the said Grammar School do nominate, elect and appoint *Richard Willetts of Wollaston Junior* to be Usher of the same school from Michaelmas last and to enter upon the School House at the same time, in the room of the said John Gaunt, observing the Orders of the said School. and to be discharged at the Governors' pleasure for the time being if they think that he shall not behave himself well, and he shall not go away or withdraw himself from the service of his place in the said School without giving six months notice thereof, under the penalty of forfeiting six months salary, which the Collector for the time being is ordered and authorised to Defaulk and Detain by not paying him the six months salary according. Witness our hands the fifth day of September 1763.
Thos. Saunders, Thos. York, John Hill, Edw. Russell, Nich. Parker.

Pausing only to remark that the governors certainly seem to have learnt the lesson of Wentworth's sad dereliction of duty, we go on to notice an interesting hint about the new usher. In the parish register of St. Mary's Oldswinford in an entry under the date 22 March 1741/2 we find the record of the baptism of *Richard, son of Richard and Jane Willetts.* Clearly this could well be our man. Like all his fellows in the service of the school at this period he is so obscure as to be almost invisible — but we shall have something to say about him later on, before he passes from oblivion to the grave. If he was indeed the infant of 1742, then he would be aged 21 when he became usher at Michaelmas of 1763 — precisely what we should expect.

In the year 1763-4 the school's rent-roll amounted to £89-3-6d; the headmaster's and usher's salaries were respectively £45 and £25, and the balance in hand on 18th June 1764 was seven shillings and a penny three farthings! The accounts at this time were in the hands of Humphrey Moseley, the elder of the two ironmongers whose service initiated the system of paid and permanent 'Deputy Collectors', starting in the year 1729 (see page 7). Humphrey Moseley went on until 1770: he was then succeeded by William, presumably his son, who continued as Deputy Collector until 1820, an astonishing example of long service by men of the same family. William indeed, in an entry written onto the opening page of the second governors' minute-book (which dated from the year 1800) claimed to have been collecting the rents from the year 1751! This would have given him a span of almost 70 years at the time when he was superseded in 1820; and if we consider this to be incredible, we must assume either that he simply made a mistake in recollecting when he started, or else that he started collecting the rents on his father's behalf twenty years before he formally succeeded him as Deputy Collector. This he could well have done.

There is one curious — indeed, mysterious — matter to be recorded from the 1770's. In the first year of William Moseley's stewardship the accounts, dated 27 May 1771, show a credit balance of fourteen shillings and fourpence: this follows several years when it varied from a matter of shillings to a maximum of £3.10.1d. The arrears of rent recorded at the same time amounted to £52.16.1d on a rent-roll of £89.13.6d, again a figure not very dissimilar from those of the preceding several years. After this quite suddenly in the following years, as William Moseley gets going, the arrears are reduced from sums of around £30 or £40 or even £50, to sums ranging between £20 and £30. The balance in hand went up from a credit of mere shillings or the like, or even a deficit, to an average credit over the next eleven years of no less than £37.6.6d! The total 'turnover' shown on both credit and debit sides of the account goes up from a figure of £100–£120, as in the previous decade, to one of £150–£160 under William Moseley. There is no overt explanation for all this, and one is left to assume that it was simply that 'the firm was under new management', though this, we feel, would hardly satisfy any even moderately competent accountant. We shall see later that in another thirty years or so the improvement in the school's finances became so marked and so well established that it revolutionised the value of both the headmaster's and the usher's emoluments. But this was not to be in the Rev. Charles Harris's time.

It is an odd comment upon the featureless and level monotony of his forty years that one picks out from that whole stretch of time one entry, and only one, which breaks the surface, as it were, of those still waters and leaves a little ripple behind. In the account of 1761-2 — almost mid-way through the long tedium of that quiet voyage — we find our one surprise, and our one glimpse of the continuing truth that there was still life and vital humanity — in the playground and amongst the boys. (Why do we hear so little about the boys?) The item which we greet with so much pleasure reads as follows:

Cash received of ye boys tow'ds ye broken windows   1-6d.

If we know anything about schools, that levy must have been imposed by the headmaster. So the Rev. Mr. Harris probably *was* 'reverenced' by his pupils. At any rate they must have known that he was there!

One noticeable feature of the St. Thomas's period is the remarkable length of service of the four successive headmasters. From 1745 to 1858 is 113 years; so the *average* span of the four was 28 years in office. Charles Harris actually lasted for 37 years, and one is moved to the thought that so many generations of boys went through the school in his time that in after-life there would be no-one — literally no-one — of their boyhood acquaintance, and indeed virtually no-one in the town and district at all, who would remember any headmaster of the grammar school other than Charles Harris. It is all the more tantalising to us now to find that the headmasters of the St. Thomas's period appear to have matched their length of service by their virtual anonymity. The word, of course, is strictly quite inaccurate, since we know all their names: but they remain for all that virtually unknown.

John Pattinson, Charles Harris's successor, stayed for 26 years; so by the time of his depature in 1808 it would have called for a memory as long as the life of the oldest normal member of the community to go back beyond him and his immediate predecessor. What is more, he left behind him in 1808 the same man as usher whom he had inherited from Charles Harris in 1782. For Richard Willetts — who incidentally achieves the status of 'the Reverend' in the records, so, degree or no degree, he was admitted to orders — *the Reverend* Richard Willetts outstayed his second headmaster, who was eleven years his junior, and died after a year with his third in the year 1809, at the age of 67. Stability, like what we have called anonymity, was certainly the order of the day in those times.

Another curious thing is the speed with which successors were found to take the place of the departed. Perhaps the double appointment made this a very desirable 'shop'.

In 1782 a governors' meeting was held on 14th November, and the minute reads:

Stourbridge School House: Nov. 14th 1782.
We the Governors of The Free Grammar School of King Edward the Sixth in Stourbridge aforesaid — Do unanimously elect

nominate and appoint the Revd. Mr. John Pattinson, M.A., now or late of Queens College in the University of Oxford — Head School Master in the room and in the stead of the Rev. Mr. Charles Harris lately deceased, upon the salary of Forty-five pounds per Annum — Witness our hands the day and year above written.

                Edw. Hickman   Thos. Hill
                John Wells   W. B. Collis
                Jno. Pidcock   Fran. Stokes
                Rob. Foley   Joseph Cox

This was the occasion, be it remembered, when the Rev. Robert Foley, who was rector of Oldswinford, advertised the vacancy of both the headmastership of the grammar school and the ministry of the new church to be at the disposal of the governors (see page 104-5). John Pattinson was his choice for the church, and it may well be that on 14th November the Governors were simply concurring, for whatever reason, in that choice, already made. There were objections, as we have said, but the trouble appears soon to have blown over.

The new headmaster is described by Foster as:

Pattinson John, s. of Thomas, of Holme Cultram, Cumberland, Pleb., Queens College. Matriculated 19 Nov. 1773, aged 20; B.A. 1778, M.A. 1782.

So this time we have no local man — far from it; and John Pattinson was unusually late for those times both in his university career and in his first post. He had graduated only four years before and was now aged 29. To the best of our knowledge he spent the whole of his professional life in his joint appointments at Stourbridge, and was to be no more than 55 when he came to leave them in 1808.

He must have been appointed very soon after the death of Charles Harris. Not that we can rely too precisely upon the phrase 'lately deceased'; but in the school accounts for the year in question the executors of the Rev. Mr. Charles Harris receive payment of £18.15.0d, which implies five months salary, while the Rev. Richard Willetts gets, in addition to £25 being his salary as usher for one year in full to Lady Day, an additional payment specified as:

    ditto — one Quarter for officiating as Head Master   £11.5.0d

and the new headmaster appears in the entry:

THE ROYAL FOUNDER

KING EDWARD VI

THE PORTRAIT PAINTED BY WILLIAM SCROTS, OR STREETS, IN 1552 OR 1553, PRESENTED TO THE SCHOOL IN 1875; LOST TO SIGHT UNTIL DISCOVERED IN THE MASTERS' COMMON ROOM IN 1958 (see page 14 following).

1 Portrait of Edward VI

The two 'foundation deeds' of 1430 (see p. 25). The deed of gift from Philip and Jo
Hayley is on the left, the quitclaim from William Hayley on the right. An outline
translation is given below each.

Let men present and future know that we (Philip Hayley of Stourbridge and Joan m
wife) have granted and given... to William Smyth, clerk...etc., etc.... (*the list of
trustees, as on page 49*) a parcel of land with its appurtenances in Stourbridge, as it
newly marked out and on which a new chapel is already built... to have and to
hold...etc.... to the aforesaid William...etc., etc.... in witness whereof we have put o
seals to this present deed, in the presence of John Penne, Thomas Benet, Thomas
Pulter, John (?) Peny, Thomas Rudgetts and others... given at Stourbridge on the
Sunday next before the feast of the Lord's Ascension in the eighth year of King He
the Sixth.

II Deed of Gift

all men know... that I William Hayley have remitted and released and for me and
heirs for ever have quitted claim to William Smyth clerk...etc., etc.... all my right
claim which I have, have had, and in future shall be able to have, in a parcel of
d in Stourbridge, as it is newly marked out and on which...etc.... in witness whereof
ve put my seal to this present deed in the presence of Thomas Pulter, John
y, Thomas Rudgetts and others... given at Stourbridge on the Sunday next after the
st of the Lord's Ascension in the eighth year of King Henry the Sixth.

The original Chantry seal, once the seal of the Wool Staple of the City of Lincoln (see p. 24), attached to a lease of school property.

IV The School Seal

...larged photograph of the seal. The word LINCOLN can be read
... the top left quadrant of the legend which encircles the image of the
...rgin standing on a wool-sack.

...e Black Box, the original muniment-chest of the Chantry,
...erited (like the seal) by the Grammar School and still
...like the seal) in the possession of its modern successor.

V The Black Box

Below is a copy of 'A View of Stourbridge' from Nash's Worcestershire, Vol. II op p. 207. The letters A, B and C mark respectively the School tower and cupola, St. Thomas's church and the windmill which stood behind the houses on the brow of R Hill. The view was certainly taken from the bottom of the town near the old wharf, actually in the area of Wollaston, where the river and the canal come closest togethe

Opposite, top, is an 1868 print of W. J. J. Welch's new school of 1860. The victorianised masters' houses are on the right. On the left is Green Close House, residence of the Hickmans. The spike on the fleche crowning the school tower bear an ornamental metal 'tag', pierced with the date 1861.

Opposite, bottom, is the watercolour drawing of the school houses, as in Professor Bate's book (see p. 38). The usher's house on the right was rebuilt like this in 1699 the head's house on the left in 1704–8, both by a builder named John Ellis, who wa paid £43. 10s. 0d. for the one and £103. 16s. 6d. (in four instalments) for the other.

VI Nash's view of Stourbridge

VII The School Front 1868 and the School Houses c.1700

REV. GIFFARD WELLS, M.A.,
Sidney Sussex College, Cambridge,
HEADMASTER 1833–1858.
From a painting by J. C. Vidgen-Jenks,
A.R.C.A., made from an old photograph
in the 1930's.

REV. W. J. J. WELCH, M.A., M.D.,
St. Catharine's College, Cambridge,
HEADMASTER 1858–1885.
From a photograph.

MR. RUPERT DEAKIN, M.A.,
Balliol College, Oxford,
HEADMASTER 1885–1905.
From a photograph.

MR. J. E. BOYT, M.A., B.Sc.,
St. John's College, Cambridge,
HEADMASTER 1905–1934.
From a photograph.

VIII Portraits of four headmasters 1833–1934

Rev. Mr. Pattinson one Quarter in full to Lady Day   £11.5.0d

So we conclude that Charles Harris lived and worked for five months after Lady Day — to the end of August or thereabouts, that the Autumn term was covered by the usher (while the headmastership was being advertised and the post filled), and that the Spring term of 1783 was John Pattinson's first spell in office. In this account, incidentally, the rent-roll totalled £92.16.10d, out of which the normal allowance for the two masters' salaries was £70, and for William Moseley £5, leaving little enough for maintenance of the buildings, legal expenses, management and contingencies. By 1792, however, the rent-roll had reached a total of £120.16.4d, and this was only the beginning of a startling process of increase which was to have far-reaching effects on the school. Moreover, we begin to see signs that the world is changing. In 1792, again for the first time, the Governors pay for an Insurance Policy. The grand cost of the first annual premium was £1.11.9d, so we have hardly yet reached the commercial sophistication of the high Victorian era. But in a sense this modest little item marks the death of an old social order and the birth of a new one. At the same time the accounts show for the first time a mysterious item which reads:

Paid for lamps ...   £2.11.6d.

The following year's account, dated 27 May 1793, is a little fuller, but no less mysterious:

Lamps — Revd. Pattinson (*no amount entered*)
do — Rev. R. Willetts   6.0d

In the accounts of 16 June 1794, however, light begins to dawn, as we read:

Lamps & Scavenger, Revd. J.P.   11.3d
    do.   R.W.   6.0d

So we now realise that we are entering upon the era of civic improvement and are at the dawn of municipal services.

Amongst other items round about the same time we find a payment for the expenses of 'Revd. Mr. Pattinson and W. Moseley' on a three-day stay at Worcester (including the hire of a chaise), the purpose of which was 'to settle rents' — an interesting comment on the nature of the headmaster's duties even at this date; there is another item for "Exps. attending the Auction letting Houses at Worcester", and yet another for "Expences 2 days to Hagley on Land & Window tax". In the 1780's and 1790's there are records of much increased expenditure on buildings and their maintenance: in six accounts from 1785 onward the average is almost precisely £25 a year. The insurance premiums recur; so do the charges for lamps and scavenging, for window taxes, the poor levy, the church wardens' levy, and so on. Details are jejune and sketchy, but it becomes clear that what we have called the birth of a new social order was indeed under way.

But as human nature does not change, so the old ways died hard; and in the accounts for 1790-91, followed by a minute of 16 June 1794, we find ourselves suddenly back in the world of Mr. Browne and Mr. Crane. It will be remembered that what made Mr. Browne stand up and spit fire at his governors was their kindess to his hated usher, Mr. Crane. The demure brick houses in which the Rev. John Pattinson and the Rev. Richard Willetts were now living were in fact the legacy of that bygone academic feud. Was the dog-in-the-manger then still alert and ready to snarl, lurking under the clerical robe and the academic gown? We have wondered, and so far wondered in vain, what sort of people these men really were, the Rev. John Pattinson and the Rev. Richard Willetts. We know that one came from far away in the north country and was about 38 years old in 1791, while his usher was a Stourbridge man, aged about 50, doubtless an Old Boy of the school, with 27 years in its service behind him, as against his headmaster's less than ten. How did they get on together? It could have been an uneasy relationship. How can we ever know?

In the account of 20 June 1791 we may perhaps get a hint. On the credit side there is an item showing receipt of ninety pounds in cash from a Mr. Wall for a lease — doubtless an entrance fine for one of the school's properties. On the debit side, tucked away unobtrusively and out of its place at the very bottom of the column, comes this entry:

To expences in Building Two additional Rooms
to the school house   £90.0.0d

So the governors were still up to their old tricks. Ninety pounds in hand, and they could not wait to splash ninety pounds out! But this tells us also that they must have been on good terms with their headmaster, and that John Pattinson, so one would think, must have been an acceptable person. For the reference to the school house certainly meant the headmaster's house. The proof of that comes a little later in the minute-book:

> Ordered that the Rev. Richard Willetts be allowed two pounds ten shillings per Annum from Lady Day 1790 for Compensation to him in lieu of the Rooms built by the Governors for the Revd. J. Pattinson during the said R. W. continuing Usher — and the further sum of Fifteen Pounds to Mr. Willetts and Twenty-seven Pounds to the Revd. J. Pattinson — being part of the surplus money in the hands of the treasurer. June 16 1794
>
> Edw. Hickman   Joseph Cox
> Rob. Foley   John Causer
> Franc. Stokes   Jno. A. Addenbrooke

That was a pretty generous 'Compensation' to balance an expenditure of ninety pounds, and one wonders, but wonders in vain, what lay behind it. It is true that the governers were always careful to stick precisely to the habitual proportions between the emoluments of the head and those of the usher. But this seems to be carrying the principle to extremes, and one wonders whether Richard Willetts had protested that he was not getting his fair share, or whether possibly his boyhood friends on the governing body, of whom he may well have had some, were being forward to promote the interests of their old school fellow and the town's native son. Or was he indeed perhaps being cantankerous?

Leaving that question aside for the moment, we note that the improvement in the school's finances, still unexplained, seems to have established itself to their satisfaction sufficiently for them to take special measures to deal with 'the surplus money'. Moreover, after two further years, in 1796, William Moseley's salary as Deputy Collector, was raised from five pounds to eight guineas a year. The balance in hand reported in the account of 1794 amounted in fact to no less a sum than £68.0.11d, the rent-roll reached £125.5.4d, and the total figure at the foot of both sides of the book came to £230.11.0d, almost a hundred pounds more than the usual figure of most of the preceding years. So the financial revolution was a reality, though the reasons behind it remain a mystery. Another strange and unexplained item occurs in the 1791 account, on the very same page as the record of the £90 windfall and the £90 expenditure on Mr. Pattinson's house. The standard formula of acceptance of the account — "We governors of the free Grammar School do allow this account ... etc ... etc ... " is enlarged by an additional clause, which reads —

" ... and do order that no Moneys be expended without the Consent & Approbation of the Governors or a Majority".

This entry gives us much cause for thought. For it comes very strangely at this particular point, so much so that one cannot fail to connect it directly with the expenditure of the ninety pounds on the additional rooms. We have tried in vain to reconstruct the situation and to see, especially in the light of the governors' later decision to 'compensate' Richard Willetts, what actually had happened — who did what, and with what motive! We are driven to speculate whether one possible solution is to suppose that John Pattinson, possibly with some support from one or more of the governors, but certainly not of a majority, had 'jumped the gun' in ordering the extra rooms to be built and then sent in the bills to the Collector for the year, Francis Stokes, who proceeded to pay them. It is impossible to be sure, but one may perhaps think that this would make more sense of the subsequent proceedings than any other suggestion.

This, of course, is no more than conjecture, and it serves to drive home the point that our picture of John Pattinson and his regime is really very hazy indeed, shadowed with questions unanswered and darkened by uncertainties unresolved.

The questions and the uncertainties become even more obtrusive and leave us peering even more helplessly into the dark, as we come towards the last years of the century and the end of John Pattinson's time. On 29 May 1797 the Governors held a special meeting at the school, only two weeks in advance of the annual audit of Trinity Monday. The minutes recording this meeting are written only three pages after the record of the governors' special action in 'compensating' Richard Willetts for the ninety pounds spent on the headmaster's house. Yet this is what we now read:

May 29th 1797. At a Special Meeting at the School.

It is the Opinion of the Governors now present that the Revd. Richard Willetts Usher of the School has grossly misbehaved by

Improper Correction of Edward Ash a scholar — that he be and now is admonished for the same, and that upon a Second Charge being Established against him his Salary be withheld & he be discharged from his Ushership.

Order'd That in future no Corporal Punishment be inflicted but by the birch Rod — and the Rules and Orders be printed upon a Board and hung up in the School

Ordered That the hours of School from Lady Day to Michaelmas be from seven o'clock to twelve & from two to five — & from eight to twelve & two to five the other half year.

Ordered That the Masters not attending the School regularly their salarys be withheld.

     Rob. Foley Jno. Addenbrooke
     Tho. Hill   John Causer
     Franc. Stokes Edw. Oliver
     Joseph Cox R. Worcester

It is to be noticed that this minute has been countersigned by the bishop of Worcester; so it is clear that the Governors intended to make their new statutes as formal and official as possible. In fact they were in later times printed on large paper, and in this state formed an exhibit in Chancery in a suit concerning the school in 1851. This large-paper set of rules consisted of the William III Statutes and Orders of 1702, printed in full, with the 1797 minute from the governors' minute-book attached as an appendix, evidently accorded the same status as the rest.

 It is clear that the occasion of the new rules which became a permanent part of the Statutes and Orders of the school was the gross misbehaviour of the usher, Richard Willetts. What he had actually been doing remains a mystery. Evidently he had inflicted corporal punishment, evidently he had not used a birch-rod, or cane. The mind boggles over pictures of sadistic practices. But the explanation most likely in modern times would be that he had simply lost his temper, probably under the provocation of impudence, knocked the boy down, and very likely given him a black eye! Perhaps we had better leave it there. But if it was so, it will perhaps affect our mental picture of what sort of a man the Rev. Richard Willetts may have been. We begin to get a hint of irascibility and a whiff of the cantankerous. But before we are carried away by imagination, let us not forget to ask ourselves why on earth the governors were moved to include in their revised rules not only a prescription about corporal punishment, but also a change in the hours of school which in effect made lessons start one hour later than before throughout the year.

That will have to do for Richard Willetts and the mystery of his gross misbehaviour. It is somehow characteristic of the shadowy uncertainties of that dimly lighted world of the St. Thomas's period. Whatever Richard Willetts had done, the governors went on paying him the 'compensation' of his enhanced salary, though no further distributions of 'surplus money' were made for several next ensuing years.

What we must also ask, but ask in vain, is what had the masters, one or both, been up to, that prompted the governors to re-state the rule that if they absented themselves from duty, their salaries would not be paid? We do not know the answer, but it surely must be true that something had occurred in the way of an unauthorised absence from duty; otherwise the presence of the last clause in the 1797 minute is meaningless.

It is certainly significant that the account of 4 June 1798, admittedly some years later than the mysterious minute, shows that John Pattinson did indeed suffer a diminution of his salary received. The entry reads:

To Revd. Pattinson Salary 1/2 yr. due Michs. last   £22.10.0d

At the same time Richard Willetts was paid, as in the normal way, £27.10.0d for a full year up to Lady Day. What is more, in the next year's account in May 1799 Pattinson received a full salary of £45, but only that, with nothing to make up the missing half of the previous year, and again only to Michaelmas instead of to Lady Day.

That is all we are able to say, and there is no explanation in the book. Indeed, that is the point at which the first Governors' minute-book comes to an end, and the first pages of the second book are taken up with various summaries and preambles which lose sight of the consecutive story of the governors' activities. This makes it impossible to be sure, but it does nothing to weaken our conclusion that John Pattinson had been quietly docked half a year's salary, presumably because he had at some stage stayed away from school. This may be presuming upon insufficient evidence, but without some such explanation it is impossible to explain the loss of half of Pattinson's salary for 1798.

The first thing to emerge from the early pages of the new book, when it gets under way, is a considerable, even startling increase in the total income from the school's rent-roll. In 1802, 1803 and 1804 it came to £125.11.4d; but in 1805 and 1806 it was £185.6.4d, and in 1807 no less than £296.18.8! Side by side with this goes a string of irregular and inexplicable amounts for the salaries of the two masters. It has proved impossible to reconcile the recorded figures with the official salaries in force, and the eventual termination of the confusion has to be taken on trust in the account of June 1805, where Pattinson is credited with £90 for *two years salary due and in full* up to Lady Day last, and Willetts £34.7.6d for One year and a quarter (which would be the correct figure) *also in full to Lady Day last.* It is best to assume that the failure to reconcile is due to one's own error, since it is quite certain that neither John Pattinson nor Richard Willetts would have sat down quietly to an accidental underpayment. But the impression remains that at one stage John Pattinson had lost salary because he had not given full service. He may, of course, have been suffering from the problem of ill-health which seems to have afflicted the headmasters from time to time during the St. Thomas's period, as we shall see. In his case nothing is recorded. His early retirement in 1808, on the other hand, does nothing to contradict the impression that he may have been losing enthusiasm for his work. Considering what the governors were proposing to do in the matter of the emoluments of the two masters during the last two years or so before he resigned, his resignation is still more surprising, except on the assumption of ill-health or disinclination. The story begins with the minutes of a meeting of 18 December 1806.

> It appearing to this Meeting that the Annual Rents and Revenues of the Possessions belonging to this School have within this few years increased very considerably and that it is expected a further increase will in a short time take place, and that the Population and Trade of Stourbridge and Parish of Oldwinsford and Neighbourhood have also of late very much increased.
>
> Resolved unanimously by us the Governors present that it would be of great benefit and advantageous as well to the inhabitants of the town of Stourbridge and Parish of Oldswinford as to others

his Majesty's subjects of the Neighbouring Parts (at whose humble Petition and for whose especial Benefit the Letters Patent or Charter of King Edward the Sixth the Founder of this School was granted) if the English Language, Writing, Arithmetic, Geography and the Mathematics as well as the Latin and Greek Languages were taught in this School

Ordered That a draft Form of good and wholesome Statutes and orders be forthwith prepared to Enable us the said Governors to augment the stipends and Salarys of the Headmaster and Usher of the said School for the time being and also to provide an English or petty school House adjoining or near to the present school, and also to provide an additional Master or Assistant and to allow him a proper and suitable stipend and Salary so as to carry into effect the Benefits stated in the above Resolution, and also concerning and touching the order, Government and direction of the said Master and Usher and such additional Master and Assistant and the stipends or Salarys of such Master Usher and Assistant and other things touching and concerning the said schools and the order and Management Preservation and Disposition of the Rents and Revenues Appointed or to be Appointed for the support of the same Schools and that the draft or form of such intended Statutes and orders shall be laid before us at our next meeting for our Perusal and that the same when sealed and approved by us shall be laid before the Right Reverend the Lord Bishop of the Diocese of Worcester for his Approbation and Consent pursuant to the said Letters Patent or Charter of King Edward the Sixth, and that such other Devices ways and means be had and taken as Councill shall advise for obtaining the Benefits stated in the said Resolution and for legally and permanently establishing such statutes and orders and making the same binding and conclusive so that the same may be acted upon for ever hereafter.

    Thos. P. Foley
    Thos. Hill
    Jos. Robins
    John Pidcock
    Francis Walker
    John Causer

> We the Undersigned Governors being unavoidably absent from the above mentioned meeting do hereby signify our full consent and approbation to the appointment Resolution and order before written.
>
> Thos. Homfray
> Jno. Addenbrooke

Attached to the accounts of 25 May 1807 comes the 'follow-up':—

> Ordered that the draft of the Statutes and Orders now produced for augmenting the Head Master and Usher's salaries and for allowing a salary to a writing master and providing a new school be laid before Counsel to enquire how and by what means the same can be legally carried into effect.

This, of course, was quite revolutionary! The effect of the changes proposed would have been quite simply to create a new school. So one can say that the governors were clearly intent on ushering the school into the modern world; to put it another way, it becomes clear that they were aware of the crippling effect of what we have called 'the dead hand', and that they were taking steps to break its hold. It is typical of the governors' methods of recording their proceedings at this time, that they give no overt signs of any anxiety about any decline of the school's position, or of any loss of what is called in today's jargon, its 'viability'! The revolutionary proposal comes out of the blue, and it comes as a bombshell. Nor do the governors give the slightest indication that they had had any discussions with any other parties, such as the headmaster and usher, who might be presumed to have an interest! The masters' views are not mentioned, their concurrence with the wishes of the governors is simply taken for granted. We are not even told that they had been informed of what was afoot; but it is safe to assume that John Pattinson and Richard Willetts must have known what was going on. What their reaction was remains for the moment obscure.

However, the drift of the governors' intentions is clear enough, and their proposals, let it be repeated, were quite radical. One wonders whether the Stourbridge governors were aware of the famous Leeds Grammar School Judgment given by Lord Eldon in 1805? This effectually quashed, by legal process, an attempt by the governors of that school to do very much what the

Stourbridge governors were proposing to do now, in 1807. Lord Eldon had ruled that the Founder's wishes, expressed in the foundation Charter, were paramount and inviolable. The headmaster at Leeds had, not unnaturally, since he was the beneficiary of the classical monopoly, taken the strongest exception to his governors' proposals, and had won the day. One wonders what line John Pattinson was taking in this. But the records are entirely and infuriatingly silent. We do, however, notice with admiration the very considerable skill of the Stourbridge governors in declaring that their prime and original purpose was to bring about the augmentation of the headmaster's and usher's salaries. Everything else was put forward as a concomitant subsidiary to that first aim. This was in fact what they proceeded to do, and they were not content with half-measures. For directly following the signatures appended to the last minute quoted is a further record which was written half a year later, on 17 December 1807:

> December 17th 1807 — Ordered at a meeting of the Governors — That William Moseley do pay to the Revd. John Pattinson fifty-five pounds and to the Revd. Richard Willetts Thirty-two pounds ten shillings, in addition to the last year's Salary.
>
> Thos. P. Foley   Tho. Homfray
> Jno. Addenbrooke John Pidcock
> Jos. Robins   Francis Walker

At that stage, then, it appears that the revolutionary proposal is takings its course towards realisation. But this turns out to be far from the simple truth. For stuck onto the same page, so as to lie over the last-quoted order, but pasted onto the page only at its top, is a sheet of letter-paper. It is written over in ink, in the same handwriting as the entry in the book, probably that of William Moseley, and is in the form of a resolution. But it bears no signatures. It is characteristic, in fact, of the rather slovenly and careless way in which the minute-book was being kept at the time of these crucially important proceedings. The inserted paper reads as follows (and we notice first of all the date):—

> At a meeting of the Governors of the Free School of King Edward the Sixth held this day February 23rd 1809, it is ordered with the consent of the Right Revd. the Lord Bishop of Worcester, that the annual sum of *£150* be paid to the Revd. Joseph Taylor, the

Head Master of the above School — and the annual sum of *£90* be paid to the Revd. --- Reed the Usher of the said School for their respective salaries, being the usual and customary proportions viz. five eights to the Head Master and three eights to the Usher — and that the Usher for the time being of the said school shall instruct the Boys two afternoons in every week in writing and accounts as well as in the Classical learning.

So there, it seems, was the outcome of the proposed revolution. The mountains had travailed, and here was born the absurd little mouse. Here was no new school, no writing-master, no additional Assistant, no English Language, no Geography, no Arithmetic, no Mathematics. Here was the revolution cut down to size — two half-days a week in the junior school given over to writing and accounts, and that in the hands of the Usher! Here also, it is true, as the governors had promised, was the augmentation of the masters' salaries — and if this was indeed intended as a bribe, it was certainly large enough to command attention, if not to guarantee success. A rise in salary from £45 to £150, and from £27.10.0 to £90 was a rise indeed!

But what has happened to our headmaster and our usher? Where is John Pattinson? Where is Richard Willetts? who is Reed? For we know already who Joseph Taylor was. He was the third of the St. Thomas's headmasters, and he succeeded John Pattinson in 1808. We now see that our inserted minute has been inserted in the wrong place in the book, and is dated a year *after* Pattinson's departure.

Sure, enough, on the opposite page of the minute-book to the pasted-in note we begin to see what has been happening. Here are the minutes, again rather hurriedly written, of a meeting of the governors held on 16 April 1808, almost a year before the order for the new salaries and the teaching of writing and accounts. This is what it says:

At a meeting of the Governors held at the school the sixteenth day of April 1808 the Revd. John Pattinson gave in his Resignation, of which the following is a copy:

Gentlemen,
    I hereby resign the Headmastership of the Free Grammar School of King Edward the Sixth in Stourbridge in the County of Worcester.

Given under my hand this 16th day of April in the year of our Lord one thousand eight hundred and eight.

J. Pattinson

ordered That all moneys in hand, together with all profits arising from Rents due at Lady Day last be divided between the masters in proportion to their salary of forty-five pounds to the headmaster and twenty-seven pounds ten shillings per Annum to the Usher, Deducting what was in hand when Mr. Pattinson was elected headmaster into the school.

Ordered that the governors do meet on Tuesday next at 12 o'clock to elect a new master in the room of the Revd. John Pattinson.

So that was the end of John Pattinson as headmaster. He did not wait for his threefold increase of salary. He must have been unenthusiastic indeed about his work. He may, of course, have been fleeing from the revolution. He may have been quite unable to stomach the idea of a petty school, of a writing-master, of lessons in the English Language, Arithmetic, Geography and the Mathematics. In other words, he may have objected totally to the governors' attempt to bring the school into the modern world. He could hardly have objected to the new salaries!

It is infuriating that we simply do not know what made Pattinson resign when he did. We have no means of telling what precisely was happening. The evidences which gave us chapter and verse for every move of the Tudor governors in their dealings with Richard Alchurche in 1595, and which guided us step by step through the labyrinth of the two-year battle which led to the appointment of John Wentworth in 1705, have simply dried up. The governors' minute-book has survived, but it does not give us the information which we want.

However, what we do know is that Pattinson went, that he was succeeded by Joseph Taylor (actually appointed within a week of Pattinson's resignation!) and that a year later Richard Willetts died, to be followed by an usher named Reed. We know also, as it happens, by virtue of one fortuitous break in our covering cloud of non-witness, enough for us to hazard an intelligent guess as to who was responsible for cutting the revolution down to size, or for turning back the tide of the inexorably advancing modern world.

Before we come to that, however, let us bid a more satisfactory farewell to John Pattinson. His letter of resignation, copied in a hurried minute into the governors' book (on the same day that he wrote it) and accepted without a word or sign of regret or a single friendly reference to his twenty-six years of service, is surely a sad and inadequate end, as well as an obscure one, to that obscure and shadowy stretch of time which saw his lifetime's labours. Let us turn, then, before we leave him, to a news item from Berrows Worcester Journal, carefully copied by an unknown hand into the pages of the first volume of H. E. Palfrey's great set of scrap-books, now in the County Record Office at Worcester. They originally constituted what remained of the fabled 'Milward Evidences', those relics of the family muniments and memoranda of the great Wollescote dynasty who bore that family name. The news paragraph reads as follows:

> 1813. The following truly distressing accident happened on Monday afternoon near the Halfway House on the road from this city to Kidderminster. As the Rev. Mr. Pattinson of Bath was proceeding from Ombersley to Stourbridge, his horse took fright at a cart loaded with fern, and after galloping a short distance, Mr. P. fell with great violence upon his head; some persons upon the road immediately conveyed him into the Halfway House, where every attention was paid to him, and a messenger sent with all speed for Mr. Jukes, surgeon, Stourport, whose assistance, however, proved unavailing. After Mr. P's decease, Mr. Jukes discovered that the scull was not fractured, and had no doubt but his death was occasioned by the rupture of a blood-vessel in the head. An inquest was held upon the body yesterday by Mr. Hill, Coroner; verdict — Accidental Death ... Mr Pattinson was formerly master of Stourbridge School; he was much esteemed by his numerous and respectable friends, who are filled with the deepest grief for his melancholy death.

The paragraph is annotated in the margin by its unknown transcriber — 'My Schoolmaster', — a better epitaph than anything that the school could summon up for him.

John Pattinson resigned on 16th April 1808. The Governors resolved on the same day to meet on the Tuesday following to elect his successor, On 19th April 1808 they met as arranged and proceeded to elect the Reverend Joseph Taylor, vicar of Snitterfield. So the whole operation of changing heads was completed in three days.

This leads one to wonder whether they had not perhaps made up their minds already, and whether Pattinson's resignation had been perhaps 'in the wind' before it became a fact. Certainly they could not have gone through any process of advertising, summoning candidates, pursuing references and making further enquiries, in the space of three days. That is quite impossible. We know that Joseph Taylor also became minister of the new chapel, as well as headmaster of the Grammar School: unfortunately we do not know the precise date of his appointment to St. Thomas's, so we are left to wonder, once again, whether his succession to the chapel was already settled when the post at the school fell vacant. But the whole process was so brief, so quickly over — indeed so *hurried*, that one must assume that Joseph Taylor was already standing in the wings, as it were, and waiting only for his entrance-cue to take the stage. He must already have known what was afoot. Nothing else can explain how he came to be appointed on the Tuesday following Pattinson's resignation on that Saturday in April of 1808.

We are unlikely ever to find the evidence which will prove this suggestion, but commonsense is in its favour and in fact requires that it should be true. But be it true or false, Joseph Taylor takes the stage as the third of our four headmasters of the St. Thomas's period. He was a man of 34 at the time, listed in Foster as:

TAYLOR Joseph, s. of George, of Bowes, Yorks., gent. Matriculated at St. Edmund Hall 14 Nov. 1793, aged 19; B.A. 1797: M.A. from King's College, Cambridge 1802. Headmaster of the Grammar School and perpetual curate of Stourbridge. Vicar of Snitterfield until his death 2 May 1833.

Why he transferred to Cambridge we do not know, but in the Cambridge lists Venn gives the same information as above, with the added note that he was aged 59 at his death, died at Stourbridge and left a son George. His death is referred to in the Gentleman's Magazine for 1833 (i,649), where we again read the doubtfully accurate description of his ministry of St. Thomas's as a perpetual curacy, and the added note that he was a magistrate; and that he had been collated to Snitterfield in 1802, the same year that he became M.A., by Dr. Hurd, the Bishop of Worcester.

Miss Edwards in her history of St. Thomas's Church tells us that on 1st November 1808 the two surviving trustees of the church requested the bishop to license the Revd. Joseph Taylor, M.A. Vicar of Snitterfield, Warwickshire, *the candidate who had been nominated and elected by the inhabitants of Stourbridge*. We are not, however, told the date of this election, but we do learn that Joseph Taylor was musically inclined. It was in 1809, soon after his arrival, that the church abandoned its barrel organ and invested in a 'finger organ', which was inaugurated in March of that year by a performance at which it was stated that "the amateurs of sacred music experienced the most exquisite delight". Five years later in 1814 Joseph Taylor published *A Collection of Psalms and Hymns for the Use of the Congregation of St. Thomas's Church in Stourbridge,* by the Revd. J. Taylor, M.A., Vicar of Snitterfield and Headmaster of Stourbridge Free Grammar School. We notice that at this time the church was beginning to be called St. Thomas's, and we are interested to see that Joseph Taylor described himself as the holder of his two *other* offices, his church at Snitterfield and the Stourbridge school, and ignored his ministry of St. Thomas's, for which his book was being produced! This is strange, and we have no explanation of it.

These few, and in the historical sense unimportant details are completed by a tribute paid to him after his death by W. B. Collis, a member of a prominent Stourbridge family (a descendant and namesake of the W.B. Collis who was a governor of the school briefly from 1778 to 1779). He wrote as follows:

"There was no individual, whilst living, that I felt more esteem and regard for, or any one to whom I labour under deeper obligations. And I trust that I shall ever entertain a lively sense of his kindness towards me, and the most profound veneration and respect for his memory."

Such, then, are the few glimpses that we catch, amidst the shadows of the St. Thomas's period, of the third of our four headmasters of that period. He was to guide the school for twenty-five years, another example of what appears to be the easy longevity of the heads from Charles Harris to Giffard Wells; and he was to leave little enough behind him by way of recorded achievement or activity. He does, however, have one striking claim on our attention: it was during his regime that the school reached absolute 'rock bottom' as an educational institution. This will become clear as we go on with his story.

We are now pointed towards what we called 'the one fortuitous break in our covering cloud of non-witness' (see page 130). We were referring there to a document from the Harward and Evers archives, whose survival and eventual discovery were both striking examples of our good fortune — all the more so because our researches have been for the most part singularly ill-rewarded as far as this period of the school's history is concerned.

Our document is the exception which proves the rule. It is a small manuscript notebook, of a type common in schools, quite cheap and ordinary, of about the size of those which we used to call 'vocab.-books' when I was at school. It differs from those of my time in being made of unlined paper throughout its 48 pages, and in having a marbled cover instead of one of some grey or tan-coloured cartridge-paper. Considering its age it is well preserved — so much so that one wonders what magic has kept it intact for the better part of two centuries.

Its contents are not obviously valuable or strikingly interesting. The first full 'opening' presents the start of a copper-plate clerk's copy, evenly and monotonously written out on left-hand pages only and extending to just over fifteen pages, or about two-thirds of the way through the book, of the school's foundation charter of 1552. This is clearly identified in a title or heading on its first page:

Translation of the Charter of Stourbridge Free Grammar School

The ensuing text just goes steadily on from beginning to end, uninterrupted by any extraneous matter, *except for four notes*. Strictly speaking these are simply the four numerals, (1) to (4), entered in each case on the right-hand or blank page, opposite to an underline or a marginal upright line in the text on the left-hand page. The points so marked start with the word 'Grammer' (so spelt!) in the school's title, and include reference to the powers of the governors to appoint a headmaster and usher and to make statutes with the endorsement of the bishop of the diocese, their status also as a corporation and obligations as individuals in suits of law, and that passage of the charter which establishes the school's 'licence in mortmain'. In other words, here we have a lawyer's notes; but it would be a very clever man who could deduce from them what legal point was the object of the lawyer's attention. But we do not need to be clever; for on the next left-hand page after the end of the translation of the charter, written out in the same hand, is a *Quaere* from a solicitor asking for Counsel's opinion and extending only to one question of seven lines. This is followed by Counsel's opinion in reply, still in clerk's copperplate, set out at the length of about a page, or 33 lines.

This, of course, is the nub of the whole thing. Before we detail its contents, let us complete our description of the writings in the notebook. The final few pages contain a *List of Governors* (headed in those precise words) with their dates, from 1688 to 1792. We remember that the first surviving governors' minute-book starts at 1688 — so someone else had been consulting it. The handwriting of these names is now anything but copperplate — much freer, larger, blacker, bolder and entirely individual. It is clearly the same as that of a brief inscription entered on the first page of the book, by itself. This says:—

> To John Pidcock Esqr.
> Platts —
> with the Revd. J. Taylor's
> Kind Regard.

So we now know that this book — charter copy, solicitor's case for Counsel, and Counsel's reply — came from our third headmaster of the St. Thomas's period, and was directed by him to one of his governors, John Pidcock of the Platts.

The substance of the question to counsel tells us what we wanted to know. Here it comes:

> Qu. Have the Governors of this School a power under the preceding charter to appoint a Writing Master at the expence of the Foundation, the profits of which are now £290 pr. Annum, in addition to the two present Classical Masters?

If we were to read no further, we should surely already at this stage suspect that we were on the way towards finding out who or what was responsible for cutting the revolution down to size and for turning back the inexorably advancing tide of progress into the modern world (see page 130). For that was precisely the same question as was asked in the Leeds Grammar School case. So it looks as if, just as at Leeds, so at Stourbridge it was the Classical Master who put in his spoke and stopped the modern bandwagon from rolling!

We go on to read what Counsel's opinion on this subject was. It is straightforward and seems logical and sensible:

Counsel doubts if the Governors can of their own authority appoint a writing-master at the expense of the Foundation.

But he thinks that the Court of Chancery would probably do so, if it should appear that the income of £290 is more than enough to support the two Classical masters.

He isolates as the central point at issue the question — *If the £290 is enough to leave money to spare for a writing-master, is a writing-master wanted*?

He says he does not know enough about the circumstances, *and in particular the numbers in the school,* to give an accurate judgement.

But he does not believe in any case that £290 is in fact too much for two Classical Masters, and he concludes *that for that reason the Governors cannot pay a writing-master out of it.*

This is, of course, fascinating stuff. The signature of Counsel — R. Richards — means nothing to us, but the date of his opinion is of crucial importance, — 22 October, 1807!

This date at once stops us in our tracks and bids us reconsider our premature conclusions. For if we were crediting Joseph Taylor with the achievement of getting the legal opinion which might halt the march of progress, we must clearly now think again. Joseph Taylor was not appointed to the school until 19 April 1808, six months *after* the date of Counsel's opinion on the propriety of paying a writing-master out of the funds of the foundation. This opinion had clearly been given in the time of John Pattinson.

The only plausible explanation which will fit these facts is to suppose that it was Pattinson who set himself to check the governors' headlong rush into revolution and the modern world, and he must have set to work to get counsel's opinion in or before October of 1807. It was on 25th May of that year that the governors ordered that counsel should be consulted to find a legal way of changing the character of the school. We found reason to think that Pattinson was losing enthusiasm for his work, Now we seem to have discovered with fair certainty what we had before only suspected, that the governors' proposed changes were indeed anathema to their headmaster. Hence his move, recorded in the marbled notebook, in October 1807, if not before. Two months later, on 17 December 1807, the governors ordered a large extra payment to both headmaster and usher. We found ourselves surprised that Pattinson had resigned in the following April without waiting for his threefold increase in salary. We now see, if we can put ourselves into his place at the time, that he was committed to a stance of total opposition to his governors' plans. He must have felt himself unable to carry on in this situation, and he resigned.

This reconstruction might well explain also what we realised was the quite unnatural speed of his successor's appointment. It now begins to look as if the liaison was between Joseph Taylor and John Pattinson, rather than between Joseph Taylor and the governors. The marbled notebook, we now conclude, while it was certainly Joseph Taylor's instrument for winning over at least one of his governors to his own point of view (for it was certainly he who presented this legal bombshell to John Pidcock of the Platts), had come to him previously as his legacy from the hands of his predecessor John Pattinson. We do not know exactly when the book was presented to John Pidcock, though we conclude that it was most likely in the latter half of 1808. Certainly by February of 1809 the situation had radically changed; for it was then that the Governors, with the consent of the bishop, ordered that the usher should instruct the boys two afternoons every week in writing and accounts.

However, we have not yet finished with this strange episode of the writing-master. First we must refer to the minutes of a governors' meeting of 8 October 1808 — six months after Joseph Taylor's appointment as headmaster, but four months before the decision to cut down their reforms to the two afternoons a week of lessons by the usher in writing and accounts.

October 8 — 1808 At a Meeting of the Governors held at the School House

We the major part of the Governors of the said school do hereby elect appoint and nominate during our pleasure only Michael Beesley to be a writing and accounting master at the said school at a Salary not exceeding Thirty pounds per Annum, he the said Michael Beesley observing and obeying the Rules of the School and attending two days every week at the said school.

        Tho. Hill   Tho. Homfray
        John Causer   Francis Walker
        Jno. Addenbrooke
        Jos. Robins

It is to be noted that six of the eight governors signed this order, the order, the missing two being the Rev. T. P. Foley and John Pidcock. Two months later, on 22 December 1808, the governors ordered "with the Advisement of the Right Revd. Foliot, Lord Bishop of Worcester", that from Michaelmas last the annual salaries should be £150 to the Rev. Joseph Taylor, £80 to the Rev. Richard Willetts, and to Mr. Michael Beesley, during the time he shall attend as Writing Master, the annual stipend of £25. This time those who signed included John Pidcock. So the progress which we have presumed of the campaign of Joseph Taylor, with the collaboration of John Pidcock, to persuade his governors, begins to recede from probability. We have to look around us for further evidence or for straws in the wind that will help us towards a feasible explanation of what was happening. For the moment we are bound to accept that our explanation of the course of events from the meeting of 18 December 1806, when the governors unveiled their revolutionary plans, to that of 23 February 1809, when they decided merely to make the usher teach writing and accounts on two afternoons a week — our story of this period of twenty-six months, fraught with the most fateful issues for the future of the school, is uncertain and obscure. Two further discoveries, however, from the governors' minute-book bring us some help in our search.

FIRST We find that in fact no payment was ever recorded in any of the annual accounts to any Mr. Michael Beesley as writing-master. He simply drops out of view as if he had never existed. So he at any rate can safely be set aside from our narrative and forgotten. The revolution, it seems, was indeed doomed to be cut down to size.

SECOND Meantime on 13th June 1808 the annual accounts include the following payments to John Pattinson:

1807	28 Oct.	Pd. to Rev. J. Pattinson	22.10.0d
	21 Dec.	to do. more	55.0.0d
		To do. for Councillor Mr. Richards opinion	2.2.0d
1808	9 Apr.	To Rev. J. Pattinson	50.0.0d
	9 May	To do.	50.0.0d

This certainly sets the cat among our pigeons. For not only were the governors loading Pattinson with bribes in the form of extra salary in the years 1807 and 1808; but they also in December of 1807 actually paid him the cost of getting counsel's opinion (and an adverse opinion, at that) about the propriety of their paying a writing-master. This certainly confirms our belief that it was indeed Pattinson who moved to get that opinion; but it also raises the probability that after Pattinson had got the opinion he presented it openly and officially to the governors. The official recording of the reimbursement, on 21 December, of his two guineas, together with details of the purpose for which that reimbursement was made, seems to indicate beyond doubt that the discouraging opinion had been officially passed on to the governors before the end of 1807. Quite clearly it did not have the effect desired by Pattinson, and on 16 April 1808 Pattinson had had enough and decided to resign. He passed on his legal ammunition to Joseph Taylor, and Joseph Taylor at some stage, and for reasons which we do not know, sent it with his Kind Regard to John Pidcock. Six months after Joseph Taylor's appointment, on 8 October 1808 the governors were still intransigent and moved to appoint Michael Beesley. Why they proceeded in the next four months or so to change their minds, abandon the idea of a writing master, and cut down their reform to a mere fraction of its original force, remains a mystery. But on 23 February 1809 came the new resolution, — to make the usher teach the writing and accounts!

As for the part played by Joseph Taylor and John Pidcock in this retreat, we cannot be sure of our facts; for the governors' minutes are woefully incomplete (as we have seen in the case of the dropping of Michael Beesley), as well as untidy and disorderly during the last years of William Moseley's long service. But we have one more port of call, so to speak, on this rather uncertain voyage of discovery. It will take us right away from our own archives onto much surer ground, though it will not clear up all uncertainties. It takes us also forward in time by a quarter of a century, to the year 1833, the very year of Joseph Taylor's death, though that is entirely a matter of coincidence. In that year was published the great Report of the Commission for Inquiring Concerning Charities in England and Wales — a monumental record of a monumental task. In volume XV of that report, on pages 569-75, comes the report on the Stourbridge Free Grammar School. It is comprehensive, enormously competent and well-informed, and also for our purposes extremely informative. This is the part which interests us here (on pages 573-4):

"It will be seen from the statutes that the school was in its original foundation a free grammar school, it being ordered that no boy should be admitted to learn writing and accounts only. *This regulation, however, shows that such instruction was not excluded*; and there are several early entries in the minute-books, from which the same inference arises. This subject was more particularly taken into consideration in 1806; and in 1808 a writing-master was appointed, with a salary of £25 a year.

In 1809 it was ordered with the consent of the Bishop of Worcester that the usher for the time being should instruct the boys two afternoons in every week in writing and accounts as well as in Classical learning. A quarterage was paid by the parents of the children for such extra instruction.

Under this arrangement the school appears to have flourished for some years, there being at one time near 50 boys in the school, of whom above half (including six or seven boarders) were entered under the headmaster. They were principally the sons of neighbouring gentlemen and the more opulent tradesmen in the town, and in several instances went from school to the universities.

About the year 1813 one of the then governors objected to the payment for instruction in writing and accounts, as well as to the admission of boys into the upper school, without previously passing through the lower. From this period the headmaster admitted no more boys on the terms of paying quarterage, and gave up taking boarders. Mr. Homfray, who had then just been appointed Usher, had a few children remaining with him, who continued to pay him a guinea a quarter. *But the school soon ceased to be attended,* and for several years *there was no scholar at all:* there were, however, afterwards occasionally one or two boys in the lower school for a short period. The school has continued much in the same state within the last twelve months, when a few boys have attended. *At the time of our inquiry these were four boys in the upper and four in the lower school.* Of the causes which have led to the decay of the school we shall have an opportunity of remarking at the close of this Report, when we shall have learned the result of some proceedings which were in progress at the time of our inquiry."

The report then gives figures to show that the average expenditure on the charity for six years past was £414.15.8d, of which the masters' salaries accounted for £322.13.4d for doing, in effect, nothing!

We shall come back later to the 1833 Charities Inquiry Report and the 'proceedings' to which it refers. For the moment let us only say that we are glad to find confirmation of our theory that one governor was found (though not until 1813) to stand in the path of progress and to halt the revolution. Whether that one governor was John Pidcock of the Platts we have no means of knowing. But if we are inclined, unless and until some fresh evidence suggests some other candidate for the honour, to accord it to him, let it be recorded also, that if he deserves it he was also responsible for the disgraceful fact that for no less then twenty years, from 1813 to 1833, there were either no boys at all or a pitiful handful at any given time in the school. In 1820, for example, in Bentley's Worcestershire Directory (p.166) we read, "The school is handsomely endowed, has two respectable houses for the residence of the masters, whose salaries are liberal, *but there are no scholars.*" In the same publication for 1837 (p.13) we learn that *"about six boys are at present on the foundation"*. In 1833, as we have just been told, there were eight.

This is what we meant when we said of the Rev. Joseph Taylor that it was during his regime that the school reached absolute 'rock bottom' as an educational institution. It is an astonishing thought that he served as headmaster for twenty-five years, and that for most of that time he had either no pupils at all, or fewer than ten. This was an extreme example of the blighting effect of what we have called the 'dead hand'. One can only wonder which of the two evils John Pattinson would have found the lesser if he had stood his ground and taken his threefold increase in salary. Was it the teaching of writing and accounts by his usher? Or was it the total dereliction of the school until it became an echoing and deserted shell?

We have not quite finished with the story of the Rev. Joseph Taylor. Remembering that the Charity Inquiry report gave 1813 as the year when the action of one of the governors effectively brought the school to an end, we turn to the governors' minute-book under that fateful date, to see how the governors recorded such a catastrophe. The answer is as simple as it is surprising: they simply ignored it. But perhaps this is not so surprising when we recollect that the governors minutes never at any time took any notice of the real business of the school, the business of teaching and learning. Lands, buildings, leases, repairs? — Yes! — Governors, headmaster, ushers? — Yes! Boys, books, lessons, scholarship? — No, certainly not! So it was, and so it went on; with the result that when there ceased to be any boy, any teaching, or any learning, it made no difference at all to the record of the governors' activities.

The year 1813, however, throws up one piece of information of great interest to our search for a closer acquaintance with the Rev. Joseph Taylor. There are only four minutes of proceedings entered in the book for that year, and their substance is as follows:

1) On 19 March the governors appointed *Jeremiah Caswell Homfray* to be usher in the place of the Rev. Joseph Read, resigned. This Jeremiah must be the son of Francis Homfray by his second wife Catherine, daughter of Jeremiah Caswell of the Hyde, Kinver. The Homfrays were a family of ironmasters, originating from a place called Wales, near to Rotherham, and first resident in the Stourbridge district in the early years of the eighteenth century. Francis Homfray's youngest brother John married Mary, the daughter of Jeremiah Addenbrooke, and their son John Addenbrooke Homfray inherited Addenbrooke money and estates and in 1798 by royal licence changed his name to John Addenbrooke Addenbrooke. He was elected a governor of the school as J. A. Homfray in 1792, and was still on the governing body as J. A. Addenbrooke in 1813, when his cousin was appointed usher.

(2) On 14th June the annual accounts were adopted on Trinity Monday.

(3) On 23 June appears the following minute, in William Moseley's handwriting:
At a meeting of the Governors held at the School House in Stourbridge this 23rd of June 1813 the Revd. Joseph Taylor gave in his Resignation, of which the following is a Copy:

To the Governors of the Free Grammar School of King Edward the Sixth in Stourbridge in the County of Worcester,
Gentlemen,

In consequence of my intention to reside at my Vicarage in Snitterfield I do hereby beg leave to resign into your hands the Headmastership of the free Grammar School of King Edward the Sixth in Stourbridge in the County of Worcester.
     I am, Gentlemen, Yours sincerely,
       Jos. Taylor
Dated at Stourbridge
the 22nd day of June 1813

Signed and delivered by the Revd.
Joseph Taylor in the presence of
    Willm. Moseley.

Below, this, written in a new hand, much clearer, firmer, and evidently that of a younger man, we read:

> At a meeting of the Governors held at the School this twenty-third Day of June 1813. Whereas the Revd. Jos. Taylor hath by a letter under his hand bearing date the twenty-second Day of June inst. resigned the place of Head Schoolmaster of the free Grammar School of King Edward the Sixth in Stourbridge, We the major part of the Governors of the said school Do elect nominate and appoint the Revd. John Morley A.M. of Woodbridge in Suffolk Head Master of the school aforesaid to succeed the said Joseph Taylor, He the said John Morley being to observe the Rules and Orders of the said school.
>   Signatures of seven governors

(4) On the next page but one, following the accounts of 6 June 1814 and therefore entered out of due order, is the following:

> At a meeting of the Governors held at the School the Thirty-first day of August 1813 — Whereas the Revd. John Morley A.M. has by letter under his hand bearing the date the 10th day of this inst. August resigned the place of Head Master ... etc. etc. ... We the major part of the Governors of the said School do elect nominate and appoint the Reverend Joseph Taylor A.M. of Stourbridge Head Master of the said School to succeed the said John Morley, he the said Joseph Taylor being to observe the Rules and Orders of the said school.
>   Signed by all eight governors

Pasted onto this page are two letters, one the resignation of John Morley, dated 10th August 1813, the other the original letter of resignation of Joseph Taylor (exactly as cited above) dated 22nd June 1813.

This is the entire record as the minute-book presents it. What we are to make of it would be hard, if not impossible, to say, were it not for yet another example of our familiar serendipity.

The bare facts are these:-
On 22nd June Joseph Taylor resigned. He was replaced *on the spot*

by a Rev. John Morley, apparently from Suffolk, who is otherwise unknown to us. About three weeks later Morley resigned. After another fortnight Joseph Taylor was appointed again. The school, which we understand from the 1833 Charity Enquiry report had been in recent years 'flourishing' was shortly to decline into the lowest possible state of decay, that of having no pupils at all.

Did Joseph Taylor, then, like Pattinson before him, feel so strongly that writing and accounts were not for him that, like Pattinson again, he felt that he could face it no longer and simply resigned? Did the objecting governor, also mentioned in the 1833 report, succeed in his objection soon afterwards and manage to return the school to its old ways? Who was Morley? How could the governors possibly choose him at no more that twenty-four hours notice? Why did he in his turn resign?

The governors did not rate such matters as important enough to be recorded in their minutes, and on this occasion their reticence almost reduces us to impotent silence: almost! — let us repeat the blessed word, but not quite. For during the actual writing of the present section of this history, almost but luckily not quite too late to be taken into account in our attempt to get behind the apparent facts to the mysterious motives, there came to light from an old folder, full of miscellaneous material of greater or lesser relevance to our story, accumulated over the years and in many cases faded from the memory, a substantial newspaper article, evidently printed in the County Express in its old days as a traditional local journal. The article in question proved to be a scholarly description of the friction and upheaval caused in the town of Stourbridge in the past by the link between St. Thomas's Church and the Grammar School. The author stated that he had at his disposal "a bundle of old documents shown to the County Express by Mr. H. E. Palfrey, F.S.A." Using these, he was able to throw a flood of light upon the Taylor-Morley incident of 1813. The relevant paragraphs read as follows:

"... Taylor continued as minister and headmaster of the Grammar School until 1833. But it would seem that within a few years of his appointment there was some question of his resigning his appointments at the church and school in favour of the Rev. John Morley, *vicar of Wasperton*, which was the parish next to Snitterfield. On June 23rd 1813 Morley did in fact tender his resignation of the Wasperton living to the Bishop of Worcester, and a Stourbridge meeting elected him to be minister. But many people in Stourbridge it seems were not prepared to have a change. "The Rev. Joseph Taylor wrote from Stratford-on-Avon on June 25 1813 to Henry Roberts of Stourbridge. 'I am truly sorry for the uproar, and afraid we shall have some trouble.' On the reverse side of this note the Rev. John Morley wrote on the same day, 'Mr. Taylor having read me your letter which he has just received, I cannot help feeling and expressing great regret at the clamour which has been so unjustly and ungenerously raised in the town. It is pretty clear that personal hostility against me has nothing to do with it, and that a desire on the part of certain persons to separate the church from the school, *and to reduce the latter to a mere commercial establishment*, has caused all the opposition to my election.' Mr. Morley's note concludes as follows: '... unless I exert myself in advancing the credit of the school, it is a positive fact that I shall not gain a farthing in any other way by the exchange. Nay, I shall be a loser, for my vicarage is of more value than Stourbridge school by £20 per annum, and my curacies at Ipswich are of more value than the new church by £15 per annum.''

The author of the article draws the following conclusion:

> "From this it would seem that Taylor, who is known to have neglected his duties as head of the Grammar School, and probably could not devote much time to St. Thomas's because of his commitments at Snitterfield, had come to an arrangement with Morley that Morley should exchange his Warwickshire vicarage for the combined positions of headmaster of the school and minister of St. Thomas's. But the local opposition prevented the move, and the Rev. Joseph Taylor continued in office until 1833."

This is, of course, quite invaluable as an explanation of what was going on. The article was unsigned, but one would readily ascribe it to the pen of Mr. H. J. Haden, that indefatigable and unrivalled student of the history of Stourbridge, whose efforts have repeatedly been of inestimable value in the search to dredge up the casualties of time from the waters of oblivion. If this information indeed came from him, then we owe him yet one more debt for his unrivalled contribution to the labours of research.

The Mystery of the Cupola

This was the precise time in the history of the school which saw the physical destruction — or rather, partial destruction — of its buildings by fire. It is an odd coincidence that this came about when in any case the school as an institution of learning had ceased to function. In earlier pages we told the story of the water-colour picture from Professor Bate's book on Samuel Johnson. On that picture, behind the two masters' houses, rebuilt in the time of Mr. Browne and Mr. Crane (1699-1705), appeared the mysterious tower and cupola whose history we tried in vain to elucidate. It was that very tower and cupola which was destroyed by fire at a time very close to Joseph Taylor's resignation in 1813.

In his 1948 pamphlet history of the school, Mr. George Burley wrote:

> "A correspondent writing to the Stourbridge Observer on 11th February 1865 says, 'on Whit Tuesday at midnight in 1813 the Free Grammar School grand and noble charity, was destroyed. This conflagration I witnessed, and saw the bell fall, which smashed'.

Mr. Burley commented that he had been unable to confirm the destruction of the 'grand and noble charity', and added, "I think that the correspondent's memory must have played him false after a lapse of 52 years."

However, Mr. Burley goes on to say that a news item from the Stourbridge and Dudley Messenger of July 1st 1814 seems to prove that there had been a fire of some kind. This item reported the completion of a new cupola at the Grammar School, erected by the Coalbrookdale Company and thirty feet high above the battlements, made of cast iron. "It is perfectly safe from fire — the last cupola was burnt down." So the correspondent of 1865 was in the main right. The cupola and tower *were* destroyed by fire and the bell *was* smashed. His only mistake was in the date, and we have two-fold proof of this. In 'The Reades of Blackwood Hill', that monumental work of Johnsonian genealogy, we are told on page 150 that the author had been informed by Mr. Freer, of the family which owned and occupied Green Close House at the time of which we are speaking, "that when his father William Leacroft Freer lay dying at Green Close in 1812, the school was nearly destroyed by fire, and the invalid had to be carried away out of danger." It is most unlikely that Mr. Freer's memory of that date could be at fault, and we can accept his testimony. Moreover in the governors' minute-book, at the foot of the annual accounts of John Pidcock as Collector — presented, of course, by William Moseley — on 15th June 1812, we read:

> "We also direct that the Tower and Cupola be rebuilt and a new Bell put therein, and that an Estimate and Elevation be first made for our inspection."

Nothing could be more conclusive than this. The fire was at that time a fact, and the governors were dealing with its effects. Whit Tuesday in that year was 19 May, and Trinity Monday was 25th May. So the Trinity audit was being held precisely three weeks late, quite possibly because of the fire.

The minute-book has nothing else to tell us about the fire, but the Black Box contained an interesting and pretty complete record of the governors' correspondence with the Coalbrookdale Company, together with the company's accounts for designing, manufacturing and installing the cupola. Mr. Burley had seen the local newspaper report, dated 1st July 1814, about the completion of the work. All, efforts to track down that newspaper have come to nothing, but we cannot doubt its authenticity.

The two fold mystery remains as we recorded earlier. First, where was the site of the tower and cupola? It was a massive structure, towering above the school houses, visible all over the town and far beyond. The cupola itself was thirty feet in height. The original schoolroom, a small *cella* or chapel with a pitched roof, even if we allow for the two extensions to its length which we suppose housed the Hickman library, simply could not have carried it. Yet there is nothing else to be seen on the architect's drawing of the old buildings as the time of the great rebuilding of 1860 which could be remotely considered as suitable for the base of the tower.

So we come to our second question. When was the first tower built, and when was the second, that of 1814, demolished? The governors' minutes are so limited and selective in what they record that we are thrown back on a despairing search through the surviving builders' and tradesmen's accounts. Here we are on uncertain ground, since all we can look for is evidence of unusually large expenditure: specification of the work concerned is uniformly conspicuous by its absence. But references to the existence of the tower, the cupola or the bell keep cropping up, and they prove to be valuable.

Working, first forward and then backward, from the year 1812 through the accounts and the Black Box papers and other surviving records has been a tedious process, and its results cannot claim any certainty. However, in the forward process we find negative results until we reach the year 1857-8, very close to the great rebuilding. Here there is a payment to John Scott, who was a mason, of £116.6.0d. This is an enormous bill when we remember that the total of all building and maintenance costs for many whole years during this period was less than half that sum; it is more than three times as big as any other such account of the time. So this might well conceal the record of the removal of the tower and cupola. Two years later, in 1860, when the architect made his drawing of the existing buildings, there was no sign of a possible base for a tower of the kind shown in the watercolour.

Going then in the other direction, backward from 1812, once again the minutes are incomplete and the archives inevitably haphazard and sporadic. Even so, we do find references to the 'school bell', the 'belfry', and the 'cupiloe'. We need not give a complete list here, but a few examples will show what we mean.

1797		2 cwt. sheet lead for cupola
		15 of white paint for ditto
		7 cwt. 2 qr. 27lb of sheet lead to tower.
		work at free school tower by order of Mr. Moseley.
		altering passage to clock and scaffolding round etc.
1788		Bell-rope, omitted before.
		To the care of the bell, 2 yrs, at 1/6.
		to the blacksmith's bill for repairing the iron work to the bell, a new stock to ditto.
1785		Painting the cupiloe
1784		A new part to the belfry floor.
1783		Ironwork for ye bell.
1782		A door jamb to Belfrey door case.
1782–3		Hanging the bell, repairing the wheels, bracing the frame, fresh capping the clapper of Bell in Cupiloe.

There is no need for further quotation. Clearly the purpose of the tower and cuploa was to serve as a housing for the bell, and the bell was considered to be important. Significant entries on the same lines can be found going back to 1763, where we find the following:

    1763   Mending ye Belfry door lock.

In other words the belfy — and that must mean the tower — certainly existed in 1763. Before that the records, it is true, are scantier. But they contain *no* references to bell, belfry, tower or bell-rope. In the circumstances this *must* be significant for our enquiry. So we conclude tentatively that it is at least reasonable to date the first tower and cupola to about the year 1760, and the destruction of the second (the replacement of 1814) to about a hundred years later, in 1857.

Endpiece to Joseph Taylor

We left Joseph Taylor on 31st August 1813 (see page 143), newly reinstated as headmaster of the school after his resignation. We know from the Charities Inquiry Report of 1833 that soon after the 1813 incident "the headmaster admitted no more boys on the terms of paying quarterage, and gave up taking boarders ... the school soon ceased to be attended, and for several years there was no scholar at all ... The school has continued much in the same state within the last twelve months, when a few boys have attended. At the time of our inquiry there were four boys in the upper and four in the lower school."

We repeat this passage from the 1833 report to bring home to the reader the melancholy and astonishing truth about Joseph Taylor's headmastership. We earlier described the school under him as "an echoing and deserted shell", and so indeed it must have been. The destruction of the tower and cupola by fire was made good, as we have learnt, by the governors with commendable speed and efficiency, and at considerable expense. In 1815 we read in the minute-book a sentence appended at the end of the annual accounts:

"The Governors of the free Grammar School do allow this account and nominate the Rev. T. P. Foley Cashier and Thos. Hill Esq. Assistant And do likewise order that the Library be repaired."

No-one could possibly tell from reading the Governors' minutes that there was anything amiss with the school; one can only wonder what on earth was the purpose or point of rebuilding the tower and cupola, and now of repairing the library, when there were no boys to be summoned by the bell or to read in the library. It is a ghostly and weird situation, when one sits back and takes it in — and it was to continue in much the same state for the astonishing period of twenty years. The imagination of Charles Dickens might perhaps have done it justice: but surely no one would have believed in the possibility of the picture, even if Dickens had spread himself and summoned up all his powers to shroud the school in dust and cobwebs like some bizarre cross between Dotheboys Hall and the house of Miss Havisham!

But the governors went steadily on, playing their solemn game of business-as-usual, or, perhaps more accurately, of make-believe. Incidentally, the order to repair the library, following on the rebuilding of the tower and cupola, suggests that the two were, as we suspected, separate structures. Nothing further is mentioned about the library repairs, just as nothing further was said about Mr. Michael Beesley the mythical writing-master. But after a further five years, on 29 May 1820, there was a very important meeting. At long last the long, long service of the Moseleys had come to an end, and it was carefully recorded that the Governors "do order that Mr. John Perry of Stourbridge be and is hereby appointed (in the room of the late Mr. William Moseley deceased) deputy or under Collector of the Rents issues and profits of this school at a salary of fifteen guineas per annum And that he do give bond with two sureties to the Governors in the penal sum of Five Hundred Pounds for the due and faithful performance of his office." This, of course, reminds us of what were the really important things to those eight Stourbridge worthies in the year 1820. We had been forgetting the Rents, issues and profits! But the trustees must not forget them, and indeed they did not. So the records go on — every penny received, every halfpenny spent — duly and faithfully set down, by a new Secretary (still an ironmonger in Stourbridge High Street, but no longer a Moseley) in a new hand.

John Perry seems to have made a good job of his stewardship. The balances in his hands steadily increase, to be doled out in the precise proportions of five and three to the Rev. Joseph Taylor and the Rev. J.C. Homfray. On 18th June 1821 John Perry, and all his Governors with him, dividing £75 between the two masters, allotted £45 to Mr. Taylor and £30 to Mr. Homfray. But the arithmetical error was not allowed to pass uncorrected. One year later, on 6 June

1822, the governors ordered that £80 be divided between them: but they also decided "that five pounds be paid to the Revd. Joseph Taylor to make his share equal to the Rev. J. C. Homfray of last year."

So careful were the authorities of the school to see that everything was done exactly as it should be! In 1823 they decided to pay the sexton of Oldswinford church half a guinea a year for "cleaning the seat and taking up the books belonging to the Governor". That was the year when one of the Governors named Joseph Robins died, and was succeeded by Henry Roberts. This latter we identified as the first of four solicitor-governors who acted as unofficial legal advisers before the practice developed of employing a lawyer as clerk to the governors in the modern sense (see page 8 above). We now see that after Joseph Robins' death the governors' accounts included several payments to his executors, including one for the very considerable sum of £42.10.10d. Accounts amongst the Black Box papers show us that this money was due for legal work going back many years into the time of William Moseley. After the old man's death in 1820 the Governors were faced with an accumulation of unpaid bills from different sources — tradesmen, workmen, and so on. He had evidently become not just an institution in his later years but also something of a law unto himself). The big account due to Joseph Robins prompts us to look for him in the local records, and he emerges as a Stourbridge solicitor, whose son William later became a local banker, resident in Hagley, and in his time to become High Sheriff of the County. Joseph had been elected a Governor in 1802 and it is now clear that he in fact *preceded* Henry Roberts as the first in the line of unofficial legal advisers to the school. We learn also that his grand-daughter Mary, co-heiress with her sister of William Robins, banker and High Sheriff, was married to the Rev. G. D. Boyle, vicar of Kidderminster, whom we met (see page 15 above) when we were telling the story of how we recovered the portrait of Edward VI.

However, we must not be distracted from our story of the Governors' charade. It is almost literally meaningless and of no importance, when you set it against the fact that the school meantime was entirely or nearly devoid of boys. But the governors went on solemnly doing their job — collecting the Rents, issues and profits, maintaining the empty fabric, doling out the surplus money to the under-employed masters. In 1827 the rent-roll amounts to no less than £420.4.8d. The balances in hand, after all payments were running at £84, £99, £194, and so on. In March 1831 the distribution to Mr. Taylor and Mr. Homfray amounted to £144. Then at last in 1832 we come to a year of incidents.

First we go back to the Charity Inquiry Report, from which we quoted a promise from the commissioners that they would comment on the reasons for the decay of the school when they had learnt the result of some 'proceedings' which were in progress at the time of their inquiry. It is time now for us to see what these proceedings were. The Report tells us. The four last paragraphs read as follows:

"Shortly before the time of our examination a meeting of the most respectable inhabitants of Stourbridge had been called to take into consideration the state of the Grammar School, and a committee was appointed to inquire into the causes which had tended to reduce it to its present neglected state. Their report, which was soon after presented to the governors, imputed it mainly to the misconduct of the undermaster, and the committee suggested that it would be of great advantage, and tend to the permanent efficiency of the school, if a master were appointed to teach English, writing and arithmetic, and added, that if the governors did not feel justified in appropriating any part of the funds for that purpose, the expense would be cheerfully borne by the parents of the children.

"This report was presented to the governors. A meeting subsequently took place between them and the committee, and we are informed, that since the period of our inquiry, the undermaster has resigned his situation upon terms which have met with the concurrence and approbation of the Bishop of Worcester, and that his place has been filled by a person competent to teach writing and accounts, for which instruction he is to receive a quarterage from the boys.

"The school has been repaired, and more conveniently fitted up for the reception of the scholars.

"It appears to us very desirable that the statutes should be carefully revised, with the consent of the bishop, and adapted to the existing circumstances of the population; and we have no doubt that, by the advice and judicious interference of the governors, this school may be re-established with the most beneficial results to the town and neighbourhood."

It is a remarkable fact that what we have here, in March 1832, is little if anything more than a restatement of the governors' minute of their meeting of 18 December 1806 (see page 126 above). It had taken almost 26 years, mostly years of dereliction and decay, to bring the governors back to their resolve that there should be a revolution. But this time they were not alone: they had the bulk of responsible opinion in the town behind them.

We can in fact set down the official record of that meeting of the most respectable inhabitants of Stourbridge, referred to in the Report above. It is to be found in the Milward Evidences (or the Palfrey Scrapbooks) in the County Record Office at Worcester, on page 277 of Volume 1, where we read as follows:

> At a general meeting of the inhabitants of the Township of Stourbridge and the Parish of Oldswinford for the purpose of taking into Consideration the present state of the Free Grammar School of King Edward the Sixth, held the 3rd day of March 1832.
>
> Wm. Robins Esq. in the chair.

It was unanimously resolved:

> Upon the motion of Mr. George Bate, seconded by Mr. Causer THAT the Free Grammar School in this Town has of late years been almost without scholars, and thus rendered useless for the purposes for which it was founded.
> Upon the motion of Mr. R. Scott, seconded by Mr. Freer THAT a committee be appointed to confer with the Governors and to consider what measures can be adopted to restore the Utility of the school.
> Upon the motion of Mr. J.H. Dixon, seconded by Mr. W. H. Hickman THAT Messrs. Richard Hickman Robert Scott W.H. Freer Thomas Bate William Orme Jeremiah Mathews George Bate Thomas Penn Edward Rogers Thos Mansell Chas. John Wragge William Hunt Junr. Francies Rufford Junr. Paul Mathews Edward Causer Joseph Pitman Joseph King and John Collis be appointed such a committee, with power add to their number, and that any five of them shall be empowered to act.
> Upon the motion of Fra. Rufford Junr. seconded by Mr. Thomas Mansell THAT the thanks of this meeting be given to the following who proposed the meeting — Richard Hickman,

Robert Scott, Wm. M. Freer, Thomas Bate, William Orme, Jeremiah Mathews and George Bate.
William Robins. Chairman

The minutes are in manuscript (all in one hand) and on paper, and in the Palfrey scrapbook they are accompanied by a folded and addressed slip, in clerk's copperplate, of invitation to a committee meeting at the Talbot on the Monday next after March 20th at 10 a.m.

We notice that the chairman of this meeting was none other than the William Robins whom we have mentioned as a banker of Stourbridge and son of the Joseph Robins who had been a governor of the school from 1802 until his death in 1813. The names of the other gentlemen concerned would certainly repay the researcher into the making of modern Stourbridge, but apart from two Hickmans, a Scott, a Freer, a Rogers, a Hunt and a Collis, all names which have occured in our previous pages, we cannot linger over them here.

We come next to the official record of the departure of the usher. Needless to say, the governors' minute-book contains no indication or inkling of any meeting of the governors with any outside party, no hint of a breath of criticism of the usher, let alone any suggestion that it was the usher's shortcomings which had ruined the school — since as far as the minute-book was concerned the ruin of the school is simply not recognised. The substance of the minute is as follows:

Meeting of 9 July 1832.
1. J.C. Homfray resigns his post as usher on the terms set out in a written memorandum sanctioned and approved by the bishop and attached verbatim here.
2. The memorandum says that the Governors have proposed the terms, and the usher has accepted them, subject to the bishop's approval. He is to resign his post and give up the house attached to it. in return he is to receive a 'retiring salary' of £80 a year, payable half-yearly at Midsummer and Christmas, for as long as he lives.
    The governors have already submitted the memorandum by a deputation to the bishop, and his written approval is set out in due form at the foot.
3. The governors now appoint John Malsbury Kirby, B.D., as usher in place of J.C. Homfray, at a salary of £70 a year. (a) He is to teach the lower boys the classics up to the stage of

Phaedrus' Fables. (b) He is also to teach them writing and arithmetic two days in every week. (c) He is to be paid one guinea a quarter by the parents of every boy who learns writing and arithmetic. (d) He is at liberty to take up to six boarders, who are to be educated along with the boys on the foundation. (e) He is to give six months notice of leaving, or to forfeit six months salary.
4. The new usher signs a written acceptance of the post and an acceptance of the terms set out above.

So "the desire of certain persons to reduce the school to a mere commerical establishment" (see page 145 above) had at last triumphed over the desire to preside over an empty and echoing shell — and the school was embarked at last upon the long, slow, painful voyage from decay and disuse towards prosperity, public usefulness, and in the end academic distinction. But, truth to tell, one can hardly accept the proposition voiced by those "most respectable of the inhabitants of Stourbridge" which ascribed the ruin of the school to the deficiencies of the usher. He may indeed well have been a 'total loss' — we just do not know. But it required no bad usher to bring the school to ruin in the conditions of those times. and however brilliant a success any usher might have been, he could never by his own efforts have kept the school's head above the swirling waters of the new industrial society by teaching a programme devoted mainly to the ancient classics. Jeremiah Caswell Homfray was a scapegoat, and the cloud under which he departed covered a multitude of sins that were not of his commission.

Not that he came off badly in the financial sense. He was guaranteed his full official salary for life — a prime example of what was often the cheapest and best course for a governing body to take (see page 111 above). We should probably also reflect that he may well have owed his post to his relationsip to the John Addenbrooke Homfray, later Addenbrooke, who served as a governor from 1792 to 1837, and to the John Addenbrooke Addenbrooke Junior who served from 1827 to 1836. Had this happened in the time of Alchurche, or even of Wentworth, we should doubtless have had some pretty clear indications surviving in the records of what was going on. Not so in the year 1832. Mr. Homfray took his departure, and with it his pension, and his successor took a ten-pound cut in his salary — all without any expressed comment or explanation.

But the pension did not last very long. On 19th December of the same year J.C. Homfray died. His executors were paid £40 for a half-year's 'salary' and from 21st December Mr. J.M. Kirby went onto his full salary of £80 a year.

If this was progress, then things were getting on. And next, as if to satisfy the impatience of those who were looking forward to reform, we are told that "The Rev. Joseph Taylor ... having applied for and obtained the Governors' permission to retire for the space of six months from the 13th May next, for the purpose of re-establishing his health — and having proposed to appoint the Rev. Charles Tookey to officiate for him in the school during his absence... the governors resolved to accept Mr. Tookey as a fit and proper person to take Mr. Taylor's place, and to live in the house, — with the express proviso that he give it up at the end of the six months."

We pause only to wonder what exactly Mr. Tookey would find to do when he came to take over the school; we look in vain for any sign of his name in the annual accounts, and conclude that either he never came, or he was not paid out of the foundation funds.* And on the next page of the minute-book in the minutes of 3rd June 1833, we read that Joseph Taylor had died on 2nd May last, eleven days before he was due to start on his long holiday, and that a bonus of £80 was to be divided in the usual proportions between his estate and the new usher, the Rev. J. M. Kirby.

So Joseph Taylor's long spell was over. The way was clear for a new regime; and it can truthfully be said that the hopes expressed by the Charity Inquiry Commissioners "that the school may be re-established with the most beneficial results to the town and neighbourhood" were no longer doomed of necessity to inevitable frustration.

---

*The 1833 election material tells us that The Rev. Charles Tookey was a parson at Wolverley. Joseph Taylor was going to recompense him for his work as substitute by giving him the curacy at Snitterfield, worth £65 a year! But the arrangement fell down because the leave of absence offered by the governors was too short to make all the necessary furniture removals worth while.

An End and a Beginning:
Giffard Wells (1)

Before we resume our narrative, let us take a glance at the evidence for recovery under Giffard Wells. For the recovery did begin in his time. That evidence is to be found in an article written in the year 1922 and printed in the then newly inaugurated school magazine, the Stourbridge Edwardian. It was entitled 'Notes on the History of the School', and the editor announced that it was to be the first in a series of articles. The author was the then headmaster, J.E. Boyt (1905-34). He was as good as the editor's word on his behalf, and contributed about a dozen articles on the school's history. Readers may recall that we said that in his 1948 history Mr. Burley paid tribute to two people's researches — H.E. Palfrey and J.E. Boyt. The time for us to speak of J.E. Boyt has at last come.

To the present writer J.E. Boyt's part in the search for the school's history has always been rather mysterious. George Burley wrote in the school magazine in 1951 that he first heard of the Black Box about 1925, when the then headmaster — the late J.E. Boyt — told him that he had first been informed about it on his appointment in 1905. I gathered from Mr. Burley that J.E. Boyt never gave up his belief in the lost records and the Black Box which contained them. The strange thing is that those records — the whole mass of them — certainly emerged from the offices of Travis and Sheldon in 1913 (see page 10) and were carried across the road to Harward and Evers' offices, whence long years later they came permanently to light. J.E. Boyt *must* have known of their existence at the time — and in any case a reading of his articles in the magazine makes it clear beyond doubt that he had certainly studied very many of the documents which were supposed to be lost and which later came to light in the so-called Black Box collection. There is no other way in which he could have known what he put into his articles.

J.E. Boyt did not always record where he had got his facts from. One can often deduce their origin from one's own studies of the archives; but on the topic of the number of boys in the school at different times — in which he was always greatly interested — we have until recently been unable to check his figures, because we did not know their source. Now, however, there has emerged from the archives the first register of pupils ever compiled (following an order of the Governors in 1839) (see page 167 below). It was actually to be found in the Black Box collection, but was there wrongly catalogued as an attendance-book, which it certainly is not. It is a very basic and elementary record of names-on-roll, covering the years 1840-1859. For our present purposes it confirms J.E. Boyt's figures and is indubitably the source of his information — one more of the 'lost' archives. Its figures give simple proof of the recovery of the school from the pit of dereliction into which it had fallen under Joseph Taylor. There were eight boys in the school in 1832, we remember: Giffard Wells took over in 1833. Here are J.E. Boyt's figures from 1840 to 1858:

Year	No. of Boys	Year	No. of Boys
1840	17	1850	41
1841	25	1851	23
1842	24	1852	29
1843	31	1853	53
1844	27	1854	51
1845	22	1855	33
1846	23	1856	25
1847	22	1857	25
1848	30	1858	37
1849	26		

There is some fluctuation here; but the average for the first ten years is 25, for the remaining nine years 35, and for the whole period about 30. The Charities Inquiry commissioners considered that the school 'flourished' when the numbers approached 50. Our conclusion is that Giffard Wells did what John Morley had intended to do in 1813, that is to say, "to exert himself in advancing the credit of the school".

The new headmaster, appointed on 26 June 1833, is described in the minutes as simply the Revd. Giffard Wells M.A., of Sidney

Sussex College, Cambridge. The date is eight weeks after Joseph Taylor's death; so this time there was no 'instant replacement' practised, as before. In fact the governors voted a special payment of five pounds to John Perry, for his extreme trouble over the election of a headmaster, and for the first time we have the evidence of a full-scale operation on businesslike lines to attract good candidates, investigate their credentials and find the best man.

Much of the evidence survives. It was packed roughly in a slatted orange-box: the contents included a mass of newspapers containing the advertisement for the post, and a considerable number of applications, in envelopes of all shapes and sizes, mostly addressed to William Hunt Esq., but some to John Perry, Ironmonger. There were many printed brochures of accumulated testimonials, some of them quite substantial pamphlets, as well as miscellaneous letters of enquiry and so on. This material has now been reduced to order, and includes two original copies of a list of candidates, containing thirty names, with personal details and governors' notes. The whole dossier, never yet read with more than cursory attention, would repay study. Its value to us now is that it gives one more proof that the school was entering the modern world.

The successful candidate is described in Venn's Cambridge lists as: WELLS Giffard. Admitted sizar at St. John's July 1819, son of Jonah Smith Wells, stock and share broker, of Islington, Middlesex: b. 22 Oct. 1802; schools, Tonbridge, Westminster, Merchant Taylors. Mtc. Mich. 1820, migrated to Sidney Jan. 22, 1822; B.A. 1824, M.A. 1827. Headmaster of Stourbridge School 1833-58; P.C. of St. Thomas' Stourbridge, Worcs. Subsequently of Stoke, nr. Guildford, where he died Aug. 1876.

So here was something more like 'a modern man' than his predecessors had been; here was a London stockbroker's son, a 'public-school type' (except that the public schools in the sense implied by that phrase had hardly yet come into being). We should like to know what he had been doing in the nine years since he graduated, for he was now aged 31. The material in the 1833 election dossier gives us a partial answer. He had been living at Barford House near Warwick, had acquaintances of ten years standing at Leamington, and was well-known and popular as a preacher in that town. We also learn that he had influential friends! For there are two pressing letters to William Hunt from none other than the Earl of Stamford at Enville Hall, urging the claims of Giffard Wells to the Stourbridge headmastership.

He is the first headmaster of whom we possess a likeness — rather a distinguished and authoritative-looking man, if we can trust the timeworn oilpainting which survived on the school premises in the company of the portrait of the royal founder. St. Thomas's church also published a portrait, for of course Giffard Wells was the last of the four men who filled the double role of headmaster and minister. He was appointed to the church after an election in July of 1833, i.e. when he was already headmaster of the school. Miss Edwards tells us that on the morning after Joseph Taylor died four candidates were ready to announce themselves, and that they included not only Giffard Wells but also his usher J.M. Kirby. It was hard to understand how Giffard Wells could have been in the lists at this stage, since he was not elected to the school until eight weeks later. But this is now explained. The election dossier includes a pamphlet issued by Giffard Wells on the day after he was elected headmaster. Addressing the inhabitants of Stourbridge he says that he now has the honour of addressing them, *not as before, with the hesitation of a stranger,* but as Head Master of the Grammar School .... So he had been conducting his campaign for some time already.

An extract from one of Giffard Wells' handbills is illuminating, if not exactly elevating:

> "Can the Rev. Mr. Kirby deny saying that he had never made any application for the Head Mastership of the School, nor had ever intended to do so, while at that very moment he knew that he had formally applied to the Governors for that appointment? Can Mr. Kirby deny that in consequence of his own false representations, prevarications and falsehoods (now discovered) Mr. Lister has retired from his Committee, and withdrawn his support from him?"

That was not the best of notes for the two masters to strike at the start of their joint service at the Grammar School. It looks as if there was no love lost between them from the outset. One wonders what afterthoughts may perhaps have come to the mind of any of the governors who may have heard this unpleasant exchange so soon after appointing Giffard Wells to the school. But in fact, strange as it may seem, the new headmaster had already every reason for confidence that he need have no fear of upsetting his governors by thus casting public insults at his usher. For at the very same meeting when he was appointed, the governors went on to another item of business, which was recorded in the minutes immediately after the appointment.

> "A complaint having been made to us by the parents of some of the scholars that the Revd. John Malsbury Kirby has not applied himself with all diligence to the teaching of such scholars and that they have not profited under him by reason that their exercises have not been grammatically corrected by the said John Malsbury Kirby, WE the major part of governors do hereby in pursuance of the 18th Statute and Order ... admonish the said John Malsbury Kirby, and he is this day admonished accordingly."

One can only call it astonishing on the governors' part to lump this business in with the appointment of the new headmaster, and one can only think that any outside observer at the time would have come away with only one impression, that of the threat of disaster.

In fact, however, everyone seems to have taken Mr. Kirby's dereliction of duty and his consequent admonition very much as a matter of course, and no consequences appear, so far as our records go, to have immediately followed. There is, however, evidence of an occurrence soon after the incident of the usher's admonition which might well be in some way connected with it. On 28 September 1833 (i.e. when the autumn term following had just about got well going) the governors adopted three new Statutes and Orders — formal rules for the conduct of the school, — had them inscribed on fine paper, signed them and had the whole document countersigned by the Bishop of Worcester in token of his approval. This is a remarkable echo of the proceedings of 19 May 1797, when three new rules were adopted and later attached to the William III Orders, as described on pages 122-3 above. Then, as now, the bishop formally counter-signed the new rules: then, as now, they had been immediately preceded by the admonition of the usher — in 1797 of Richard Willetts, for 'improper correction of a scholar', now in 1833 of John Malsbury Kirby for 'not having applied himself with all diligence to the teaching' of his scholars. This is so strange a repetition as to look like a pattern of events and a pattern of behaviour. Even the nature of the new rules on the two occasions is similar. In 1797 there was a rule about corporal punishment, accompanied by a change in the hours of schooling and a check on unauthorised absence by the masters. Now let us look at the rules of 1833:

AT A MEETING of the Governors of the Free Grammar School held at the school on Saturday the 28th of September 1833, THE following Orders were made, subject to the approbation of the Lord Bishop of the Diocese.

FIRST THE Scholars shall be at school from 7 till 8 and from 9 till 12 o'clock in the morning and from 2 till 5 in the afternoon from Lady Day to Michaelmas, and from 8 till 9 and from 10 till 12 o'clock in the morning and from 2 till 5 in the afternoon from Michaelmas to Lady-day Except on Wednesdays and Saturdays when the Scholars are to leave school at 12 o'clock and not return in the afternoon.

SECOND THAT in future no holydays be kept except upon Ash Wednesday, Easter Monday, Easter Tuesday and Whit Monday. And that the Midsummer vacation shall commence on the Friday before the 7th of July and continue from the next succeeding Monday for six weeks and no more. And that the Christmas vacation shall commence from the Friday before Christmas and continue from the next succeeding Monday for four weeks and no more.

THIRD THAT upon the Thursday next before the day fixed for breaking up for the Midsummer vacation a public examination of the Scholars shall annually take place in the School Room by a graduate of the University of Oxford who shall be requested to report to the Governors the proficiency of the scholars.

Here we find once again a change in the hours of schooling, and a firm reminder that the holidays are not to be lengthened without authority, which can be seen as merely a different formula for the rule that the masters might not absent themselves without leave. This is very much like the pattern of 1797.

There can be little doubt that the three new rules of 1833 must have owed much to the influence of Giffard Wells. They came in his very first term and on the face of it they were closely concerned with matters on which his opinion was indubitably the one which mattered. It was no small thing to take one hour out of the unbroken spell of five hours of morning lessons. It was an even greater change to proclaim two half-holidays every week. More revolutionary still was the institution of two lengthy annual vacations, six weeks in summer, four in winter (though there is reason to believe that the summer holiday had been prescriptive by custom, though strictly unofficial from time out of mind — to allow the boys to help with the harvest). It was a very clever touch to word this liberalisation of the annual programme as if it were a restriction — "for six weeks *and no more* ..." and "for four weeks *and no longer*". We have suggested that Giffard Wells looked more like a "modern man" than did his predecessors: these new rules certainly were more like rules for the modern world than any that had been in force before.

The new pattern of the school day, week and year might as well have belonged to 1933 as to 1833: in 1733 it would have been unthinkable.

So we begin to think that we can detect right at the start of Giffard Wells' regime the scent of change and the atmosphere of reform. If we are right, this would be basically the reason why the school began to climb slowly out of the pit of ruin. Change and reform were of the order of the day at this period in the history of English education. Much more was to come, and to come very quickly, but the first four decades of the century had already seen the seeds of change lodge themselves in the unwelcoming earth and yet germinate, thrust up their spikes, and spread their drift of green across the landscape.

The most extraordinary thing about these new rules — not the most important or the most significant thing, but speaking in precise terms the most extraordinary — is the source from which we learnt about them. For the governors' minute-book entirely ignores the meeting of 28 September 1833, the adoption of the three new rules, their reference to the bishop and the signification of his approval. As far as the school's official records were concerned the three new rules simply do not exist! We have had to comment before on the incomplete and inadequate record which the minute-book at this period provides, but this is the crowning example of this inadequacy. We are quite at a loss to explain the reason for it and must be content simply to record it as a fact.

We owe the recovery of the three orders to a piece of good fortune. The document containing the record, a fine large-paper copy, unsealed and not stamped but signed by seven of the eight governors and countersigned by the bishop, was included in the large bundle of papers described on pages 45-6 above, concerning the chancery action of 1851. It is endorsed as an exhibit in that case by Skilbeck and Hall, the governors' London legal agents at the time. It was produced on the governors' behalf by Rowland Price, whom we have met several times. The Chancery case dossier came to light very late in the long process of our researches. It could well have stayed unnoticed amidst a welter of undifferentiated and unimportant Victorian 'office-fodder'. But by good fortune it was so bulky as to attract special attention.

There is one postscript to add. The third of the new rules was the most original of the three, and arguably the most important. The idea of a compulsory external examination of the boys was clearly in effect, and probably in intention, the first foreshadowing of an entirely new determination on the part of the authorities to check on the efficiency of the school. For almost three hundred years it had been a case of gentlemen keeping a friendly eye on gentlemen. Not so in the new world. Following so closely after the arrival on the scene of Giffard Wells it looks very much as if this first step into the modern world was taken with the guidance and under the prompting of the new headmaster. We shall see later that his views carried more weight with his governors than those of his predecessors had done; but even without further confirmation we have seen enough by now to set up the name of Giffard Wells, though tentatively, at the head of that roll of honour on which we shall inscribe a list of the creators of the modern King Edward's School.

Whether this tentative impression is correct or not, we find during the first five years of Giffard Wells' regime further indications that the school was looking up under his management. There are also signs that he was not always an easy man to get on with, perhaps the hint of an imperious temper which we thought we detected in his portrait. Let us look into the minute-book again. It is unforgiveably haphazard and incomplete but for the time being it is all that we have. Our eye first lights on an entry of 22 February 1836: here we learn that an application has been made by a man named Richard Eaton, a miller, of Lutley in the parish of Halesowen, to have his boy admitted on the foundation. The governors rightly decide that the boy is disqualified by his place of residence for this; but agree that he can be admitted as a 'Stranger', since he lives near enough to keep the hours and regulations of the school. But they then have to go on to state that they have searched the school records but cannot find the amount of the 'accustomed salary' payable by Strangers. So they have *consulted the master*, and fix the 'salary' at four guineas a year, payable quarterly.

Lutley was not very far from Stourbridge, and there is no evidence here of the school's achieving widespread fame. But at least it is now achieving the respect of those who lived near enough to know of its local repute, and this is a far cry from the days, not long past, of no scholars at all.

The next item of significance, and a further testimonial, as it were, to Giffard Wells, comes on 22nd May, 1837. Here the Governors state that 'Master Frederick Fisher' after being educated at the school, has gone on to Cambridge University, and has applied for the scholarship of three pounds per annum (see page 68 above), and also for the arrears that have accumulated for some years past. They decide that it would not be proper to pay over the arrears but that these could be invested in the public funds, and master Frederick Fisher can have the extra interest as well as the three pounds!

This is the incident which we referred to when we were describing how the scholarship was originally set up in 1692. 'Master Fisher' is the only beneficiary recorded throughout its whole history from 1692 until it was extinguished in 1876. No one can say whether there were ever any others; we can be sure that there were very few; for there were very few parents able or willing to keep their boys at school long enough to enable them to go to the university. So not only had Giffard Wells nursed Frederick Fisher through long years, but he must have got him far enough advanced beyond the mere rudiments of Latin and Greek to enable him to take his place in a college. Considering all we know and can reasonably deduce about the school in the early part of the nineteenth century, we have to count this as in many ways the height of its achievement. It is true that one swallow does not make a summer, but even one swallow is an infallible sign that winter has come to an end. One cannot help wondering what the governors of 1837 thought about the news that one of the boys had gone on to Cambridge. We have no inkling at all whether they even gave it a thought.

One other incident, trivial in itself, bears witness perhaps to the quality of the new headmaster. On 31 March 1836 there was a special governors' meeting called by request of the two masters, for the purpose of settling a quarrel between them. Giffard Wells had made a boy in the usher's class stand out for making a noise. Kirby had objected and sent him back to his seat, and had then expressed himself strongly to the headmaster in front of all the boys. The Governors' decision was as follows:

> RESOLVED THAT the head Master is justified under Rule the 16th in interfering with the undermaster's class, but that Mr. Kirby is not justified in his conduct towards Mr. Wells upon that occasion; and that Mr. Wells be called in and recommended as to his future conduct in school hours, and that Mr. Kirby be called in and admonished for his conduct towards Mr. Wells; and he is, in pursuance of the 18th Statute, admonished accordingly.

The governors come out of this very well. The Rules of 1700 make it quite plain that the usher is to be "at all times directed for his method of teaching and other observances by the chief schoolmaster". So J.M. Kirby was wrong by the book as well as by commonsense, and Giffard Wells doubtless knew that he was working by the book. The governors used their discretion in giving him what amounted to a tactful hint not to push matters to extremes; they then backed him to the hilt, and J. M. Kirby got his second admonition in the space of the four years since his appointment. According to the rules one more would have meant his dismissal. As for Giffard Wells, the incident points to the sharpness of temper which we thought we had seen indicated; but it also suggests that he was earning his governors' confidence in the right sort of way, and that there was now the right sort of assumption that they and he were on the same side.

He must have been responsible for several pieces of practical 'management' during the years which we are considering. In his very first term the governors decided that 'a Timepiece be purchased and put up in the school in such a situation as the masters shall think fit'. So the school then had a clock, at a cost of eight guineas, after about twenty years without — for since the fire of 1812 there had been none. How a school can function without a clock is a matter for the educational theorists — but when it came to the practical problem, it must have been Giffard Wells who found the practical solution. Then in 1836 it was resolved to make a catalogue of the books belonging to the school, and to put a copy in the school chest. So the Hickman Library was at last organised so that it could be used without the risk of being whittled away by loss and theft. Then in 1839 it was ordered that in future there be kept in a book or books a list of the boys on the school roll, with names and ages, dates of admission and classes, — brought up to date twice a year and available at every governors' meeting. It seems elementary, but it had never before been done!

These are small things in themselves, but taken together they strengthen the impression that here at last was a hand on the helm which we can recognise as that of a modern 'management' man.

Again in 1839 came the hint of a quarrel between the masters. Kirby had asked permission for two of his private pupils, boarding in his house, to be admitted as Strangers. The governors stated that as Giffard Wells had given his certificate of consent, they could be so admitted on payment of the appropriate fees. Then, however, came the stumbling-block. When they read over their resolution to Giffard Wells, he refused his certificate, so they cancelled the resolution! Here then is the evidence of another debacle and another 'misunderstanding' — and almost certainly of another disagreement between Giffard Wells and his usher. One beings to wonder whether the wretched Kirby might be moving into a situation where he was threatened with yet a third and final admonition.

It was not to be — and for the most final of reasons. Within little more than eighteen months J.M. Kirby was dead.

This is a sad story; we are indebted for many of its details to a lady whose great-grandfather was J.M. Kirby's second son, born about the year 1828. Kirby himself died on 1st December 1840. There is a large memorial tablet to him and his two infant daughters, who died at about the same time, now to be found on the southern boundary wall of the churchyard of St. Mary's at Oldswinford. They died of 'an infectious fever', probably typhus. J.M. Kirby was not only usher at the grammar school but also chaplain to the Union workhouse in the town. Early family letters say that it was through visiting the workhouse in time of epidemic that he came to his early death. He was born at Rugby in 1795, educated at Rugby school and admitted a sizar of Queens' College, Cambridge as a 'ten-year man' at the ripe age of 27 in the year 1822. His great-great-grand-daughter dates his B.D. degree to 1832, shortly before he came to Stourbridge. His widow went to live after his death at an almshouse for clergy widows near Hungerford, together with at least some of her six young sons. There she died in 1868.

A sad story, indeed, rendered even sadder by a reading of some papers from the school archives, originating in the Wheeler-Kynnersley collection. They tell in detail the story of the complaints made against the usher in 1833. There are three papers, pinned together. The first is a large foolscap sheet, written out as follows:

> To the Governors of the Free Grammar School of King Edward the Sixth in Stourbridge
>
> The undersigned inhabitants of the Town and neighbourhood of Stourbridge take leave respectfully to represent that a serious complaint having been made by certain persons hereunto subscribed of the incompetency of the Under Master to hold his situation in the school, such complaint has been admitted by the governors to have been so fully established that they have thought it their duty to admonish the Undermaster thereupon.
>
> That the incompetency of the Under Master which has been so visited by the admonition of the Governors amounts to an ignorance so gross and is allied to such a degree of presumption,

that there can be little hope of any amendment in the Under Master nor room for the slightest confidence in him on the part of the Inhabitants — his scholars can only deride him, and instead of deriving benefit from his instruction it would be better for them wholly to absent themselves from a school where instead of being taught correctly they are deprived of the little knowledge which they might before possess.

Under these circumstances the undersigned beg respectfully yet earnestly to submit to the Governors that nothing remains but at once to discharge the under master from his situation, and leave him to take any measures which he may think it expedient to adopt.

The undersigned inhabitants beg to assure the Governors that they may rely upon their zealous support in carrying the above recommendation into effect.

July 1st 1833

	R. Hickman*
	Geo. Bate*
	W.H. Freer*
Robert Scott*	James Payton
Thomas Bate*	J. H. Dixon
Sophia Hornblower	C. Gaine
W. B. Collis	C. Morgan
Joseph King*	M. Matthews
? Orme*	Edw. Biddle
J. Downing	Wm. Perring
John Collis*	? Brookes
Robt. Loverock	Joseph Pitman*
John N. Bland	Fra. Perks

Received July 11th 1833

It is difficult to deny that this is an extremely unpleasant document. The admonition of the usher on 26th June had been the governors' perfectly correct and adequate response to the original complaint. According to the school's Statutes that was the most they could do; and in doing it they gave a very reasonable and accommodating reply. The petitioners were clearly looking for trouble, and there is certainly an element of vindictiveness in their second attack — for it was no less than an attack, and a vicious one — upon the unfortunate usher. We notice several names in the above list — and we have marked them with an asterisk — which occurred amongst the

169

names of the committee which hounded J.C. Homfray out of the school in 1832. There was evidently a very active and very belligerent anti-grammar-school lobby in the town. Two of them were to become governors themselves — Richard Hickman in 1835, Joseph Pitman in 1844 — which suggests that the governors at this time were by no means deaf to the voice of criticism and by no means averse to 'the wind of change'. We shall soon find evidence to support this view.

For the moment let us be glad for J.M. Kirby's sake that he escaped the misery of dismissal and unemployment, with his vast brood of children to maintain. An impudent and peremptory note from the same signatories to the governors, demanding a copy of the minute which recorded the admonition of the usher, was met by a courteous but firm refusal, and an equally firm negative to the original presumptuous demand for the usher's immediate dismissal.

J. M. Kirby's death led directly to a development of the greatest interest and importance in the history of the school.

Giffard Wells (II)

When we started the chapter on the headmastership of Giffard Wells we entitled it "An End and a Beginning". It is now time to justify the title by the story of what happened in 1840-41. As a preliminary we quote from Blond's Encyclopaedia of Education (London 1969) on page 245, as follows:

> "Efforts to break the dominant hold which Greek and Latin acquired in the grammar school culminated in the appointment of a Royal Commission in 1819, which in its 20 year survey examined 28,480 endowments* .... Its reports prompted a select committee in 1835 to recommend that a permanent board should superintend charities. *In the case of grammar schools an Act of Parliament in 1840 allowed governors and trustees to apply discretion in the matter of compulsory Latin and Greek.*"

We now turn to the minutes of a governors' meeting of 21 December 1840. These open by stating baldly that the death of the usher, the Revd. James Malsbury Kirby, having occasioned a vacancy for the post of undermaster, several applications have already been received. Then follows a resolution of the governors, as follows:

> RESOLVED THAT previous to the election of a successor to the Rev. J.M. Kirby, the Rev. C. H. Craufurd, Francis Rufford, William Hunt and George Grazebrook — i.e. four out of the eight governors — be appointed a committee (*with the assistance of the headmaster, the Revd. Giffard Wells*) to frame a code of

---
*This was the commission which reported on the Stourbridge school in 1832.

Rules and Regulations for management of the school, *so as to embrace the teaching of other useful branches of Education as well as the Greek and Latin languages*, making it more beneficial to the Township of Stourbridge and Parish of Oldswinford and the neighbourhood. And that such Rules and Regulations when framed be submitted to the bishop of the diocese for his approbation.

The next meeting was then fixed for Monday 18th January following.

The reader will recollect that the movement towards reform had been going on for a very long time. At the end of 1806 the governors had resolved to widen the curriculum, frame new statutes, and even to build an entirely new and extra school to accommodate the new type of scholar. In 1808 they had appointed a writing-master and established the principle that parents should pay fees for the teaching of 'new' subjects. In 1813 or thereabouts, after some years in which the usher had taught arithmetic and writing, they were frustrated by the efforts of one of their number, and the school became for a considerable period of time moribund. In 1832 they dismissed their usher and appointed a new one specifically charged to teach writing and arithmetic for a fee. It was a halting and intermittent process, but the twitching limbs of reform had never entirely sunk back into quiescence. And now the departure of another usher was used to find for the governors another excuse, or another stimulus, to make yet another move for reform.

This time, however, there were two crucial new factors — one national, one local. The national one was the passing of the 1840 act (Wilmot's Act) which allowed — and consequently encouraged — governors of grammar schools to use their discretion in the matter of compulsory Latin and Greek. In 1807 the reformers had had to face the powerful obstacle of Lord Eldon's recent Leeds Grammar School judgement. In 1841 they had the support and encouragement of a recently established change in the law. The second factor was the presence of a very different headmaster in the person of the Rev. Giffard Wells. So far from lurking in the background and seeking counsel's opinion to stop the reformers in their tracks, Giffard Wells was to be the assistant, expert and active, of those appointed to draft the reformed statutes. These two changes were to transform the situation.

Once embarked upon their projected programme of reform, the governors moved with notable speed. On 18 January 1841 the new set of statutes was ready; once read out it was immediately approved, and it was resolved to send a copy to the bishop, in the care of a deputation, for his approval. The rector of Oldswinford (C. H. Craufurd), William Hunt the solicitor and George Grazebrook, *together once again with Giffard Wells*, were requested to attend upon the bishop whenever he should think fit. The meeting took place on 28 January, when the bishop's signature of approval was appended to a large parchment copy of the new Rules and Orders. On 15 February 1841 the governors formally resolved that they should be adopted, signed, and a printed copy hung up in the school. This was eight weeks to the day after the first mention of the reform. Several copies of the 1841 Statutes survive in the school archives. The original parchment is there, endorsed as an exhibit in chancery at the time of the 1851 suit. One of the printed copies is similarly endorsed. The others date from 1857, and on them the governors' names have been brought up to date for that year. So clearly the new rules were considered to be 'alive', rather than merely something for the archives! The new rules make an interesting and impressive document and are a tribute to the skill of those who framed them. They are ingeniously calculated to fulfil the purposes of reform, and in particular of the 1840 Act (actually referred to in Rule 17), and yet to preserve the original character of the school sufficiently to make it manifestly a grammar school. In other words, someone had used his brains to work out a formula for getting the best of both worlds, both that of the King's Royal Grammar School and that of the 'mere commerical establishment'. We cannot prove who that someone was, for there were five men charged with the task. But from what we know of the new headmaster we are inclined to believe that we can detect his hand. Certainly he wrote a letter to the governors on 9 March 1841, which is significant of his attitude. This is what he said:

Gentlemen,
    I have given, as you know, every consideration to the rules lately drawn up by you, and approved on the 28th of last January by the Bishop of the Diocese as Visitor of the Stourbridge Royal Free Grammar School, and consider them calculated to render the institution most generally beneficial. I have therefore as Head Master much pleasure in lending aid to their introduction into and

observance in the school, and shall be very glad to give my full consent to them, whenever the Governors may think right to require me so to do in the manner prescribed by the late act of 3rd and 4th of Victoria (referred to in rule 17), being "an Act for improving the condition and extending the benefit of Grammar Schools", to which Act I in this instance especially refer, because tho' I always have been and shall be desirous to act cordially with the Governors for their improvement of the school, I feel it my duty towards myself and any one who may be my successor as Head Master to reserve all the privileges and authority by such Act granted in favour of every Head Master of a Grammar School.

I have the honour to remain,
Gentlemen,
With great respect
Your Obedt. humble servt.,
Giffard Wells,
Head Master

March 9th 1841.

There is no certainty here, but it seems fair to say that this letter is in itself an exercise in the art of looking both ways and of getting the best of both worlds. It is clear also that the writer was fully familar with the terms of the act of 1840, and he gives the impression that he was working in accordance with that act. Whether we are reading too much into Giffard Wells's letter the reader must decide for himself; but we feel justified in remarking that at least its tone and contents confirm the impression we have tried to convey of Giffard Wells as a man of a decisive and authoritative character, skilled in affairs, highly intelligent and well able to look after himself. There was a great contrast between the situation of the school at the time of Joseph Taylor's death on 2nd May 1833, and now at the time of this letter in March 1841. It is difficult not to believe that this contrast was largely due to the contrast between the character and qualities of Joseph Taylor and those of his successor.

So as we come to look at the new Statutes and Orders, we have their purpose and that of the 1840 Act uppermost in our minds. There are 26 rules, following a substantial preamble which clearly states that it is 'expedient' to "extend the system of Education to other useful branches of Literature and Science, in addition to the

Greek and Latin languages", and which specifically makes it clear that the governors have made these new rules for the school "with the assistance and consent of the Reverend Giffard Wells, the Head Master thereof".

Rule 3 states that the teaching shall, besides Greek and Latin, embrace writing and arithmetic, the first four books of Euclid, the first part of algebra, and also history, geography and English composition. Rule 4 lays it down that Classics shall be the main object of instruction and shall also be the criterion of proficiency by which boys shall go up to higher classes or shall be placed in the school on admission. Half the teaching hours shall be devoted to Classics, one quarter to writing, arithmetic and mathematics, and one quarter to the rest.

This is an essentially simple but ingenious way of achieving reform without destroying the character of the grammar school. The present writer remembers that Mr. H.P. Jones, who was Chairman of the Governors in the 1950's, used to recount with great pride and satisfaction that even as late as his own days in the school, in the early years of this century under the authority of Rupert Deakin (1885-1905), he himself was constantly at loggerheads with the headmaster (whom he still remembered with a mixture of dislike and — it has to be said — contempt) and that his greatest delight was to rest with confidence upon the safety-net of his unfailing ability in Latin, which in those days guaranteed him to be always top of his class! So, even when he fled from the headmaster's physical pursuit and escaped by climbing over the playground gate, he had the satisfaction of turning and making an extremely rude gesture at his pursuer, in the full and certain confidence that classical abilities would save his bacon and leave Rupert Deakin helpless to wreak just retribution. H.P. Jones was no scholar, certainly no academic: he became a prosperous tradesman in the town and happily forgot all his Phaedrus and his Cornelius Nepos and his Latin grammar. But he remained a beneficiary of the grand old fortifying Classical curriculum, and remembered with gratitude what the Classics had done for him. It is doubtful if that sort of benefit was in the minds of Giffard Wells and his collaborators when they framed the rules of 1841: but when a man sows, he does not always know what exactly his harvest will be.

It is also laid down in the new statutes (rule 13) that no boy shall be admitted to learn writing or arithmetic or either of them, unless he also learns the Classics "and entirely conforms to the system uupon which the school shall be conducted." Here is another safeguard for the traditional values.

Rule 17, mentioned by Giffard Wells as containing a reference to the 1840 Act, is concerned with regulations to safeguard the governors against wilful absence by the masters on the Wentworth pattern. It states that if either master shall be unable to attend to the duties of the school, from illness or otherwise, for the space of one month, he shall after that time find at his own cost a sufficient subsitute to the satisfaction of the governors. *"But this rule is not intended to restrict the powers of the governors for the removal of the masters, given to them by the late Act of* 3rd and 4th of her present majesty Victoria".

It is typical of the ambiguous effect of the new Act and the new rules that Giffard Wells draws special attention to this particular clause, evidently designed to bind the masters more tightly under the authority of the governors than ever before, specifically in order to reserve all his own rights and authority as headmaster, conferred by the same act upon headmasters of grammar schools!

The new rules also reiterated the principle that 'strangers' could be admitted as feepayers (four guineas to the usher if under him, six guineas to the headmaster similarly) — provided that the headmaster would certify that the extra pupils would not prejudice the teaching of the boys on the foundation. The governors were to have the last word in the matter of these admissions, and the strangers had to live near enough to be able to keep the hours and regulations of the school. The governors were the only authority for the expulsion of any boy.

The rules included provision for a compulsory annual examination of the boys in the presence of the governors. The holidays were fixed in date and length as they had been previously. There was also a requirement that the headmaster should keep a register of all boys in the school, with ages, date of admission, classes and so on, and produce it at every governors' meeting.

The rules of payment for learning writing and arithmetic clearly had to be adapted to the new arrangements. The usher now had to teach *all* the boys writing and arithmetic — until they could go on to mathematics, which they took under the headmaster. All boys now had to pay ten shillings a year *for the use of pens, ink and pencils*. (They had to provide their own copybooks account-books and slates). The new fees went to whichever master was teaching a boy. It seems clear that this charge was a device intended to compensate the masters in a small degree for the loss of the fees previously paid for 'extra' subjects. The salaries of the masters were now fixed by the rules at £150 and £90, the rates already established, with the addition of a bonus, consisting of five eighths and three eighths of any residue left over from the school's income after payment for necessary repairs and outgoings.

In general terms much of this and the remainder of the new body of rules was a consolidation of the existing practices from the point of view of the three participating elements — boys, masters and governors. The formulae, and the format, would have been easily recognised as familiar by Wentworth, or even by Alchurche. But the essential changes in the matter of the curriculum brought the school, with all its unchanging elements still woven securely into its fabric, effectively into the modern world. It was in fact a very good example of radical reform achieved by skilful adaptation.

So the Stourbridge governors, with the assistance and consent of their headmaster Giffard Wells, had taken the necessary and radical step which carried the school into the onflowing tide of educational progress. There were to be strange backslidings and then further steps and further movements to drag the school out of the confines of its ancient strait-jacket. But if it is true that it is the first step that counts, then the Statutes and Orders of 1841 should on the face of it be accounted as the essential turning-point, the pivot on which the whole process ultimately hinged; and Giffard Wells must on the face of it be considered as not least amongst those who assembled the wheels of change and wound into the springs of reform a stored momentum of sufficient power to complete in due course the process of revolution.

That is on the face of it. But we are then faced with mysteries. We have been aware for some time that the official records of the school's history — the governors' minute-books which have been the constant companion of our researches since we came to the later years of the seventeenth century — these records have degenerated in completeness and reliability until we cannot really guarantee that we know the essentials of the story. And now that we have reached towards 1850 we are faced with an ever greater problem and a more complete deprivation: with the year 1849 the records of the second great volume of governors' minutes comes to an end. What is more, there is nothing comparable to take their place. The extraordinary truth is that the nearer we come towards the present time, the less we know about what was happening. This is as infuriating as it is topsy-turvy, but it is a fact and we have to accept it. We do have one main prop remaining to guide our uncertain steps. That is a third folio volume, bound in full leather, with a decorated and tooled label showing that it belonged to the school, and two metal clasps. It is indeed a very handsome volume, and happily for our researches far from neglibible as a source of information about the school's activities. For it contains the governors' annual accounts, presented each year on Trinity Monday from 1850 to 1909. It records information, in varying degrees of detail, about for example, the salaries paid to the headmaster and his assistants, that of the secretary or clerk to the governors, expenditure on lawsuits, building costs, tradesmen's bills for repairs, insurance premiums, charitable disbursements, costs of domestic service, management expenses, and so on. Out of all this much can be deduced about the governors' proceedings, though much will remain obscure. Even the names of the governors are recorded only if personally attending the annual audit. Even so, the account book will, we hope, have much to tell us. Apart from its information we shall have to rely on chance survivals, such as the dossiers attached to the appointment of a headmaster or undermaster, the records of the 1851 Chancery suit, the official copies and lawyer's drafts of successive Statutes and Orders, and so on.

In these circumstances we must expect mysteries, and the first of them soon confronts us. Remembering that we have several years of the governors' minutes left in the book to refer to, we turn to its last pages to find out how the curriculum changes of the 1841 Statutes were put into effect. How many new assistant masters did the governors appoint? What new subjects were introduced? How much were the extra masters paid? What sort of men with what sort of qualifications were selected? The answer is as simple as it is surprising. From 1841 till the end of the minute-book in 1849 there is no mention whatever of any additional master, no payment recorded to any teaching staff except the headmaster and his usher. These two continue to draw their statutory £150 and £90 per annum, and bonuses continue to be doled out to them from the surplus revenues. But there is nothing else. We have to conclude that either the minute-book is even more grossly defective as a record than we had suspected, or else that for some mysterious reason the great curriculum reform was for the time being at any rate entirely stultified by being completely ignored. What can possibly be the explanation of this it is at first sight different to conjecture. All we can do is to admit ourselves defeated after recording the fact that in the matter of staff appointments, *as far as the governors' minutes are concerned* the 1841 Statutes might as well never have been adopted!

It is not as though the new rules are ignored in every particular. In 1849, for example, the new rule 17, the very one which contains a reference to the Act of 1840, is called into action. Giffard Wells, it appears, had been absent from his duties through illness "for the space of one month and upwards". It was therefore ordered that he should at once find at his own cost an acceptable substitute to the satisfaction of the governors, and further "that our Secretary should communicate this resolution to him and ask him to name his proposed substitute".

If we look back in the book to the year 1838, we find that before the new Statutes were adopted they ordered things very differently. For here is a minute from that year:

12th May 1838
The Reverend Giffard Wells the Head Master having had leave of absence granted by the Governors from January last till after the next summer vacation on account of severe illness, and having applied for a further leave of absence,
RESOLVED
That the Governors will grant such further leave of absence to Mr. Wells from the end of the next summer vacation as shall be thought necessary, if his health should not be re-established sufficiently to undertake the duties of the school.

Under modern conditions two terms of sick leave would be enough to raise a few eyebrows. An application for a third term's leave of absence might well raise the question of compulsory retirement. We have no hint of the nature of Giffard Wells' illness. In those days, with typhus, cholera, tuberculosis, pneumonia and their like lying in wait to lay low the strong and weak alike, and with an expectation of life that meant less than the much less speculative expectation of falling prey to one of the countless ills that flesh was heir to, — in those days doubtless the experience of a long illness, often of an unspecified nature, followed by an even longer convalescence, was no uncommon thing. To us in the present day it must seem strange that a man in his middle thirties should need almost a year to 're-establish his health', particularly in a comparatively sheltered occupation. It is even stranger when we recall that in fact he was to live on to the then ripe old age of 74.

But so it was; and one can only wonder who managed the school during his leave of absence. The minute-book gives us no hint that anyone at all was paid to do the headmaster's work. The silence of the governors' minutes about the headmaster's illness in 1838 is another example of the inadequacy of the minute-book. We do know that the masters' salaries were paid as usual, and not only the salaries but the bonuses as well — £50 and £30 to headmaster and usher on 11th June 1838, only a month after the provisional extension of Giffard Wells' sick leave. In the matter of bonuses there is a curious and revealing incident after J.M. Kirby's death.

He had been paid three-quarters of a year's salary up to Christmas 1840 (he died on 1st December). At midsummer following the governors declared a bonus of £104, to be divided as always, five and three. But the £39 due to the usher was then further split, and one quarter of it was transferred to the share of Giffard Wells. The apparent explanation of this is that there was no usher from Christmas 1840 till Lady-day 1841, and that the headmaster took over the lower school for that one quarter. He now also took one quarter of the dead usher's bonus. One must conclude that (a) his health was now fully re-established, and (b) he had a keen eye to the main chance. One cannot help giving a thought to the usher's widow in the almshouse with at least some of her six small boys.

The matter of Giffard Wells' ill-health is of some importance, and we have therefore left it to be dealt with all at once in this place. Some time ago we spoke of the problems of ill-health which appeared to affect the St. Thomas's headmasters; but until 1838 there was not the least hint of any such problem in the case of Giffard Wells. He was 'on the job', and quite clearly in charge of the operations of the school. His governors respected his judgment and deferred to his opinion. The school had begun to gather strength under his care, and we found reason to conclude that he was a man of decision, authoritative and active. Now here he is in 1849, sick again: but this time the 'modern' regulations are catching up with the gentlemen of the old school: even the method of telling the headmaster the governors' decision has a new and ungentlemanly sound about it!

However, we have not exhausted the record of Giffard Wells' illnesses. We now turn once again to evidence which has no place in the governors' minute-book and which has survived in the Harward and Evers archives by chance. It is all contained in the dossier which concerns the appointment of an usher in succession to J.M. Kirby.

It will be remembered that he died in December 1840, and that by 21st of that month several applications for the post had already been received. But the election of a successor was delayed by the preparation of the new Statutes. When the draft for them was approved and sent to the bishop on 18th January 1841, at the same meeting the governors resolved to appoint as usher Mr. Thomas Peirce Medwin, undermaster of Hartlebury School. He signed a formal undertaking to abide by the new statutes on the same day that they were formally adopted by the governors.

T.P. Medwin was a man of 58 years of age*, non-graduate and non-clerical. He had taught both minor classics and commercial and general subjects, mainly the latter. He had had a long spell at Hartlebury and was supported by a good testimonial from the bishop. He wrote numerous letters to different people, not always clearly named or readily identified, in his campaign for the post. In one letter he cited the bishop as saying that in another school in the locality the appointment of a non-graduate, non-clerical, non-classical, non-scholar as undermaster had resulted in the rejuvenation of the school after a period of decay — clearly supporting the thesis that a commercial town like Stourbridge did not want scholarship or the Classics, but would support a 'mere commercial establishment'. Medwin remarks that he had applied at Stourbridge in 1832 and sends the testimonial which the bishop had then written for him, brought up to date by an addition dated 12 December 1840. In one of his other letters he sends a copy of this latest testimonial from the bishop, with the addition of the following extraordinary postscript:

> The following passage from Carlisle's well-known work on 'Endowed Schools' may not be thought irrelevant on the present occasion:
> "At the Grammar School of Stourbridge the number of Scholars is very trifling, being upon an average not more than *Ten* and sometimes *none*. This has been the case for more than sixty years, as Classical learning is in little estimation in a commerical town like Stourbridge."

*In 1832 he had written from Hartlebury to John Pidcock of the Platts applying for the ushership when Kirby was appointed, He then said that he had been teaching in endowed schools from the age of seventeen to fifty.

The question here is whether the postscript was the work of the bishop or of T.P. Medwin himself. He may even have left the answer deliberately in the realm of uncertainty: for the whole paper, being a copy, is in his own unmistakable hand, with the postscript following straight on after the testimonial and in the same handwriting. So either the bishop wrote it (which would be strange indeed) or (even stranger, but in the circumstances much more likely) Medwin attached it as a further persuasion to the governors that they should modernise the school — and employ him as being particularly well suited to the task.

The Medwin dossier contains three other applications which are of considerable interest:

(1) From Upper Ludston House near Wolverhampton comes one from *James R. Willetts*. He proves to be the son of Richard Willetts, our usher from 1763 to 1809, the one who was admonished for 'improper correction of a Scholar'. James Willetts says "my sole ambition is to hold the situation which under your trust my late revered father held for 50 years ... and to end my days in the house of my birth". He adds that his claims were "acknowledged to be very strong at the last election" — showing that he too had been a candidate in 1832.

(2) From Mansfield comes an application from the *Rev. R. H. Goodacre*. It emerges that *he has lived for two years as an assistant in the Stourbridge school* and so is acquainted with it. He refers the governors to Giffard Wells for testimony to his abilities, and indicated that it is now three years since he returned from Stourbridge to his native Mansfield, where he has entered into holy orders and served as a curate to his own father, the vicar of three populous parishes. *He asks whether the governors intend to avail themselves of a recent Act of Parliament,* and what alterations in that case they would want to make. William Hunt replies that he is unable to answer that question. Our own query must be whether it was this question from Goodacre, following the broad hints from Medwin, that prodded the governors into their resolution to modernise the curriculum. We cannot assume this, but the possibility is distinctly there. More important for our present purpose is the information that Giffard Wells was paying his own assistant for two years until about the end of 1837. We are accumulating a growing dossier of Giffard Wells as an absentee headmaster. We were wondering who ran the school in 1838, and we know that he was asked to find a substitute in 1849. Add the fact that he

employed an assistant (and so possibly a substitute) in 1836 and 1837, and the picture is developing. We now turn to the third application from 1840:

(3) Thomas Rogers, M.A., late fellow of Sidney Sussex College, Cambridge and evidently in holy orders, writes his application from Stourbridge. He says that he has lived in the neighbourhood for nearly four years and is personally known to the Governors. For most of 1840 he *has assisted Mr. Wells in his Church, to which he is licensed as Curate by the Bishop of the Diocese. At the beginning of the year he was also employed by Mr. Wells in the management of his school* — *"which I continued to do during his illness, until the Midsummer holidays"*. He puts his claim neatly by suggesting that as he was considered capable of conducting the higher duties of the school, he might be thought to possess the qualifications to undertake those of the second master.

So we add to our list of Giffard Wells' absences, and presumed illnesses, the first half of the year 1840. The whole list now reads as follows: 1836, 1837, 1838, 1840 and 1849. This renders our judgment of his qualities and of his contribution to the history of the school very precarious, to say the least. We had credited him with the influence which led the governors to modernise the curriculum. But we are now asking ourselves whether that modernisation was a total sham, since up to 1850 we have no evidence of any payment to any new master for the teaching of any new subject; and we are now finding reason to believe that in fact Giffard Wells, so far from being active and vigorous in the management of the school's improving fortunes, had been persistently, even chronically, either a sick man or a hypochondriac, and in either case most certainly an absentee. So our tentative conclusions are in danger of falling apart, and as we come towards Giffard Wells' last years as headmaster we can only wonder what the truth really was about this enigmatic man.

The minute-book has come to an end. The account-book which succeeds it may well be inadequate, but it is all we have, so we turn to it out of necessity. Its first account, for the year 1849-50 shows salaries paid only to Giffard Wells and T.P. Medwin, together with substantial bonuses. The same holds good for 1850-51. In June 1852 comes the first variation; Medwin has been paid only £45 — for half a year's salary up to Michaelmas last, i.e. September 1851. This should mean that T.P. Medwin is dead — and sure enough in the Trinity accounts of 1853 we find two instalments of £45, each for half a year's salary, to the Rev. Edmund Hall, who we know succeeded

T.P. Medwin as usher. He was paid from New Year 1852, and there was a payment of £11.5.0, half a quarter's salary for an usher, to the executors of the late T.P. Medwin — showing that he died in the autumn term of 1851. Giffard Well's salary, and the bonuses to him and Edmund Hall are recorded. There are no further salaries for teachers. The same holds good for the accounts of 1854, 1855 and 1856. In September 1856 Edmund Hall left, and was replaced by Richard Woods. Giffard Wells and Richard Woods were the only salaried teachers on the books on 8th June 1857. It is now sixteen years since the adoption of the new Statutes and Orders, extending the curriculum.

At this point we turn to our last godsend from the archives. We have several times spoken of the records of the 1851 Chancery Suit, discovered in the last stages of our researches. It is time for us at last to make use of them; and our best plan will be to transcribe the abstract in note form which was made at the time of the discovery of the record. There is far too much material to allow of our quoting *in extenso from the original*: but for our present purpose the main points at issue in the suit are of very great importance, and we shall attempt to present an outline, arranged in numbered sections, as follows:

(1) The petitioners are named as *Charles Skidmore Perrens* of Stourbridge, Land Agent, and *William Griffiths,* of Oldswinford, nail factor. The petition is brought under the Abuses of Charities Act of 52 Ge. III (1812) and also under the Act of 3 & 4 Victoria — Wilmot's Act (1840) 'for improving the condition and extending the benefits of grammar schools'. The object of the petitioners is *to get Giffard Wells removed as incompetent from ill-health*, and *Peirce Medwin similarly from age and infirmity;* and to reform the school and enlarge the governing body.

The petition recites the foundation of the school, the rules for appointing headmaster and usher, and various details up to the appointment of Giffard Wells in 1833. He is said to have been for ten years and more in a very infirm state of health. The number of boys under the headmaster during that time has varied from 5 to 8; the rest are under the usher exclusively and the head does nothing for them. The reason given is that Giffard Wells insists that he is obliged to take only such boys as have reached a certain stage of proficiency in learning. He has not regularly examined the lower boys. He is unfit from illness even to teach the few boys he has had. *He has for long periods employed an assistant to do his work.* There is no prospect of his health improving.

T.P. Medwin came in 1840, when already 58 years of age, and has been for some time from advanced age and infirmities incapable of doing his work properly. He has told the governors that he wishes to retire, but they have been unable to make an agreement. The school has been for many years inefficient, and the numbers very small, not averaging more than 30, for a population at the 1841 census of 17,597. After public dissatisfaction some years ago the governors remodelled the rules. *But Giffard Wells says that he is not bound by the new rules, as he was appointed before they were adopted.* The masters do not obey the new rules.

Several people have sent boys to the school in the hope of stimulating an improvement, but to no avail, so they have withdrawn them.

To make the school efficient the Headmaster and usher must be removed under the Act of 3 & 4 Victoria, cap. 77.

The system of education should be extended.

The school's revenues (about £500 a year) are badly mismanaged, with leases too long and rents too low.

The school buildings are inadequate and should be replaced.

The body of eight governors, self-elective, is too small for the enlarged population of the locality. It should have a different form of election. Only Chancery can effect this change.

This tells us a great deal, and reminds us to be grateful for its discovery. But we must certainly remember that it is entirely an *ex parte* statement, unsupported as yet by evidence. We do, however, already detect signs of the 'anti-grammar-school lobby in the town', determined and suspect of being vindictive — and we shall be looking for names that we have met before.

(2) Affidavits in support of the petition include the following:

Richard Barney of Stourbridge, Hemp Merchant, has had four sons, one at the school. It is inefficient; he has made no progress; too many holidays. He has withdrawn the boy and is sending all his sons elsewhere at great expense.

Benjamin Penney of Stourbridge, grocer — sent one son for two years but has removed him.

John Wall of Stourbridge, wholesale brewer, wanted to use the school, but enquiries show that boys make little or no progress; discipline very lax and bad. Has sent his son elsewhere at great expense;

Henry King of Oldswinford, deputy magistrate's clerk. He had two boys at the school, one two years under the headmaster. Giffard Wells absent for months at a time. Second boy after one year has made very poor progress. Too many holidays. Boys used to attend before breakfast, but not now. Head does not examine lower boys.

William Baker of Stourbridge, Millwright and engineer. Had one son at school 1844-48, but took him away and sent him at great cost elsewhere. Will not send his second son.

John Moreton Hicks of Stourbridge, architect. Wished to send his son of 10 years, but bad reports of the school dissuaded him. Of his nephews at the school one has been removed, one stays only in the hope of a late improvement.

Richard Gibson of Stourbridge, coach maker. Has a son at the school 11 months. Little progress. Too many holidays. Discipline lax. School before breakfast discontinued.

Thomas Nash of Stourbridge, builder. Sent three sons in 1850. One removed for ill-health; others make little progress. Discipline bad; too many holidays. Boys say headmaster has never examined them or taken any interest, and is months absent; the usher too old. Has removed boys to another school at heavy cost.

Henry James of Stourbridge, writing-clerk. A young man, who refers to his own time at the school — three years up to about 1847. Very frequent holidays. no public examinations before the governors either in the schoolroom or elsewhere.

(3) Affidavits against the petitioners include the following, first from governors:

Rev. Charles Henry Craufurd, Rector of Oldswinford. A governor since 1835. He says that the 1841 Orders have, so far as the masters are concerned, been strictly adhered to. His eldest son has been a pupil since January 1850 and he is perfectly satisfied. With the present income it is not advisable to try to extend the curriculum offered. There are many other schools in the parish for commerical branches of education; it is very important for the middle and upper classes of society for this school to continue as a grammar school.

The only complaint made to governors in the last ten years was in

December last, made by *Mr. W. B. Collis,* about the progress made by a child of his; it was dismissed.

The governors have had a proposal to alter the schoolroom; but they could do this out of income, without borrowing money. According to the Rules the governors may after three admonitions remove the masters — but neither of the present masters has been admonished at all.

The change in school hours (no pre-breakfast school) was made at the suggestion of parents of boys living at a distance, who had had to pay for a breakfast in the town.

Charles John Wragge of Stourbridge, Banker. Is a governor and has known the school for 30 years. It is beneficial to the town to have a grammar school, *with the lower branches of learning being taught when required.* He had a son there, but removed him as he wanted him to be a boarder away from home.

Rowland Price of Stourbridge, Solicitor. A governor since 1847. Has known the Rules and Statutes since 1830. He was clerk to Henry Roberts in earlier days. The 1841 Rules were redrawn, approved by the Bishop, published, and have ever since been acted upon.

In earlier times there was no order for the teaching of English, Arithmetic or Writing: in 1841 other subjects were added to the Classics, with no charge except for 10/- a year for use of pencils etc. The masters have kept these rules.

Giffard Wells has been occasionally absent but has found himself a subsitute. He takes Medwin's boys, one class each week to check their progress. They go up to him when they can deal with Phaedrus, Cornelius Nepos and Latin grammar. Medwin is not infirm. He has taught Price's son privately for nine months and is always regular; he has never been ill for three years past.

The number of boys is greater in proportion to the population of the parish than in the free grammar schools of Birmingham, Bromsgrove or Bridgnorth. Average for four years past is 35.

Price then lists other schools in the town, and says that it is a great advantage to himself and others in the Middle Class to have it kept as a grammar school, with liberty for the boys to learn the lower branches, as now.

He repeats Craufurd's statements about the masters' houses and the school buildings. He says there is no probability of increased income for about fifteen years.

He defends the governors' record on leases and rents, and also their record as interested and active trustees.

These three testimonies tell us that the governors considered that *the 1841 curriculum reform required essentially only that writing and arithmetic should be added to the Classics — taught, of course, without fees.* This was fundamentally what the Wilmot Act of 1840 had been after, and this it was which made the school acceptable to the generality of parents in a commercial community. So they felt justified in ignoring other subjects, and by arranging for the 'lower branches' to be taught alongside the Classics to all the boys they satisfied their consciences about fulfilling the demands of the 1841 rules and 'extending the benefits' of the grammar school. Here at last is the explanation of so much that has baffled us in the regime of Giffard Wells.

So even at this late stage the archives have produced in our hour of need yet one more godsend, in the shape of the Chancery Suit record. Nor is its contribution to our story by any means yet exhausted. We now come to a fourth section of this voluminous record.

(4) The affidavit of *Thomas Peirce Medwin* of Stourbridge, the usher who is one object of the petitioners' attack. He admits to being 69 years old and confirms that he came to the school in February of 1841 at the age of 58; He claims as former pupils the Duke of Beaufort, the late Earl of Durham and his brother, and several other noblemen! He says he has always obeyed the rules of 1841 and that no complaints have ever been made on this score in ten years; that he has never been absent from school throughout that time; that the only one complaint made against him, in December last, was dismissed. He considers himself capable of continuing to teach. He did think himself entitled to a retiring pension after being so long a schoolmaster, but not on grounds of infirmity; and the governors' reply was that they were unwilling to dispense with his services. The headmaster has taken one class a week of his boys. The school holidays have been no more than is usual, and in any case he has himself no power to grant them. He points out that neither of the petitioners had had any son at the school. He produces a testimonial from 21 parents, and a certificate from Thomas Cooper, surgeon, his 'medical attendant' for ten years, to the effect that he is unusually active for a man of his age, and is not incapable. He also produces a letter written to him in December 1849 by William Norris of Stourbridge, Doctor of Medicine, which gives him the writer's

warmest thanks for his teaching of his son for several years at the school, and for setting him such a good example of promptness and attention to his duties.

(5) Affidavits from various parents make it clear that many of the middle classes look upon the grammar school as an essential advantage in bringing up their children. These statements include two from a father and his son, the latter of whom has obtained "a respectable situation" as an Accountant-clerk and who is clearly grateful to the school for enabling him to do so. William Robins the banker, son of Joseph Robins, lends his voice with the rest.

(6) Observations on the affidavits in support of the petition (see Section (2) above) are illuminating:
On *Griffiths* and *Perrens* the comment is that from the habits of life of Mr. Griffiths and his station in society and from his having no relation in the school, it is not likely that he knows anything more of the school than that there is a free school in Stourbridge and that it has two masters in it. *Mr. Perrens* is a young surveyor and auctioneer *entirely under the control of the solicitor to the Petitioners, whose petition it really is. It is understood that the petitioners are guaranteed from all costs by their solicitor.* General comments simply deny that there has been any breach of trust or of the 1841 rules, except in the matter of annual examinations, which have not been held because of the cost. The masters' health is considered to be acceptable. As for numbers, there are at present 33 boys, more than in the free schools of Birmingham, Bromsgrove, Bridgnorth or Kidderminster. As for the extension of the system of education, that now available extends from the time a boy can read to the construing of Greek plays and so on. Several gentlemen have gone from the school direct to Oxford or Cambridge. The school has been of great benefit to the town and neighbourhood, except for a few years before the appointment of the present headmaster. The other complaints — of financial mismanagement, poor buildings, bad repair, and so on, are answered on the same lines, mainly by a combination of simple denial and reassurance.

(7) Observations on the affidavits of complaining parents are designed to discredit them and to undermine their bonafides.
John Moreton Hicks is said to be "one of the most drunken, disreputable vagabonds in the kingdom". And as for the nephews

to whom he refers, their father says that he removed them "for private reasons" — and as to the witness's own son, unless his relations had supported him, he would have been in the workhouse before now.

Benjamin Penney's son left the school three and a half years since, and he made no complaint then. The other son stayed only five months, and did *not* go to another school, but his father took him into his shop at once.

Richard Gibson's son has been at the school only 11 months, and is very unruly and ignorant.

Henry James is a writing clerk to the petitioners' solicitor: his father sent five sons to the school, and both he and his older brother make affidavits for the masters.

Henry King is a clerk under the petitioners' solicitor and has no ground for complaint, having had one son at the school for six years and another for two, and never complained.

The general effect is to suggest that the petition is a put-up job, and the petitioner's witnesses little more than a gang of frauds.

The case against the petition was clearly very competently handled, and it is no surprise to us to learn that on 31 May 1851 the petitioners gave notice of their intention to abandon the petition, which was promptly dismissed by the Court with costs. The killing blow, no doubt, was a statement by one *Edward George Lewis* of Stourbridge, otherwise unknown to us. He states under oath that he had discussed the case with the petitioner Griffiths, who openly admitted that he was "not a voluntary but a solicited petitioner", acting under the persuasion of *William Blow Collis,* extensibly solicitor for the petition but in reality its prime mover. Griffiths owed him a favour and was repaying it in this way. The other petitioner Perrens was similarly placed. Neither of them had any interest in the petition, and they would be glad to see the end of it.

It is difficult not to feel some satisfaction that the 'put-up job', as we have described it, had failed. William Blow Collis decided to cut his losses — which must have been not inconsiderable — and the school went on teaching its Classics, together with its 'lower branches of learning', to the sons of the middle and upper classes of the locality, its number of pupils more or less settled for the time being around the thirties, its headmaster still regularly an absentee and finding at his own cost his own deputy, but still apparently enjoying the confidence of his governors. As for Thomas Peirce

Medwin, he too, for all his 69 years, lived to fight another day — but in his case, as we have seen, not for very much longer. For as between Giffard Wells and T.P. Medwin nature ruled with an impartial hand. The invalid lasted much the longer of the two — until, in fact, the year 1876 and the age of 74. But he did not last as headmaster; and that was due, in an indirect way, to the advent of Richard Woods. This we shall see in our next chapter.

Over the Threshold

Peirce Medwin's death, late in 1851, brought into the school the Reverend Edmund Hall. He stayed in office as usher for four years, and left behind him a 'Task and Lesson Book' which shows him to have been a very nice man, kind and humorous, and gifted with the ability to draw attractive little sketches and vignettes to enliven the pages of his uneventful chronicle. We know a little about him because of the accidental circumstance that he was maternal grandfather to the wife of T.W. Watson (headmaster 1934-51). Mrs. Watson told us that he was born near Salisbury, studied as an undergraduate at Peterhouse, Cambridge, was ordained during his time at Stourbridge and served as curate at St. Thomas's Church. He died in 1910. He was reputed to be connected by blood to the Dr. John Hall who married Shakespeare's daughter Susannah. When he died, one of his daughters found in an old trunk a "book of punishments" from his time at the school; and as it contained the names of boys who had become locally prominent and respectable men, and who were still alive, she thought it best to destroy it! This sad story only emphasies the extraordinary good fortune which has attended the survival of the great mass of archives to which we have made such copious reference in the course of our study.

Edmund Hall's departure brought upon the scene a man named Richard Woods. He was almost a total nonentity and we know almost nothing about him; and yet in a way he became the unwitting agent who nudged the school "over the threshold" from the old into the modern phase of its history.

Richard Woods came to Stourbridge after five years as undermaster of the grammar school at Worcester. A non-graduate and a layman, he was the successful one out of no fewer than 69 candidates! Many of his rivals were graduates and in orders, with far more to offer on paper than he had. He must have had excellent testimonials. He proved, however, to be undoubtedly an awkward customer, a niggling "commonroom lawyer", a stickler for the letter of the law — which he often misinterpreted — and an inflexible and grossly harsh disciplinarian. For his activities in this last field he was, within months of his appointment, first at odds with his headmaster, whose justified criticisms he resented and rejected, and soon afterwards the object of a concerted series of complaints from aggrieved parents — no less than eight letters, backed up by a very articulate and determined deputation consisting of twelve of the most respectable inhabitants of the town and district. This was in the Spring of 1857, and so in his second term as usher. He was accused of brutality in thrashing a boy named Joseph King*, and of petty tyranny over all the boys in his charge, specifically for his method of punishing small boys by making them 'stand out' in the middle of the schoolroom and literally *do nothing* for the duration of the punishment.† In the case of one Thomas Wall* the 'standing out' lasted on one occasion for four days, and on another occasion for five days, on end! If this seems inconceivable to the modern reader, let him be assured that Richard Woods not only inflicted the punishment but admitted it, and not only admitted it but justified it at length in his written defence. As for the caning of Joseph King, the doctor who examined him listed a horrifying series of injuries which he maintained might, if repeated, have left the boy a cripple for life. Richard Woods argued that the boy had deserved it, because he refused out of obstinacy to give an answer which he certainly knew.

There is an extensive dossier about this case, which spread itself over several months of the year 1857. This was partly due to the absence, yet again, of Giffard Wells, who was recuperating from yet another spell of ill-health, this time in the salubrious air of Brighton. He must have been away for some months, since the incidents complained of took place in March, and in his letters in July Giffard Wells disclaims all knowledge of the caning, because it occurred after the period of his absence started. Joseph King gave evidence

---

*King and Wall are names which both occur in the list of affidavits which were given in support of the 1851 petition.
†It was this 'method' to which Giffard Wells took exception.

that when he was caned it was stated by a Dr. Swann, who was present, to be 'cruel treatment'. This Dr. Swann, we conclude from the evidence, was Giffard Wells' deputy at the time. Later on, however, the governors, after an abortive attempt to get the Charity Commissioners to send an inspector to conduct an inquiry, eventually and with reluctance had to ask the headmaster to examine and to make a report on the complaints, as required by Rule 7 of the 1841 Statutes, — and to let them have it for a meeting of 3rd June. At that stage Giffard Wells excused himself, submitted a medical certificate and instructed his present substitute and deputy to do the work for him. The deputy by this time proves to be none other than the Reverend W.J.J. Welch, who was also officiating as curate in charge of St. Thomas's Church, and who was destined, of course, to become in 1858 the new headmaster of King Edward's School in succession to Giffard Wells.

For the governors had in fact been convinced at long last by the difficulties of dealing with the Woods affair in the continued absence of their headmaster, that the school could no longer go on like this. So on Trinity Monday of 1857 they resolved:

> THAT it is in the opinion of the Governors essential to the interests of the school that the Head Master do resume his duties immediately after the expiration of the Midsummer holidays continuously, and that if he be unable so to do, it will be advisable to make arrangements for his retirement and the appointment of a suitable successor.

So it was undoubtedly due to Richard Woods, unwitting as he was, that the regime of Giffard Wells came at last to an end. As long as there were no problems, the school could get along satisfactorily with an absentee headmaster. But when trouble came, as it certainly did with the arrival of Richard Woods, the governors had to face the fact that the situation was not really acceptable, and Giffard Wells had to go.

John Harward, who had conducted all the correspondence for the governors throughout these months, sent Giffard Wells a copy of a resolution adopted by the governors on 30 June 1857. This was an offer of an annuity for life of £100, to be paid out of 'the bonus fund'. This gave it priority over other expenditure after the official salaries and necessary outgoings. The offer was subject to the approval of the Charity Commissioners, and Giffard Wells lost little time in accepting it. John Harward then embarked upon the task of getting the Charity Commissioners to agree. In a letter to W. H. Freer dated 12 March 1858 he reported that he had been successful in this.

His letter states that the Charity Commissioners considered that they had power to dismiss Mr. Wells from Office as being from ill-health incompetent, and that the terms were matters for the discretion of themselves and the governors. They thought the terms proposed were more liberal than the school's income could really justify, but they were not disposed to raise any obstacles. They proposed to make the £100 per annum a primary charge on the future headmasters' bonus. But if that bonus was not sufficent to pay the whole pension in any one year, the balance only, with no interest, was to be payable out of future bonuses.

On these terms the ailing Giffard Wells took his departure and tottered off to Guildford, where he proceeded to survive for no fewer than 18 years, until 1876. We are left to wonder what could possibly have been the matter with him. Our only clue is the so-called medical certificate which he sent from Brighton. It is in fact a letter from a Dr. Dill, and it reads as follows:

My Dear Sir,
I regret exceedingly that you ever were involved in the unpleasant correspondence which has recently occupied your mind and pen. It has not only retarded your recovery, but positively thrown you back, so that you are only now gaining the state of health and strength of the nervous system which you had acquired before it commenced. As you ask my opinion, I must give it to you fully and candidly, and therefore I think it only justice to you and myself to say that if you are subject to a continuance of annoyance* and worry, you will not be in a state to resume your duties at the time you contemplate in August.

So it now looks as if it all comes down to "the state of health and strength *of the nervous system*". If this means what we suspect that it means, then it was no wonder that the invalid survived and drew his pension for a further eighteen years: and we are left to stifle the persistent thought that what Giffard Wells the invalid brings irresis-

*Giffard Wells adds his own gloss on the word 'annoyance' — "Dr. Dill simply means the annoyance the correspondence occasions me in my present State of Health".

tibly to our mind is the fashionable hypochondria of a previous age, "the sickness of those whose minds or bodies ail something, but they know not what", that is to say, in a word, 'the vapours'.

But vapours or not, sick man or hypochondriac — and we have no means of telling which is nearer the truth — Giffard Wells took his departure in 1858. Whatever his weaknesses, however small a proportion of his twenty-five years in office he managed to devote — or perhaps not to devote — to the management of the school, it still cannot be gainsaid that he left it in a far healthier state than when he came to it at the end of Joseph Taylor's time. The stranglehold of the dead hand on the curriculum had been broken, the sacred cow of Latin-and-nothing-but-Latin was dead, the "lower branches of learning" were an integral part of the curriculum, available to all pupils without charge. Moreover, the number of boys had risen from below ten to almost forty. Several gentlemen had gone from the school direct to Oxford or Cambridge. The principle had been established that the masters, if for any reason they proved to be incompetent could be dismissed. Giffard Wells had gone; Richard Woods was officially reprimanded on the strength of W.J.J. Welch's report to the governors in his capacity as deputy headmaster; and though Woods wrote a typical quibbling letter of protest, arguing that the governors were acting *ultra vires* in a matter of school discipline, which by the statutes must lie solely between himself and the headmaster, reprimanded he remained; and before another year was out, he too had gone — perhaps dismissed, perhaps resigned, but certainly departed.*

So the decks were cleared and the ship sailed on, into the last great stage of the four-hundred-year voyage which we set out to record, from 1552 to 1950. There is still almost a century of progress ahead, an astonishing development, a vast expansion and enlargement of both form and function, an acceleration of change parallel to that of the changes in the country at large — such changes as no other century in the history of mankind has witnessed.

The story of that century, to do it full justice, calls for a book in itself, longer by far than the story of the three centuries and more that have brought us to this point. But that book cannot come from the present writer's pen. We have told how we opened up the treasure-house of the school's early archives. We have now passed by the whole scope of those archives, and there is nothing compar-

---

*See the special Note on p. 197.

able to take their place. We have four headmasterships to record — those of Welch, Deakin, Boyt and Watson — a massive building programme, new statutes, a new currciculum, an enormous expansion of numbers, a proliferation of assistant teachers until there were more masters in the school than there had once been boys. It is a formidable task to cover such a canvas; and with the records now at our disposal, as sparse and unrewarding for the 19th century as for the sixteenth they were rich and full, we shall have to be content to fill in our picture with the broadest sweeps of the brush, and to deal in decades rather than details, abandoning the minutiae which we cannot in any case gather up from the dark corners of the Victorian waste-paper-basket, and concentrating on the large achievements, the long vistas and the broad views.

SPECIAL NOTE

*We have several times remarked, perhaps petulantly, but if so not without good reason, on the progressive drying up of our sources of evidence as we have made our tentative way towards modern times. We eventually, it will be remembered, spoke of the moment when we ran out of consecutive and formal records altogether. That moment came with the ending of the second great volume of governors' minutes at the year 1848. For much of our narrative thereafter we have had to rely on 'educated guesswork,' — on the use of intelligence, familiarity with the world of schools, and, in the last analysis, commonsense. Our habit of serendipity had in the long run, it seemed, lost its force.

Or had it? In October of 1987, six months after this book was finished, and had been revised, again revised, and finished again, there came into our hands a leather-bound ocatavo volume labelled MINUTE BOOK, which proved to contain the official governors' minutes of the Stourbridge Grammar School covering the period from January 1850 to March 1876. It had been found under an old sink in the ruins of an outhouse at the rear of Harward and Evers' office premises, shortly to be demolished, in the autumn of the year 1963. Its finder was Mr. Jack Haden, and in his keeping, safe but forgotten, it had resided for 24 years.

Was Mr. Haden, then, yet again the agent of our serendipity, or was he the agent of the gremlins who were at work, making sure that the labour of our researches and the travail of our composition should not come to an end without one more late obstruction and one last but very uncomfortable jolt? We leave it to our readers to decide.

Here, happily, we have only to report that a rapid but careful reading of the minute-book is entirely reassuring. We do not need to embark upon any revision or re-writing, since our reconstructions and conjectures are in the essentials proved correct. Two examples only must suffice.

(1) We said above that the usher Richard Woods was "perhaps dismissed, perhaps resigned." We now find that in fact he resigned, but not before he had been reprimanded a second time by the governors — on this occasion after a formal complaint from the new headmaster accusing him of "want of punctuality and inefficiency in his mode of teaching."

(2) We state below (p. 203) that "we simply do not know who was primarily responsible for the 1862 reforms." But-we add that "the odds are that it was W.J.J. Welch." We now read in the minute-book that on 15 October 1858 "The Headmaster's proposals for an alteration in the Scheme of Education were considered." At a further meeting early in 1859 Mr. Welch's scheme was again considered, and referred to the Charity Commissioners, who sent it back with the statement that they wished to raise no objections.

The Last Phase
(I)

It is a great pity that we do not know more about W.J.J. Welch. It is also surprising, since to any objective observer, viewing the whole range of the school's history from 1858 to 1950, it must appear as a truth beyond argument that in the whole panorama of progress, and indeed of almost total transformation, the longest steps — the giant strides taken in the ten-league boots — came in the first ten — even in the first five — years. The difference between the school of 1858 and that of 1868, or even of 1863, was so complete that no one who knew it on only one of those dates would have found anything familiar about it on the other. It had become, in fact, in a few short years a new institution. What happened after that first transformation was by comparison inconsiderable, a matter of enlargement, addition and variation, change of scale and change of detail. But the first changes were radical — "root and branch".

So it seems extraordinary that when, in the fulness of time, the school reached the zenith of its development and achievement, those who looked back from the 1950's invariably limited the range of their historical perspective to the five decades of the current century: what went before that, it seemed, was a sort of undifferentiated chaos, void of landmarks, empty of personalities and sunk in oblivion. The modern history of the school, as they saw it, began with J.E. Boyt; when Boyt came, it was a little school: when he left, it was a great school. As such, it was his creation. So what happened before Boyt was comparatively insignificant. Rupert Deakin's name cropped up occasionally: Welch was totally forgotten.

This is not difficult to explain. First, it was more than a normal lifetime since Welch's departure. Then, most of those who knew and loved the school at the time, from H.P. Jones and H.E. Palfrey downward, knew it and loved it from their own liveliest recollections of it. Many of the older ones, of course, had been boys there before Boyt's time, at the turn of the century. But the whole of their adult lives, as Old Boys, parents or governors, intervened between the present and those old, dead days, and in their collective reminiscences almost blotted them out. As for Welch, no one could remember him at all.

It happened also that the great J.E. Boyt was indeed a giant — a formidable scholar (14th Wrangler at Cambridge in his time), a formidable disciplinarian and a formidable man. What is more, it is probably fair to say that he was one who recognised, and admired, his own formidable qualities. So it was natural that inside the school his name and fame still lingered, and whispered in every corner of the buildings long years after his physical presence had gone from the scene. Be it remembered also that many of the teaching staff had been appointed by him, and not a few of them were his pupils. So it quite naturally appeared as a truth of common knowledge that the modern King Edward's School was J.E. Boyt's creation.

Even so, it is a pity that we do not know more about W.J.J. Welch. He was appointed headmaster in 1858. By 1863 the school had in the first place been rebuilt physically at great expense and by public subscription. Secondly it was being governed under a new set of Statutes and Orders which brought into effect the abortive revolution initiated by the 1841 statutes, and so rebuilt the school as an educational institution.

With an eye to the principle laid down by the Greek historian, that it is men who make a city and not walls empty of men, we shall pass over the new buildings and concentrate our attention on the new Statutes. Let us remember as we do so that the 1860's brought to its flood the incoming tide of reform in the English schools. The Newcastle and Clarendon Commissions had enquired into the state of the elementary schools and the nine 'great' public schools respectively. Now, from 1864 to 1867, came the work of the Taunton Commission, which was appointed to deal with the remainder. That remainder consisted chiefly of the endowed schools, and the Taunton Commission was more popularly referred to as 'The Endowed Schools Commission'. It reported on 2nd December 1867, having thoroughly investigated the condition of nearly 800 endowed schools, amongst which was King Edward's School,

Stourbridge. Over the country as a whole it found a great deal that was bad enough to be scandalous, and a total situation of administrative chaos which appeared to be manifestly impervious to piecemeal improvement. It therefore recommended the creation of a central consitutional body under a minister of the Crown, together with local authorities subordinate to this central body, and paralleled by a Council of Examination empowered to inspect schools and also to examine and register teachers. These were the recommendations: but the Endowed Schools Act of 1869 which followed was content to set up a makeshift expedient in the shape of a body of three commissioners, appointed for a limited term of office and empowered to deal with endowed schools only. The chief of this Endowed Schools Commission was Lord Lyttelton, who had been a prominent member of the Taunton Commission. The new commission was empowered to make new statutes and rules for individual schools and to alter the constitution of their governing bodies. It operated for about four years, from 1869 to 1873, and it established no fewer than 235 new school schemes. In this process it effectively changed the face of secondary education in England, aiming especially at two objectives — to equalise the provision of educational endowments as between boys and girls (an aim in which its success was very limited indeed) and secondly to introduce modern studies to supplement and often to replace the ancient Classics. In pursuing its aims it antagonised a good many interests, and in 1873 the government decided to terminate its existence. This was done by an amending Endowed Schools Act of that year, which passed the Commission's powers over to the Charity Commissioners, in whose-hands they remained until 1900.

With this outline laid down we can see that those who reformed the Stourbridge Grammar School were certainly swimming with the tide. Indeed, the extraordinary thing is that they actually anticipated the Taunton Commission's work by two years, so that when the assistant commissioner reported on the school in the second half of 1864, he opened like this:

"After having remained for some time in a depressed state, this school has lately been started afresh with handsome new buildings and a new set of rules, framed by the governors with the consent of the bishop of Worcester as visitor."

It is clear that the phrase "started afresh" implies a full justification of our claim that the new statutes rebuilt the school as an educational institution. The proof comes if we make an outline analysis of the 1862 rules compared with those of 1841.

In the first place the opening preamble, stating that it is expedient to make new Statutes and Orders "for the better management and discipline etc .., so as to extend the System of Education to other useful branches of literature and Science in addition to the Greek and Latin languages, etc." is repeated verbatim. So is the statement that the governors have had the assistance and consent of the headmaster; this time his name is not Giffard Wells but William John Joseph Welch. The reader who has followed our story from 1841 onward could be forgiven for raising a cynical eyebrow at this point. Is it pious hope? Is it solemn claptrap? Is it perhaps this time something more?

There are 23 new rules, as against 26 in 1841. Eleven of the new ones reproduce eleven out of the previous set, though in a totally different order. Then there are four new rules which present slight, but in total significant, changes, all of them tending to increase the authority of the headmaster. The old rules had given the authority to allow the boys' leave of absence to the head, but in the junior school to the usher. The usher was now ruled out of this matter, and the headmaster became the sole authority. So too in the case of expulsion, whereas the power to order this had resided exclusively with the governors, the headmaster was now enabled to suspend a boy for a flagrant offence and to have him temporarily removed until the governors could rule. The headmaster also remained the ruling authority in matters of methods of teaching, discipline and other "observances in the school". But his control was now extended over other 'Assistant Masters' besides the usher, and all of them were bound to accept his instructions, in cases where they demurred from his opinion, until the dispute could be referred to the governors. Finally, the act of worship at morning assembly was now to take the form of a prayer and a reading from scripture, both selected by the headmaster, in place of the prescribed prayer laid down in all previous rules and orders since the foundation.

That leaves eight rules, in which we find substantial and important changes. First, the teaching establishment is now officially expanded; there are to be a headmaster and usher, as provided by the Charter, but also *such additional or Assistant Masters as the Governors shall from time to time appoint*. This leads to a detailed prescription of the new course of education, which is to include Latin, Greek, English, Scripture, Elements of Theology, Writing, History, Geography, Arithmetic, Mathematics, elements of the Natural and Moral Sciences, and, when practicable, the French and German Languages, Drawing and Drilling. This would be a very fair prescription for a school curriculum in our own day — unless, of course, it were doomed to become "a custom more honoured in the breach than the observance". Another of the new rules, however, offered a safeguard against this stultification; for after laying it down that the subjects of instruction would be varied in each individual case according to the judgment of the headmaster, so as to adapt them as far as practicable to prepare the boys for their future pursuits in life, and after going on to insist that every boy should learn Latin, and should go on when sufficiently advanced to learn Greek, the new Rule 6 then really cuts loose from the school's ancient ways and adds that *in addition to or instead of Greek a boy may take one or both of French and German, if his parent requires this in writing to the headmaster.* Furthermore, the headmaster may allow a boy to take up French or German before he is ready for Greek.

It must at this point be stressed that to lay down the principles of individual curriculum and parental choice at one and the same time in an English grammar school in the year 1862 was a quite extraordinary exercise of educational foresight, outstripping the pace of national progress in this field by decades. It is a great frustration of our wish to know what exactly was happening here, that we simply do not know who was primarily responsible for the 1862 reforms. The odds are that it was W.J.J. Welch, but more than that we cannot say.* One cannot help thinking that the chief of the three Endowed School Commissioners-to-be — none other than Lord Lyttleton up at Hagley Hall! — must have regarded the changes with an interested and welcoming eye. But that is mere inference.

A further move into the future came with the prescription that public examinations should be held twice each year, at Christmas and Midsummer, and that prizes and certificates would be awarded, paid for out of the foundation funds, in addition to prizes given by private individuals.

The financing of new subjects — a most vitally important provision — was to be effected partly out of the old general fee of ten shillings a quarter due from every boy, and partly out of new and

---

*But see the Special Note on p. 197

extra fees payable in advance by those who wanted French, German, Drawing or Drilling. The foundation income was thus reserved for its original purpose.

Finally, the headmaster and usher — *still the only masters on the foundation* — were allowed to take ten and four boarders respectively, all boarders paying the same tuition fees as foundation boys.

Such were the new statutes under which the school was "started afresh" in its new buildings, in the charge of its new headmaster. What is more, from very nearly the first W.J.J. Welch was assisted by a new usher. For before the end of 1858 the governors had to find a replacement for the egregious Richard Woods, and after advertising the post they appointed in January of 1859 a man named W.G. Goddard. He wrote his application from King's Somborne in Hampshire, not far from Winchester; but of his personal details — place of origin, family, school, qualifications, even his age — we are distressingly ignorant. We do know that he was destined to become the James Dalton of the nineteenth century. We saw (see page 69 above), that James Dalton was our usher for 43 years, from 1626 until 1669. W.G. Goddard was to run him close in the matter of length of service. for the archives contain an illuminated address presented to W.G. Goddard on the occasion of his retirement in the year 1899.

The Taunton Commission's report on the school in 1864 (Vol. XV, p.605) lists only one foundation master apart from the headmaster, Rev. W.J.J. Welch, M.A.: he is described as "William Gruncell Goddard", and is evidently a non-graduate and a non-cleric. For some obscure reason he is favoured in the report by the inclusion of both his fore-names, which is more detail than was accorded to his headmaster.

We can repair that omission. For William John Joseph Welch, admitted pensioner at St. Catharine's College, Cambridge, on 28 May 1850, was born in 1827 at Handsworth, Birmingham, the son of William Gylby Welch. He graduated B.A. in 1854, and became M.A. in 1857. So he was a Midlander, and like Giffard Wells a late undergraduate, being no less than 23 years old when he matriculated. He was ordained deacon at Worcester in 1854 and priest in 1855; was curate of St. George's Birmingham in 1854-5, and of Buckland and Stoke Mandeville in Buckinghamshire in 1855-7. The Cambridge lists give the date of his curacy of St. Thomas's, Stourbridge as 1857-8, and of his headmastership of the school as 1858-85. This takes him to the age of 58 and he then moved, presumably by retirement, to become rector of Barnoldby-le-Beck in Lincolnshire; but he lived for only one year more, and died on January 22nd 1886. Effectively, it will be seen, his whole life's work lay at Stourbridge.

All these personal particulars are essentially unremarkable. If they were placed amongst comparable details concerning dozens of his contemporaries, there would be nothing in them to mark him out as an individual in any way distinguished above the rest. The papers concerning his appointment in 1858 survive in the school archives, and it could be said that they confirm this judgement of him. There were between thirty and forty applicants, amongst whom he, of course, as Giffard Wells's substitute, was the man in possession. When the governing body met to make their choice, two out of the eight governors did not attend. The Rev. C.H. Craufurd, rector of Oldswinford, was in the chair, and when it came to the election he himself proposed the name of the Rev. John Godding, a 29-year-old candidate from Carlisle. W.J.J. Welch was proposed and seconded in opposition, and the election went in his favour *by three votes to two*, the chairman not voting. There is nothing to tell us whether the candidates, or any of them, attended for interview, or whether the governors relied entirely upon testimonials and personal knowledge. But considering that W.J.J. Welch had, according to his own letter of application, served as deputy headmaster in the school not just once but on two occasions, and that in addition to his formal testimonials he presented a handwritten recommendation couched in the warmest terms and signed by fifteen inhabitants of Stourbridge who knew him and his work personally, we can see that his qualities and qualifications could hardly have been such as to set him in any significant way above the run-of-the-mill. Indeed, when the governors sent the details of his appointment to learned Counsel in Lincoln's Inn Fields for the purpose of having the terms of his contract of service drawn to suit their somewhat stringent requirements, Counsel's first advice in reply was that they should convene a special meeting of their entire number in order to confirm the election, and should have the minute of that appointment engrossed over their signatures and corporate seal. The minute which recorded only three votes in favour of the appointment was considered to be shaky ground in law on which to found the terms of a contract such as the governors wished to be drawn. For our present purposes these details reinforce our impression of W.J.J. Welch as an apparently unremarkable man.

His brochure of testimonials shows that he had been in contention for the headship of Hartlebury Grammar School, evidently without success. He had strong support from St. Catharine's College, which had at one stage in his career elected him to a college prize and a scholarship worth the princely sum of £21 a year, on the strength of his examination results. He was the best mathematician and the second-best Classic in his year in the college: but it has to be added that when it came to the Tripos he was listed as 29th of the Senior Optimes or Upper Seconds in Mathematics. Compare this with J.E. Boyt's record, and we see that whatever else Welch was, he was not a distinguished scholar. His university teachers and the several rectors and vicars whom he had served as curate were united, and convincing, in their testimony to his kindness and conscientiousness, and to the affection which he inspired in his parishioners and pupils. One fact which emerges is that he had spent fifteen months of residence in France. It also becomes clear that he had been in charge of the Stourbridge school in 1857; for he cites a laudatory report, given after the midsummer examination of the Stourbridge boys in that year by the Rev. W. Cockin, who also wrote him a formal testimonial. Welch had been his curate at St. George's Birmingham, and the Rev. Cockin claimed also to understand the special needs of the Stourbridge school from his long residence at Kidderminster, where he had formerly been headmaster of the grammar school.

However, undistinguished or not, under W.J.J. Welch the school "started afresh" almost as soon as he took charge. The numbers proceeded to rise, slowly but persistently, from 51 in 1850 to 76 in 1869, then to over 90 by 1880; at the end of Welch's time in 1885 they stood at 95. Most of these figures were unknown to J.E. Boyt, and have come to light only with the recent recovery of a number of old *Fee Books*. The earliest of these begins with W.J.J. Welch and covers the years 1859-69. There is another for 1859-75, followed by 1869-81, 1881-94, 1894-1905 and 1905-12. These books actually provide nominal rolls of all boys in the school for the whole of this period — a mine of information not otherwise available. For our present purposes the main interest of the early fee books is that they record the advent, the names and the remuneration of the new Additional Masters, for particulars of whom we looked, and looked in vain, in the great Governors' Minute Book which came to an end in 1849. The Fee Books also provide the explanation of the puzzling absence from the annual governors accounts of any reference to additional masters. For it becomes clear that they record the financial operations of W.J.J. Welch and W.G. Goddard (the Second Master) *in account with the Governors of King Edward's School.* The details of the accounting system are complex and obscure, and would call for someone much more practised in accounts than is the present writer to disentangle them. But the system evidently works on the principle that the fees paid in by parents under various heads — the general fee of ten shillings a quarter, the fees for Drawing, French, Drilling, Singing (changed in 1865 to Chemistry, soon to be called Science) and the fees from 'strangers' — all these are entered on the Credit side. Payments out, on the Debit side, are mainly salaries of one sort or another. At the end of each quarter comes an acknowledgement of the receipt of a balance, signed over a stamp by the Clerk to the Governors, with a brief, and unhappily cryptic, analysis of the calculation. An example taken at random may perhaps make our meaning clearer.

General	Drawing	French	Strangers Upper	Lower	Drilling	Science	Total
35.10.0	5.11.0	28.7.0	3.3.0	14.14.0	3.15.0	3.17.6	94.17.6

The acknowledgement and analysis reads:—

1867 April 9th Received of Mr. Goddard the sum of Fifty-six pounds and eight shillings for the undermentioned Fees:

Half the General Fees	17.15.0
The Whole of the Drawing Fees	5.11.0
The Whole of the French Fees	28.7.0
Strangers Fees (Mr. Doughty's Boys)	5.5.0
	56.18.0
Deduct from Strangers Fees in consequence of Capitation Fees and the Fees arising from Mr. Doughty's boys amounting to more than sufficient to pay Mr. Doughty's Salary.	10.0
	56.8.0

We shall see later that Mr. Doughty was the first recorded Additional Master. He came on the scene in 1862. What the financial arrangements were is by no means clear in detail, but it is at any rate evident that Mr. Doughty's salary was a matter for internal accounting within the sphere of the Fee Book. This presumably takes it out of the scope of the governors' income and expenditure accounts. Mr. Doughty was accompanied in 1862 by a Herr Moehring. He appears to have been paid £25 a quarter, as against Mr. Doughty's £22.10.0: but Mr. Doughty also received occasional bonuses of £10. In 1868 new names appear — Monsieur C.A. de Vit, presumably for French, Mr. Jos. Kennedy and Mr. Wm. Bowen — subjects unknown. In another of the books there is a separate section, headed

Revd. W.J.J. Welch in account with the Drilling Fund.

1860	Dr.		1860		
	Fees rec'd March	£3.4.0	Mar. 26	Paid Sergt. Osborn	5.0
			Ap. 23	Paid Sergt. Osborn	1.0.0
			May 21	Paid Sergt. Osbron	1.0.0
Balance		1.0	Jun 15	Paid Sergt. Osborn	1.0.0
		3.5.0			3.5.0

The following quarter saw a balance in hand of £1.1.6, and in 1862 there was a payment to a Captain Walker of £7.0.9 for rifles! This account is then superseded by a new one, headed

W.G. Goddard in acct. with the Additional Masters Fund.

This is concerned occasionally with singing, but mainly with drilling. W.G. Goddard himself and a Mr. Hy. Simms are recipients under 'Singing' or 'Choir Fund', and payments for drilling mainly concern a Sergeant Walker, who was on the books for a good many years. Each payment to him is normally for the amount of £1.11.6, and this must represent his payment for taking drilling lessons in the school. He is also paid on one occasion for repairing belts, and there is an item in August 1868 entered as

Bird's Account (swordsticks)   1.4.0

The mind boggles! — and in the following year we come to

Repairs (swordsticks)   0.4.6

Other names occur, but Sergeant Walker goes on until the end of the account of 1875, when it seems to have been wound up. The last two entries are as follows:

Donation to Prize Fund	10.6
Balance transferred to School Cricket Club	14.10½

Taking all this in conjunction with several items for a newly-arising Gymnasium Fund (1868 onward) we begin to think we can discern the emerging features of Physical Education and School Games! We shall soon see that we are probably wrong; but at least let us record that in July 1872 the Additional Masters Fund paid the enormous sum of £22.2.6 to Mr. Welch for repairs done to the gymnasium, which appears to have been a structure of gymnastic apparatus permanently erected in the playground. Mr. Welch on this occasion must have paid the bill and been reimbursed, since he pencilled in his acknowledgement and formal receipt across the entry in the book. At about this time we come across entries showing payments to what is termed 'Flag Account', as well as more donations to the Prize Fund, payments to a 'Lecture Account', one item which says simply, and cryptically, "Bell"; and there is also "Mr. Stringer's Bill" for a clock.

In general terms what we have here is something in the nature of a Headmaster's petty-cash account, subject to audit but administered very much at the headmaster's discretion. What we also have is a series of hints, obscure in detail but clear in general trend, that the authorities of the school were beginning to accept the principle that the business of the school spread out far beyond the confines of the classroom. Once again we are tempted towards the conclusion that W.J.J. Welch begins to look like a headmaster far in advance of his times.

But, lest we pride ourselves too soon upon our discovery of a paragon let us turn first to the testimony of two who could speak, and did speak, of the school in W.J.J. Welch's time from personal experience. The time has gone by now, of course, for the historian's supreme piece of serendipity — the finding of the eye-witness himself. For it is more than a century since Welch retired, and another generation further back since he became headmaster. It is 127 years since the "handsome new buildings" first raised their impressive and eminently academic facade above the east side of the Lower High Street, within a stone's throw of the spot where Richard Madstard was "dryven to shutt his shopp windowes for salfgarde of his lief" on the day when Gilbert Lyttelton's men picked a quarrel with him in market time and "challendged him to the fielde", — and almost on the actual site of the humble quarters where Richard Alchurche "used his erectinge of figures" and pretended to tell the people of things lost, and "did keepe victuallinge and sellinge of ale in a place adjoyninge to the said schole". We have as little hope now of finding someone who knew Welch as we have of finding someone who had met Madstard or who had learnt his Latin from Alchurche. But luckily for us the school magazine — that Stourbridge Edwardian in whose pages J.E. Boyt published his articles on the ancient history of the school — came into being in 1922, which is two generations closer than we are to the world of W.J.J. Welch, half-way back indeed from our day to the beginning of his. It was in the summer term's issue of 1934, and again in the very next issue, that the editor achieved a double coup — *two* articles by *two* different writers, recording their memories of their days in the school under W.J.J. Welch!

The original words of these two articles will serve better than any further words of ours to provide a useful commentary on our attempt to re-create the school over which W.J.J. Welch presided, and which he must have played a great part in creating. We shall take first the earlier of the two reminiscences. The author's name (not graced by any preceding initials) can be found repeatedly in the Fee Book for 1869-81; it appears first in the Spring of 1871 and last in the midsummer quarter of 1876.

SIXTY YEARS AGO

Sixty years ago I was a pupil at the Stourbridge Grammar School. It speaks well for the perspicacity of the Governors that there have been only two changes in the Headmastership since my time there, especially so in view of the superlative qualities of the men they appointed to this post.

In my time the Headmaster was the late Rev. W.J.J. Welch. The number of pupils was about 70 and I do not think Mr. Welch had any desire to increase it. In those far-off days headmasters had things pretty well their own way, so long as they were *persona grata* to the governing bodies, and there was no such thing as government inspection.

When I was admitted in 1870 the old School Hall was large enough to seat the 70 or so boys, and afforded each an old oak desk. These desks carried the carving of countless initials, one set being S.J. — supposed to be those of Dr. Samuel Johnson, the lexicographer.

In my time the school year was divided not into three terms, as now, but into four quarters. The attendance fee was ten shillings per quarter, with extras for French, drawing and drilling, because these subjects were taught by visiting masters.

There were only two masters on the permanent staff besides Mr. Welch, — viz, Mr. W. G. Goddard and Mr. Doughty. The latter had the care of the Lower School.

A boy's position was regulated by his knowledge of Latin, and as I did not know any when I entered the school I was placed in the lowest class under Mr. Doughty.

Mr. Doughty was a good-looking man, dark as a gipsy, with raven-black curly hair and moustache, always neat and punctilious. As a teacher adequate but not great, though probably greater than his remuneration, for in those bad old days ushers, like curates, were wretchedly paid. He had sons of his own, who went, I believe, to the National School, presumably because the Grammar School fees, low as they were, were beyond his means.

Mr. Goddard, the Middle School Master, was appointed, I think, directly by the Governors. He was a striking personality and a born teacher; the only one of the masters, I believe, I ever learned anything from. He was the only one of the masters who took any real interest in his work, or in the school sports, or in the boys after school hours.

Mr. Goddard had the commanding appearance and character of a Roman senator. His iron grey eye under beetling brow missed nothing. He was a fine disciplinarian and whilst boys feared him they esteemed and liked him, because he was just and impartial. He was highly thought of among the townspeople also, and associated well.

I regretted leaving Mr. Goddard for the Upper School, for the Head had his favourites, and I knew I was not one of them. As a matter of fact at this time the Headmaster was taking very little interest in the school. He was chiefly occupied in studying on his own account to become a Doctor of Medicine. This necessitated his constant attendance at a medical school. It was a full-time job even in those days, and he was "walking" one of the Birmingham hospitals. This I know to be a fact, in as much as a young uncle of mine was doing the same thing at the same time, and consorted with him. How he got the Governors to consent to this sort of thing I do not know. But what I do know is that after I left the Middle School I made very poor progress.

My first lessons in Greek were at the hands of the then head boy, Paul Mathews.

When I began the study of pure mathematics, I was given a book on Euclid and told to learn the first proposition. It was a long time before I discovered for myself what the book was about. Mr. Welch offered no explanation, and woe betide the boy who asked for help whilst the reverend gentleman was studying his medical work.

Like the rest of us, Mr. Welch had his sorrows. He early lost his young wife, who left him with an only child — a daughter — a nice-looking girl, whom I used to admire. She sang in the choir at St. Thomas's church (where I believe Mr. Welch was at one time curate) and there met a young man with who she fell in love and eloped. The young man happened to be the son of our drill-sergeant.

I have mentioned the word sport, but practically speaking, as we know sport today there was none. I never saw a football at school. On Wednesday and Saturday afternoons a few of us used to trudge to Norton and play a game of cricket on the racecourse, where Mr. Goddard would occasionlly join us. Just before I left a cricket club was formed, of which I was secretary, and we made an arrangement with the town club to have a limited use of the ground at Amblecote.

A. J. MAINWARING.

The reader will have to decide for himself! Did the "superlative qualities" of the Stourbridge headmasters include in W.J.J. Welch's case the ability to "con" his governors into believing that he could devote himself to his duties in the school while walking the wards of a hospital in Birmingham? Did he remember that his contract of service, which learned Counsel had been so cautiously engaged to draft in 1858, included a clause debarring him from having any other employment or from taking permanent church duties without the governors' permission? If so, did he reconcile it with his conscience that he was embarking upon the arduous course necessary to qualify him as a doctor? Did he ever practise medicine? Should we perhaps understand him better if we knew more about the circumstances of his young wife's death? Was it this which turned his thoughts towards the healing art?

The answers to these questions are concealed forever in the sealed coffers of time. But one discovery we have made which enables us to tie up one loose end in the fabric of our story of W.J.J. Welch. His only daughter, as we have seen, eloped with the drill-sergeant's son: perhaps she was starved of attention by her father's preoccupation with his medical studies. The elopement must have been an unconscionable blow to his professional self-respect. Yet at the end of his life, in the will which he signed on 2nd August 1884, he was chiefly concerned to instruct his executors to arrange to take out an insurance policy for £500 upon the life of his daughter, to be applied for the benefit of her children. He names her as Agnes Mary Aston *Walker* — and we remember the entry in the Fee Book:

Paid to Sergeant Walker .. .. .. £1.11.6.

So A. J. Mainwarings recollections in this particular have been tried and proved correct. Let us be cautious, however, of equating accuracy of recollection in this matter with the correctness of judgement in all others. Perhaps our second eye-witness should now add his testimony, in the expectation that it will either complete or retouch the picture.

AN OLD EDWARDIAN'S REMINISCENCES

Although the School had its full complement of 90 boys in September 1878, I was admitted by the Headmaster, the Rev. W.J.J. Welch, M.A. on my father's arrival in Stourbridge. I was not too young at eleven to appreciate its royal origin and antiquity. I was inspired by the black oak wainscoting carved with the names of boys long gone from this world and with ancient dates, and was awed by the masters' desks, like thrones, on daises and surmounted by huge canopies draped with dark green curtains. The Headmaster taught chiefly in the one classroom, at the far end. I remember his sailing down the big schoolroom every afternoon to his desk in the oriel window abutting on the High Street, in cap and flowing gown, crying in a musical tenor voice, with cultured varsity intonation, "Prepare!" — the signal for the closing of school.

Mr. Welch taught us Chemistry and Acoustics, chiefly from books, for that was long before practical work or the 'heuristic' method had been thought of. We religiously learnt the symbols and atomic weights of the "70 elements". Mr. Welch also guided us across the *Pons Asinorum* — a terror unknown in these modern days. Isbister's Euclid was our textbook, and the sound logic and well-reasoned statements of the Greek sage impressed me deeply.

At the far end of the big schoolroom facing the Headmaster's desk reigned Mr. Goddard — a forensic-looking gentleman who daily passed my home deep in thought, as though continually pondering mathematical problems. He expounded the mysteries of decimals. The lifting of the lid of his desk was often the prelude to a descent from his "throne" and a perambulation round the class to whack our knees with a thick cane whenever our brains proved sluggish ... White's Grammar School Texts initiated us into Caesar; Eutropius and Phaedrus were also read. A thorough drilling in Allen's Latin Grammar proved of great value in subsequent studies.

I am recalling only the Middle Form's work. This ancient Grammar School of the boy King, as a member of which I donned a "College cap", situated in the heart of Shakespeare's England, was to me, born in South Africa, very inspiring. So were the songs we sang in class — "The British Grenadiers", "A-hunting we will go", etc.

I can remember no organised games, at any rate for the rank and file. I was proud to handle a rifle in the drill lessons in the playground. We used only explosive "caps". Sergeant Walker was our instructor. He invariably addressed us with good humour as "You sinners!" Perhaps he had acquired the habit as superintendent of the Wesleyan Sunday School. He was a kind old fellow.

Mr. Doughty, a fresh-complexioned, high-browed man, with dark moustache and mutton-chop whiskers — totally dissimilar from Mr. Goddard's clear-cut, sombre, sallow face — was the third master. It was his habit to arrive just as the 9 o'clock bell had ceased to ring, running up the stone staircase with the last boy, just in time to avoid the relentless closing of the great door. The violent mopping of his forehead afforded us wonderment and amusement at the outset of the morning's work.

W. W. SAWTELL (1878 – 80)

There are considerable variations of emphasis, to say the least, in this second account. The main thing is that we get a much better impression of W.J.J. Welch's impact upon his pupils. This time there is no reference at all to his lack of interest in the school or to his preoccupation with his medical studies. This last is easy to explain if we recall that A.J. Mainwaring attended from 1871 to 1876, W.W. Sawtell from 1878 to 1880. We can now turn to the brief biography of W.J.J. Welch in the Cambridge lists, which we have already cited. We failed to mention a parenthetic note which gives the details of his medical qualifications, as follows:

> M.A., M.B. and M.D., Dublin, 1874.

How a man could qualify for the three degrees in the same year we cannot explain without a greater knowledge of the Dublin university regulations than we possess, but the point is of no importance. What is important is the date. In W.W. Sawtell's time at the school all the medical studies were long since over: A.J. Mainwaring's years had coincided with the most strenuous period of study which the medical graduate of 1874 must have had to go through.

This leads us to the final chapter in our story of W.J.J. Welch and his headmastership. We have seen that within five years, probably less, of his appointment in 1858 he had piloted the school into handsome new buildings paid for by public subscription, and into a new phase of its history, complete with new statutes, a new curriculum and new staff. At that stage it is quite inconceivable that W.J.J. Welch "was taking little interest in the school". Nor does it seem feasible to suppose that he "had not any desire to increase the numbers", since in fact they almost doubled (from 51 to 95) in the years of his headmastership. It must be that his period of office can be divided into phases: in the first of these he was creating or helping to create the new school: in the second he was precoccupied, for reasons which are quite unknown to us, with the business of becoming qualified in medicine. This took him to the year 1874. Then came the next phase, coinciding with yet another new chapter in the history of the school. For we are not yet done with the reforms which produced the great metamorphosis of the mid-Victorian years. We have seen 1841; we have seen 1862; we now turn our attention to 1876.

It is an interesting speculation to ask ourselves why it was considered necessary to make yet further changes. Essentially the reforms of 1862, combined with the new buildings, equipped the school to move steadily forward on the tide of educational progress, in the same way as so many other of the endowed schools were destined to move — lesser schools as well as greater, the obscure as well as the famous, the little one-horse outfits, or one-stream market-town academies, as well, as the Bradfords, the Manchesters and the Bristols. They all, in a sense, "took off" at about the same time. They were all ushered into the modern world when they were enabled to throw off the throttling clutch of the dead hand of their ancient statutes. King Edward's Stourbridge clearly did that in 1862. Why then did the school need yet another reform in 1876?

The answer seems to lie in the activities and possibly in the personalities of the Taunton Commission of 1864-7 and the Endowed Schools Commission of 1869-73. We have referred to the Taunton Commission's report on the school of 1864, and it is now time for us to take a closer look at its findings.

It started, as we have said, with a reference to the new buildings and the new rules. The Report's comments urged that larger fees and the abolition of the rigid separation of the foundation funds from the tuition fees were very desirable. This conclusion is in strict consonance with the central aims of the Taunton Commissioners, to free the ancient grammar schools from the obligation to be 'free', and in so doing to end the special (and therefore privileged) position of the ancient Classics as the only free subject of study. The relevant passage is as follows:-

> The constitution which these rules embody seems to work well, but the financial arrangements, which have been left on their old footing, are complicated and have latterly caused some trouble to the governors. Being obliged to pay a fixed proportion of the revenue from endowment to the head and second masters respectively, and having at present to pay a retiring allowance of 100l. a year to a former master, they cannot take this 100l. from the general fund, but must charge it to the headmaster's share. The fee fund, moreover, is kept quite distant from that produced by the endowment, and is sometimes in danger of barely sufficing for the charges which come upon it for the payment of additional masters, since it cannot be supplemented from the endowment funds. The fee fixed — £2 annually for town boys, £4.4s or £6.6s for 'strangers', is a fee much smaller than is usual in grammar schools of this class, and very much smaller than the market price of the education given. All or almost of the boys who are in the school could well afford to pay £4. or £5 per annum; but as the endowment is large, and instruction in the school was at one time

entirely gratuitous, considerable local opposition might be expected to a proposal to raise the charge. The school is held to be still free for classics.

The new buildings meet with approval, and we find confirmation of our conjecture about the gymnasium. The Enquiry encouraged the taking of boarders.

> The school-building, erected by subscription, stands near the centre of the town, and seems very well suited for its purpose. The principal room is spacious and handsome, and there is a pretty large class-room besides, as well as a vestibule serving for a cloak-room. The playground is good, and one part of it has been covered over and fitted up with gymnastic apparatus. Immediately adjoining is the headmaster's house, in which there is good accommodation for boarders. The rules needlessly restrict the number which he may take to ten, and the second master's number to four.

Comments on the curriculum, with suggestions for further liberalisation were as follows:

> Educationally regarded, the school may be called semi-classical: every boy learns Latin, but only two were at the time of my visit learning Greek, and one of these merely because a rule requires that those who don't take French shall take Greek, and his father refused to pay the fee charged for French. The headmaster spoke of this rule as very inconvenient, and no doubt it ought to be abrogated. A class has been formed in natural science, but the parents show no interest in it, and grumble at the fee of 2s 6d. which is imposed to defray the cost of chemical apparatus and materials.

After a generally "Satisfactory" inspection-report on the effectiveness of the teaching, the report concludes with its recommendations:

> Although it is not now and is not likely to become a grammar school of the first order, sending boys to the universities, this school is doing a good deal of useful work in a plain and practical way. The superior education of the town, a thriving place of 9,000 inhabitants in the outskirts of the Black Country, is mainly

in its hands: boys of different social classes and different religious persuasions resort freely to it, and a general satisfaction is expressed in the neighbourhood with its position and prospects. What it principally seems to need at this moment is a settlement of its financial arrangements so as to give the trustees a wider discretion and make the position of the under-masters more satisfactory, — and the infusion of a little more vigour into some parts of the teaching, more particularly into that of the higher arithmetic and of mathematics.

This report was certainly not critical enough to call for any radical further reforms. Indeed it might well have turned out that the reforms of 1862, anticipating the work of the Taunton Commission and undertaken on the initiative of the school's own authorities, had in fact proved to be a mixed blessing, in the sense that they provided not enough of the medicine for a radical cure, but enough to prevent the patient from completing the dose. We have to remember, however, that the Endowed Schools Act of 1869 set up the Endowed Schools Commission with a wide-ranging power to make new Statutes and Rules for individual schools, and to alter the constitution of governing bodies. This the commissioners did, as we have seen, with such enthusiasm that in four years they established 235 new schemes. We remember also that the most powerful of the three commissioners was Lord Lyttelton. It was hardly to be expected that his list of 235 new schemes would fail to include one for the Stourbridge School which was on his doorstep. Nor did it do so.

The provision of a new scheme was in fact in the air as early as 1872, and in 1873 a scheme was put forward which proved to be abortive, and which was superseded by the one which was adopted in 1876. It is this latter to which we must turn our attention first. The document which enshrines it — formidably official, originating from the Endowed Schools Commission, and bearing the names of the approving Commissioners (Lyttelton and Hugh Geo. Robinson) over the date 13 August 1874, bears an impressive superscription in our locally printed copy, descriptive of the booklet's contents:—

SCHEMES
as approved by Her Majesty in Council
for the Management of the
Stourbridge Free Grammar School
of King Edward VI

And the Foundations incorporated therewith

Regulations Made by the Governors

List of Governors, Masters
etc. etc.

Stourbridge
R. Broomhall, The Crown Printing Office, High Street
1876

This is, as we have said, a formidably public and official document, far removed from the admittedly official but domestic and private sets of Rules and Orders of previous times, always initiated by the governors themselves and ranging back in time to the sixteenth century. Nor do its externals belie the nature of its contents. For it soon becomes clear that we have here a radical reconstruction. It builds, it is true, upon the rules of 1841 and 1862, but it goes much further than they did in reforming the school. In fact, it sweeps away the existing foundation altogether, and creates a new one from the ground up.

It declares its object first — *"to supply a liberal and practical education, by means of a school or schools at or near Stourbridge"* and it proceeds to state, in relation to the existing foundation, that *"all particulars which by the Endowed Schools Acts of 1869 and 1873 are capable of being hereby repealed and abrogated shall, so far as relates to the management of this Endowment, be repealed and abrogated."*

It adds that the Charities of Henry Glover, Mary Hickman, and Thomas Oliver, shall be united with this scheme and be a single Foundation or Trust.

Then comes what must surely be to us, who have followed the fortunes of "the King's new school", with its eight governors chosen from amongst "the most discreet and honest of the inhabitants of the parish of Oldswinford from its birth in 1552 for more than three hundred years, — what must surely be the most radical change of all. *'The existing Corporation of the Governors of the Free Grammar School of King Edward the Sixth at Stourbridge is dissolved'*". That Corporation was the most ancient institution, apart from the parish church of St. Mary, in the town and parish. It had survived three hundred years and more of the chances and changes of time and circumstance, from the peculations of Elcoxe and Bere and the rest, and the scandals of Richard Alchurche, through the crazy adventures of Madstard, past the financial crisis of the defaulting tenants in the Civil War, on to the domestic 'civil war' of Wentworth's appointment and the sorry tale of his dismissal, through the long decades of the eighteenth-century slumbers, and finally it had even come through the decades of the dereliction and ruin of the school under Joseph Taylor and had seen the school begin to emerge once more to a life of vigour and prosperity. The Corporation itself, old as it was, was still vigorous and active. Election to it's number was still a privilege, coveted and prized throughout the neighbourhood as it had always been. And now the body of eight was no more.

In its place the Endowed Schools Commission set up a totally new authority. There were to be ten governors, constituted as follows:

1. ONE was to be ex officio the Chairman of the Stourbridge School Board.
2. ONE was to be nominated by the local Bench (to serve for 5 years)
3. FOUR representative governors (to serve for 4 years) were to include TWO to be elected by the town Improvement Commissioners and TWO to be elected by the parents of day scholars.
4. FOUR cooptative governors were to consist in the first instance of members of the present governing body. SIX of the eight would serve, to be reduced by a designated process to FOUR.

There was to be no residence qualification and no religious bar. No master could be a governor. Rules were laid down for the frequency and times of meetings, election of a chairman, for a quorum, and for special meetings, the appointment and terms of service of a Clerk, for keeping minutes and accounts, and so on. The Governors were empowered to appoint agents at need, but *no agent who was a governor should be paid*. All the property of the foundation except copyhold was transferred to vest in the Official Trustee of Charitable Funds. The visitorial jurisdiction was transferred from the bishop to the Crown. Licensing by the ordinary was abolished.

Now we see what the Endowed Schools Commission regarded as the proper sort of authority to manage an ancient foundation under modern conditions. In effect they had Victorianised, municipalised and modernised. By the same token they had generalised and depersonalised. If one wished to seek one image as a symbol of the changes which they wrought, one could do worse than to say that they had destroyed or thrown away the ancient silver seal of the Office of the Staple of the City of Lincoln, and put in its place a rubber stamp!

As for the School and its management, they laid down 33 regulations, as follows:

The pupils were to be boys only, and day-scholars, except that the headmaster could take 12 boards and the second master six, on the same terms for tuition as day-boys.

There was to be religious instruction regulated by the headmaster and governors, on the strict understanding that parents could claim exemption for their sons from this and from corporate worship.

The governors were to have control over the general nature and balance of the curriculum, the length of terms and holidays, the provision and maintenance of school buildings. (They were empowered to spend up to £500 on providing a laboratory, to be built within three years, to enlarge the playground, maintain a gymnasium and otherwise improve the buildings). They controlled the number of assistant masters, the amount of money made avilable to pay them, and for plant and apparatus. In all these matters they were to consult the headmaster.

The headmaster had control over school text-books, methods of teaching, the arrangement of classes and school hours. He generally ruled over the whole internal organisation, management and discipline. If he were to expel a boy, he had to make a report in writing to the governors. He appointed and dismissed all assistant masters at his discretion, but subject to a right of appeal to the governors against dismissal. W.G.Goddard could be dismissed only by the governors, and he was to receive a salary of not less than £200 a year. All other payments for assistants' salaries, and for apparatus, were to be made at the headmaster's discretion. The headmaster's salary was to be £150 a year, *plus a capitation fee* as agreed with the governors, between the limits of £5 and £3 per boy, to be paid quarterly or termly, as the governors might decide.

School Fees. The Free Grammar School was a thing of the past. All boys were now to pay such fees as the governors might set (except in the case of Exhibitioners, i.e. free-place boys, from the local elementary schools). The fees were to be fixed within the limits of £4 and £10 a year, paid in advance to the headmaster or the governors' receiver. There were to be no extras (except for Greek, as below) and no privileges. The age limits for pupils were set at 8 and 17, unless a boy could prove that he meant to go on to university, when with the headmaster's approval he might stay to 19. The headmaster made the rules about withdrawal for idleness or incapacity.

Under the above limits any boy of good character and health was eligible to attend, if he was living at home with his parents or some person approved by the governors and headmaster, and if he could keep the hours and regulations. Applications for entrance must be made on a printed form to be sent to the headmaster or governors' agent, and the headmaster was to keep a register of applicants, who each paid a fee, limited to five shillings. The headmaster was to set an examination for all applicants! Successful entrants then were admitted in order of application. In case of excess numbers the governors could hold a competitive examination, the subjects being reading, small-text writing, the Four Rules of Arithmetic, and the outline of the Geography of England.

Curriculum. The subjects of study were to be Reading and Writing; Arithmetic and Book-keeping; Mathematics; Geography; English Language, Composition and Literature; Ancient and Modern History; at least one branch of Natural Science; Latin Language and Literature; at least one European Modern Language; Political Economy; Drawing, Drilling and Vocal Music. All this was subject to the headmaster's arrangements. GREEK, when required, was to be an extra, with a fee of not less than £3 a year: but boys on the roll on 1st January 1873 were exempt.

There were rules for an *Annual Examination*, set by an external examiner, who was to make a report to the governors, to be handed on to the headmaster.

Exhibitions (i.e. Free Places) were to be funded from the Glover, Hickman and Oliver charities, now consolidated. They covered part or all fees and were to be given on merit only. There were to be 12 in total, and exhibitioners had to have attended for two years at a public elementary school in the ancient parish of Oldswinford. The governors could provide maintenance for exhibitioners at need, up to a maximum of £30 in all per annum.

That was the pattern for the future. As it was printed in 1876, however, it had one odd feature — there were five sections, entitled —

General Scope
Constitution of Governors etc.
The School and its Management
Application of Income
General

But the sections were numbered 1,2,3,5 and 6. There was no number 4! One perhaps harbours the passing thought that even in the days of meticulous Victorian clerks, before the slapdash era of the computer had been thought of, gross and glaring blunders could be made, and left in print, to affront the tax-paying public and to pour shame upon the authorities which employed such irresponsible and incompetent dolts! And quite apart from this, one is bound to ask how the mistake in this case could possibly have originated. The answer comes when we turn to the sole surviving copy of the earlier and abortive scheme of 1873, which we referred to in an earlier section. An office stamp shows that this document, originating from the Endowed Schools Commission, was received in E.H. Freer's office on 3rd December 1872. The draft scheme is otherwise undated. It contains seven sections, and five of them are in substance the same as five in the subsequently adopted scheme of 1876. If we put the two side by side we shall at once see the points of interest in the abortive draft;

Abortive Draft	*Scheme of 1876*
1. General Scope	1. General Scope.
2. Constitution of Governors etc.	2. Constitution of Governors etc.
3. The Schools.	3. The School and its Management.
4. The Grammar School and its Management.	
5. Wheeler's Girls School and its Management.	
6. Application of Income.	5. Application of Income.
7. General.	6. General.

The abortive scheme, it will be seen, actually contemplated the establishment of a Girls' School in addition to the boys Grammar School! Doubtless that was why it became abortive. The girls school was to have been housed in the Wheeler School on Red Hill, by the side of the old Church Road which ran like a spine from the river-crossing up the High Street, over the hill and down to the church at Oldswinford. Those premises had been built in about 1710 for the charity school then set up by the will of Henry Glover; they had been administered by the governors of the Grammar School, and Glover's School had later been put together with Wheeler's School as a combined institution. Now, with the 1870 Education Act and the advent of universal public elementary education, such 'petty' schools had become redundant. So the Endowed Schools Commissioners, pursuing their pet purpose of equalising educational opportunity between boys and girls, took the opportunity of the proposed new Stourbridge scheme to kill this extra bird with the same stone. The details, however interesting, do not concern us here. We do know that the enthusiasm of the commissioners was not matched by that of the Grammar School governors: various notes on rough papers which have survived make it clear that the governors were extremely worried about the financial problems of providing and maintaining a girls' school. One note speaks of "the ancient character" of the premises. This must refer to the Red Hill premises, since the boys' school buildings were almost new. The Red Hill building was indeed no larger than a good-sized family house, and the petty school which it had housed must have been petty indeed! In later years, from 1951 to 1975, the house became once again the property of the King Edward's governors, though they did not realise that when they bought it. It served for those 24 years as the foundation's headmaster's residence. It is very difficult for anyone — and for one who called it home for that period of time it is impossible — to see how by any stretch of the imagination it could ever have been thought to possess the physical requirements for a girls' day grammar school.

So the dream of a girls' school for Stourbridge to match the boys' grammar School, remained for the time being a dream. Clause 71 of the 1876 scheme paid lip service to that dream by saying "The Governors may, if they think fit, and there are sufficient funds available for the purpose, establish a School for the higher education of girls at or near Stourbridge". So the pious hope was given a permanent expression in black and white: but pious hope it remained.

As for the Rev. W.J.J. Welch, we can leave him now in his new school under his new governing body and with his new staff. Broomhall's booklet of 1876 gives us all the details:

GOVERNORS

Colonel Thomas William Fletcher, M.A., F.R.S., F.S.A., F.G.S., J.P., Chairman; nominated by the Magistrates of the Stourbridge Division.
Major James Walker, ex officio, as Chairman of Stourbridge School Board.

REPRESENTATIVE GOVERNORS

Mr. Henry Hughes   elected by Stourbridge Improve-
Mr. Godfrey Rowley Perkin   ment Commissioners.
Mr. William Blow Collis   elected by parents and guardians
The Reverend David Maginnis   of day scholars.

COOPTATIVE GOVERNORS

The Reverend John Simon Boldero, M.A.
Henry Onions Firmstone, Esq., J.P.
Richard Leacroft Freer, Esq., J.P.
Mr. John Harward
The Reverend David Robertson, M.A.
Mr. Edward Westwood

MASTERS

Head Master — The Reverend W.J.J. Welch, M.A., M.D., F.C.S., & c.
Second Master — Mr. W. G. Goddard
Assistant Master — Mr. J. Doughty
French Master — Mr. C.A. de Vit, B.A. Paris and Ll.B. Heidelberg
Drawing Master — Mr. J.P. Bowen, Head Master of the School of Art, Stourbridge.
Drill Master — Serjeant Walker.

CLERK

Mr. Edward H. Freer, 76 High Street, Stourbridge

The Last Phase
(II)

At this point it is time for us to pause and take stock of what remains for us to do. In terms of headmasterships there are three — those of Rupert Deakin, J.E. Boyt and T.W. Watson. In terms of years there are 65. In terms of change and development one can look at the situation in two quite different ways. On the one hand, once we have passed the milestone of the 1876 statutes, with the school in its new buildings, with its new curriculum and its new body of governors, no longer 'free' and no longer in the old sense of the term a 'grammar' school, there is nothing much more to be said, because there is nothing much more to be done that can make changes as drastic as those that have already come to pass. The ancient school is as dead-and-gone as is the ancient school room. The new school is in its fundamentals essentially the same in 1885 as it will continue to be until we come to the end of our story in 1950.

That is one possible point of view. But on the other hand, when you consider the difference in scale and in the complexity and range of its activities, in the number of pupils and the number of teachers, the area of its site and the range and variety of its buildings, in all these things the outcome of those 65 years is effectively equivalent to nothing less than a total rebirth, the creation of a new school in a new world, as different from the old as is the jet-stream airliner from the penny-farthing bicycle.

The unanswered question — which point of view are we to adopt? — leaves us with an intractable problem. On the one hand, to continue with our forward-moving narrative through twenty years of Deakin, twenty-nine years of Boyt and seventeen years of

Watson, like a tape unrolling, is not a process which recommends itself as likely to command the reader's attention. There is too much of a sameness in the landscape ahead if we take that road: and in any case the world of late Victorian and Edwardian England is a world of the history text-book rather than of the story-book, a world of abstract 'movements' — progress, equality of opportunity, religious toleration, the education of the whole man, the education of 'our masters', the emancipation of the working classes — the list is endless — and the Victorian and Edwardian 'educationist', however well-intentioned, is not exactly a figure upon whom we fix in fascination our rivetted gaze. His was the world of the frock-coat, the gold albert and the gladstone collar. Here everything is stiff and creaky; here we are confined within the deal partitions of the *board-school* ("Surely they must have meant *deal* boards?"), if not of Sunday-school itself!

So the spirit may be willing indeed, but the flesh, at this prospect, in certainly weak, and we look round us anxiously to find ourselves a tolerable path through the bleak but busy landscape of our last 65 years. We cannot reasonably expect our reader, however patient, to plod on, stage by stage and year by year, until Deakin gives way to Boyt, Boyt to Watson, and Watson to the last word, which is FINIS.

Let us instead put out our hand and feel for the comforting grasp of our first guide. Let us turn to the archives! They are, these days, like the school itself, vastly more sophisticated, organised and *scientific* than they ever were or ever had time to be in the great 'years of discovery' when they first began to spill out of the chaotic and capacious maw of the Harward and Evers repository. They have been, as it were, 'civilized', and after the efforts of two young archivists who spent a whole year on the task, they now reside in a home of their own, classified, docketed, bundled, boxed and labelled, "all present and correct" to the historian's enquiring eye. What is more, they have been provided with an efficient guide in the shape of a typewritten catalogue, which allows one to know what records there are to be consulted even before one finds one's way into the archive-room itself, situated, not unfitly, in the oldest surviving piece of the school buildings, the Tudor-style tower of W.J.J. Welch's great 1860 reconstruction.

A rapid glance through the catalogue is immediately rewarding and sets us on our way. The archives are enormously rich in material which covers the 65 years of our present interest. There is, indeed, so much of it that it would be only too easy to lose sight of the wood through the screen of so many trees. But we see soon enough that there is the hint of a pattern to help us. A great many of the documents refer to changes and expansions in the physical structure of the school — its buildings, its site, its development of outlying sites. This, of course, must be so, for the great school of 1950 did not spring overnight into existence out of the 'commodious new premises' of 1860 — the school-room, cloakroom, classroom and ornamental tower. The A Block, the B Block, the C Block, the P Block and the Science Block, the art-room, woodwork-room, dining-hall, library and biology laboratory — these were not easily conjured out of some official brain onto the drawing board, and from the drawing-board onto the site itself in the shape of solid bricks and mortar. Their birthpangs were often protracted and difficult; their creation represents "blood and sweat, toil and tears". They are the concrete legacy of those Victorian and Edwardian frock-coated, gladstone-collared men, so dull and so respectable, but when it came to the practical problem so fierce in determination and so fertile in resource.

Then there are the records of the teaching staff and boys, mainly in the great collection of annual 'Class-lists' with their printed details of every governor and every master and every boy in every form — hundreds, even thousands, of names, including, distractingly enough, many whom we have known and many more whom we have been told about — the Palfreys, the H.P. Joneses, the Deakins and the Boyts, "Billy the Blower", Granny Gaskin, Daddy Scholes, Bisdorff, Amos England, Owen Evans, H.E. Halliday and the rest. There is obviously continuity here, derived from 'corporate memory' and enshrined in the unbroken sequence of steadily lengthening annual lists; but discontinuity still yawns, as between the staff-list of 1876 which we have seen, with its three masters, two visiting masters and a drill-sergeant — and that which appeared in the Class-list of 1950, displaying the names of the Headmaster, Senior Assistant, and no less than 33 Assistant Staff. How the one developed into the other by gradual stages in the course of our 65 years is not a suitable subject for consecutive narrative. That would be an exercise in the mismanagement of monotony.

Let us rather take a random shot into the archives, and examine the situation at about the end of the century, two thirds of the way through Deakin's time and a few years before the advent of Boyt. We could turn to the above-mentioned collection of annual class-lists and pick out the one we want. But here by a stroke of our persisting good fortune, even at this late hour, we turn up under another heading a letter written in 1898 which tells us far more than could any class-list. The writer was the then Chairman of the Governors, that William Blow Collis whose irreverent nickname we have mentioned. (It was to none other than the scholarly and outwardly austere H.E. Palfrey, himself once a young governor under W.B. Collis, that we owe the assurance that 'Billy the Blower' was indeed his popularly accepted soubriquet.)

The letter is a model of economy of expression, and as a description of the school in its essentials as it existed in 1898 it could hardly be improved upon. It reads as follows:

> Swinford House
> Stourbridge
> 3 November 1898.

Thomas Turner Esq.,
County Technical Offices,
Stafford.

Dear Sir,

Knowing the liberal support that your Council gives to Technical Instruction at the schools connected with the county of Stafford I am encouraged to make an application for some assistance to the Stourbridge Grammar School. A general description of the school is contained in the accompanying notes.

The Governors are now erecting at a cost of £1500 a block of buildings which is nearing completion and contains Physical and Chemical Laboratories, Museum, Library and Lecture Hall.

At the present time our educational expenses are in excess of our income and we are only able to afford the services of a science master *half a day a week*.

Would your Council help us by making a grant of say £50 towards furnishing our laboratories and say £25 per annum towards the salary of a science master whose whole services we now wish to engage?

We are in communication with the Worcestershire County Council from whom we hope ultimately to receive an annual grant, but at present they have fenced it round with such restrictions as to prevent our acceptance of it.

Your Councillor for Brierley Hill, Mr. John Addison, is one of our Governors and he will be able to give you any further information you may require.

Your obedient servant,
W. B. Collis
Chairman of the Governors

Situation etc.

The school consists of 135 boys all day scholars drawn from the middle and lower classes. The school buildings are situated in Worcestershire but they are only a few yards from Staffordshire. Both the football field and the cricket field are in Staffordshire. There are 12 exhibitions tenable at the school, and open to boys educated at a public elementary school in the ancient parish of Oldswinford. This parish includes Amblecote, which is in Staffordshire. There are two university scholarships connected with the school: two out of the last three have been awarded to boys resident in Staffordshire (Meatyard and Firmstone).

Staffordshire Scholars

For the last five years the school has had boys holding scholarships under the Staffordshire County Council. There are now 17 boys holding these scholarships and attending the school. These scholars come from Brierley Hill, Wordsley, Kingswinford, Pensnett and Old Hill. In many cases where the parents of such scholars have been poor, the Governors have provided further assistance for the boys out of the general school funds. This assistance has been given by reducing the school fees, by paying for books and stationery, or by grants of money for maintenance.

Efficiency

Boys are prepared for open scholarships at the universities, for the Cambridge Local Junior examination, and occasionally for the Civil Service and for the London University Matriculation examination. During the last ten years every boy who has taken one of the school scholarships has also gained an open Scholarship or Exhibition. In the Cambridge Local examinations no boy has failed for the last 13 years: and each of the last three years the school has had the first boy in all England in English subjects, and a larger number of boys in First Class Division Honours than any other provincial school in England. Since 1894

80 boys have passed these examinations, 63 being placed in Honours.

Staff

The school has five masters employed all day. This gives one master to each 26 boys. Last year the school was reported on by the Hon. W.N. Bruce for the Charity Commissioner and he recommended that an additional master for science subjects should be added to the staff.

Science Instruction

At present the science teaching is undertaken by Mr. J.H. Stansbie, B.Sc., F.I.C., who is an assistant master at the Birmingham Technical School. But he only comes over one afternoon each week and other scientific teaching has to be undertaken by the ordinary form masters.

———

One has to agree that 'Billy the Blower' knew what he was doing. The facts as he gives them are cogent and persuasive. The compliment to Staffordshire is neatly turned and fortified by the criticism of Worcestershire, though the contrast is not so heavily drawn as to invite a defensive reaction on behalf of public authorities in general. It is incidentally perhaps worthy of mention that the municipal record of Staffordshire in the matter of educational progress and provision was not very impressive until a long time after the date of this event. Even up to the middle years of this century the south of the county had to depend for its grammar school education upon the ancient endowed foundations at Wolverhampton and Walsall within its own boundaries and at Stourbridge in Worcestershire. An incomer from the industrial north, where the city of Bradford, for example, had had its own municipal secondary schools in abundance, with a hundred per cent free places, for decades, could have been forgiven for wondering if he had strayed into the last corner of the nordic twilight of old Mercia. His eyes told him that the fabled black of the Black Country was not nearly so black as the mill towns of the north: but it was "blacker than black" in the matter of black marks for educational backwardness!

Any such suggestion was of course most tactfully avoided by W.B. Collis, and his confidence in Staffordshire's liberality in support of "technical instruction" was indeed justified. He got his

£50 towards the cost of furnishing the science buildings and a £25 contribution towards the salary of a science master. This led towards the first appointment of a Staffordshire representative on the governing body. Two documents from Stafford tell the story. The first is a letter:

Staffordshire County Council
Technical Education Committee
County Technical Offices,
Stafford.

February 13th 1899.

Dear Sir,

I beg to inform you that at a meeting of this committee held on the 11th instant it was resolved

"That, it having been shown that there are 61 Staffordshire pupils out of a total of 129 who are in attendance at the Stourbridge Grammar School, and that there is at present no secondary education available in the Parishes of Kingswinford and Rowley Regis, a grant of £50 be made towards the furnishing of the new Laboratories at the Stourbridge Grammar School, and that a maintenance grant of £25 be made for the first year towards the salary of a science master.

"The qualifications of the science master must be approved on behalf of the Committee before his appointment is confirmed, and, so long as the grant is continued, his classes will be subject to inspection without notice."

I shall be glad to know whether the Governors are prepared to receive the grant on the above conditions.

If the grant is accepted, the question of whether or not a representative of the Committee should be appointed on the Board of Governors, in accordance with the Technical Instruction Act of 1889, will be decided when it has been ascertained what proportion the funds contributed by this Committee bear to the amount of the endowment of the school, including the grant from the Worcestershire County Council.

Yours faithfully,
Thomas Turner.

The Clerk to the Governors
The Grammar School,
Stourbridge.

The second paper is a manuscript memorandum, unaddressed, which reads as follows:

> Staffordshire County Council
> At a meeting of the Council held on Tuesday the Fifth day of February 1901 ...
>
> Stourbridge Grammar School
>
> In pursuance of Clause 1 of the Amending Scheme of 17 September 1900 *it was ordered*
> That Randle L. Mathews of Stourton Court, Stourbridge Esquire, be appointed as a representative Governor on behalf of the Staffordshire County Council on the foundation of the Stourbridge Grammar School.
> (signed) Matt. f. Blakiston
> Clerk of the Staffordshire County Council

This Randle Lamb Mathews was still a governor in 1926, when his name appears on a conveyance from 'Parkes Trustees' to the school of a piece of land "at the back of No. 8, Coventry Street" — one of many purchases recorded in the archives in this period, made for the purpose of extending and consolidating the school site. Randle Mathews is here described as a 'Leather Goods Manufacturer', but he is elsewhere designated (as in the memorandum of 1901) simply as 'Esquire'.*

As for W.B. Collis, he is differently described in different documents — usually as 'Mining Engineer'; but in 1897, when the governors were buying another piece of land 'behind Coventry Street', the designation was 'Coal Master'. The distinction is quite unimportant now: the important thing is that Collis was clearly an able and forceful man, whom one sees as a typical Victorian Blackcountry industrialist, and certainly as one of the makers of the modern King Edward's School. He became a governor first under the new scheme of 1876, when he was elected as one of the two

---

*His obituary appeared in the Stourbridge Edwardian of Autumn 1931. He died on 24 October of that year, having been then Vice-Chairman of the Governors since 1918. He was the youngest of four sons of James Mathews of Clent, all of whom were boys at the school together in the 1870's. He was born in 1860. His eldest brother Paul, born in 1855, attended from 1865 until 1873, leaving as Head Boy to go to Christ's College, Cambridge to read Natural Sciences. It was from Paul Mathews as Head Boy that A.J. Mainwaring had his first lessons in Greek (see p. 212 above). Paul died on 11 August, 1933.

representatives of the parents. He followed Colonel T.W. Fletcher as Chairman in 1893 and continued in that office until 1918. His family went back a good way in the history of the town and school. We have seen that an earlier William Blow Collis, a solicitor, was the real promoter of the great Chancery Petition against the school in 1851. This one was in fact William Blow Collis (3), 1809-58, and our mining engineer or coalmaster was William Blow Collis (4) 1839-1922. William Blow Collis (1) 1722-89, was a mercer and banker, of Oldswinford, and served as a governor of the school only briefly, from 1778 to 1779. He adopted as his heir his nephew George Collis, 1741-1811, who fought at Quebec in 1759, and in 1777 founded a wine business in Stourbridge. His son was William Blow Collis (2) 1778-1855, who went into the Church and was perpetual curate of Norton Canes. He was one of only two Collis generations out of the five which we have reviewed, who had no known connection with the school. From the school's point of view much the most important Collis was "Billy the Blower".

We have spent time and words on the Collises because it is important for our understanding of the school during the last phase of its history to realise that even as late as this, and even after the transformation of the old free school, little and local, into the modern municipalised, fee-charging giant, drawing its pupils from all over the north of its own county and the south of its neighbour, even yet there were men associated with the school and prominent in its counsels, whose interest in it was inherited from fathers and forefathers. The old 'network' of which we had so much to say in our earlier pages had long ago disappeared: but the old ties, generated by inheritance and fostered by what we have called "the corporate memory", were still strong.

One question which we cannot answer with certainty from the evidence arises from the last document quoted. The memorandum from Stafford speaks of Clause 1 of the Amending Scheme of 17th September 1900. Prolonged search of the archives has failed to find this scheme. That it existed is proved by a reference to it in the preamble to the Scheme of 16 November 1909. But the 1900 amendment has disappeared as though it had never been. We conclude that it could have had very little importance, since otherwise it must have been preserved. It was evidently, we now see, an adjustment of the 1876 Statutes, probably a sort of 'enabling clause' concerned with local authority representation on the governing body, designed to be called into effect when circumstances required it — as they did when Staffordshire contributed money towards the new science building.

We see, however, that one of the governors was already unofficially, as it were, a Staffordshire representative, in 1897. The "Mr. John Addison, your councillor for Brierley Hill" of W.B. Collis's letter, is described in one of the governors' lists to be found in a property conveyance as "Newspaper Proprietor", and he wrote to W.B. Collis himself in 1897 on the commerical writing-paper of the Brierley Hill Advertiser.

There are several themes for us to pursue from W.B. Collis's description of the school. In the annual printed 'Class-list' of 1897, the equivalent of a prize-day programme — we see that the 130 or so boys were divided into three 'schools' — Upper, Middle and Lower. There was no sixth form, as the Upper School was divided 'the other way', with Form 1 at the top. The function of the so-called forms is obscure: the division into forms within each 'school' appears to have affected only Latin: in Holy Scripture and English the whole of each 'school' was consolidated on a single list, while the 'extra' subjects — French, German, Shorthand, Greek, Mathematics, Drawing, Rifle Practice, Sword Exercise and Drilling — are betrayed as 'extra' by appearing at each level as a sort of appendix. The system on which all this was organised is impossible to understand: but the special treatment of Latin is probably due to the old practice that a boy should be placed, in school or class, according to his ability in that subject.

As for the "five masters employed all day" of the chairman's letter, they appear as follows:

HEAD MASTER
Mr. Rupert Deakin, M.A. (Oxon and Lond.)
of Balliol College, Oxford

HEAD MASTER'S ASSISTANT
Mr. G.H. Ball, M.A.,
of Trinity College, Cambridge

ASSISTANT MASTERS
Mr. W.G. Goddard
Mr. G.R. Thornton, M.A.
of St. John's College, Cambridge
Mr. J.B. Andrew
of Trinity College, Dublin.

Of these, the Headmaster and Mr. Ball were in charge of the Upper School; Mr. Goddard alone had the Middle School; Mr. Thornton took Forms 1 and 2, and Mr. Andrew Forms 3 and 4, of the Lower School.

Modern languages were in the care of Rev. L.B. Penley, B.A., of Corpus Christi College, Cambridge, Science of Mr. J.H. Stansbie, B.Sc., F.I.C., Associate of Mason College, Birmingham, Drawing of Mr. E.J. Simms, and Drilling of Sergeant-Instructor Downey, Ist. V.B., Worcester Regt. Of these we know, of course, that Mr. Stansbie attended for only one half-day a week.

Of the whole staff we have met only W.G. Goddard, and of him we know very little, but remember that he had held the fort in the Middle School since 1859. He was to retire with an illuminated address and a gratuity of £500 in 1899. Meanwhile one wonders how his position in the hierarchy had been affected by the advent of the "Headmaster's Assistant", George Henry Ball, in 1894. G.H. Ball was a graduate in Classics of Trinity College, Cambridge, born in 1869, a pupil of Liverpool College, an adequate if not distinguished scholar, with two posts of brief duration behind him when he came to Stourbridge. He was to share with Rupert Deakin the teaching of the Upper School — a new appointment with a new title. Whether he was also to be considered as Second Master we do not know, but in view of W.G. Goddard's position and long service this seems unlikely. He stayed until 1908, when he left to become Headmaster of King Edward's School, Camp Hill in Birmingham. We shall learn later that he kept in touch with Rupert Deakin for long years in retirement, as did his two children. His salary on appointment was £150, which rose by irregular increments to £225. He took duties as Boarding House Master, though how many boarders Rupert Deakin had in his house we do not know.

We know remarkably little about Rupert Deakin. He was a Midlander, the son of Andrew Deakin of Birmingham, gent. He went up to New College, Oxford in 1875 at the ripe age of 23, and was of Balliol College in 1881, aged 29. He was also a graduate of London Univeristy, in Science. He came to Stourbridge as headmaster in his early thirties, and retired from his post in his early fifties. We have discovered in the course of our researches that it was his wife who used the school's ancient muniment chest as her blanket-box. And that is almost all! In 1923, however, J.E. Boyt, in the second of his articles on the school's history in the pages of the Stourbridge Edwardian, wrote about 'some headmasters of the school since 1700', and his remarks about his two immediate predecessors are worth quoting:

> "Many of Dr. Welch's pupils now occupy prominent positions in the neighbourhood, and to his initiative is due the rapid rise in the efficiency of the school. In the second year of his headmastership an appeal was made "to re-erect the Grammar School and School House and to make the proposed building not only beneficial but also ornamental to the Town". The existing school room was "in such a dilapidated state, its accommodation so limited, its ventilation so bad and defective" that it was "quite imperative to rebuild it." It was therefore proposed "to erect a new School Room to be fitted out with all modern scholastic appliances and capable of accommodating 100 boys". Upwards of £2000 was raised, the Governors contributing £700 and the rest being given by public subscription.
> As a result of Dr. Welch's efforts the Governors bought the site of the Old Horse Inn on the north side of the school, and on this the older part of the existing school hall was built. In addition the whole front of the school was re-faced, the work being completed in 1861, as is shown by the date on top of the school tower."
> Mr. Deakin continued the good work commenced by Dr. Welch. The Honour Boards in the school today testify to the high standard of his teaching, and the present science buildings, erected in 1899, are a memorial of his energy and foresight. Mr. Deakin is still actively engaged in educational matters. For some time he resided at King's Norton and was a prominent member of the Worcestershire Education Committee. He is now living at Brighton and is still interested in the school and his old Stourbridge pupils."

Samuel Johnson once wrote that "in lapidary inscriptions a man is not upon oath," and the same might truthfully be said of J.E. Boyt's comments on his predecessor. But he seems to have had the rights of it in the matter of Rupert Deakin's pupils' successes. The Class-list of July 1900 lists eight holders of the school's two leaving scholarships at Oxford and Cambridge since Deakin came to the school in 1885. They included the top mathematical scholar of Balliol, an open Classical scholar at Christ's, an exhibitioner at St. John's, Oxford, a Classical Exhibitioner at Worcester College, a mathematical scholar at Queen's, a sizar at St. John's, Cambridge, and so on. This is a far cry from the day when "no boy has gone direct from the school to either of the universities for the past five years". Even more striking is the list of the "Highest Places in Honours gained in the Cambridge Local Junior Examinations during the ten years 1890-1900". These actually included, in 1893, the *Best Junior Boy in England and the Colonies*, out of 5386 candidates. His name was Chappell. Then there were three differently initialled boys named Brooks, who in three consecutive years each achieved first place in English out of between 7000 and 8000 candidates. Could they conceivably have been brothers? These were only the best out of a most impressive array of outstandingly distinguished results. So Rupert Deakin either knew how to teach, or knew how to get others to teach, or both.

There were considerable developments of the school site and buildings during Deakin's years, which we should not overlook. As early as 1878 the governors had bought a good-sized piece of the Green Close property, consisting of a rectangular plot containing no less than 1331 square yards with a frontage on what was then King William Street, later to be Duke Street, and therefore on the eastern boundary of the land available for the expansion of the school site. The papers filed with the conveyance make it clear that the purchase of the land was "for enlarging the playground and providing a back entrance", and it is evident also that the extension was in pursuance of the modernisation policy of the 1876 scheme. In the 1890's came a further purchase of land on the Duke Street front, consisting of the sites and redundant materials of four cottages which had descended from the Green Close estate through three subsequent owners. The total area was over 700 square yards. Meantime during the eighties the governors built the school's first laboratory, again pursuing the policy of the 1876 scheme. This building was later entirely superseded by the 1899 science block, and it became 'lost' when it was incorporated into the main-school buildings, in modern times called the A Block. It is no longer distinguishable as a separate unit, and has served various functions at different times: but it was the first specialist room ever built for the school when it first came into being.

Another 'first' of Rupert Deakin's time was the first playing-field. There is a problem here, for we have failed to find any record of its purchase or leasing. We know from W.B. Collis's memorandum to Staffordshire that it was already in use in 1898. He speaks indeed of 'both the football field and the cricket field', so that there may possibly have been two pieces. We know that the site was in Staffordshire, and this certainly means that it was in Amblecote. The first record of a school field surviving in the archives is a complex series of legal documents dating from 1919-20. At that time the school possessed a field of about four and a half acres roughly in the angle between Vicarage Road Amblecote and the main Wolverhampton Road, below Amblecote church. This had been bought from Lady Grey's estate about ten years previously, that is to say in about 1909. In 1919 the municipality of Stourbridge wanted this piece of land for the expansion of their gasworks, and when they offered to buy a neighbouring piece, of about six acres, also from Lady Grey, and to transfer this to the school, the governors were accommodating. That second piece was, of course, the Amblecote playing-field of modern times, for many years the only ground which the school possessed for organised games. It is safe to assume that the field or fields of 1898 lay close to the two later sites, but it is much to be regretted that the details seem to have, uncharacteristically, disappeared from the archives. We do know that on occasions of need in the early days of their playing-fields the governors paid a rent to the owners of the Stourbridge Cricket Ground, also situated in Amblecote, for the use of their pitches; it is therefore not inconceivable that the football and cricket fields of 1898 were provided from that source. We can say with certainty only that it was in the 1890's that the school got its first recorded playing-field, probably under the prompting of Rupert Deakin.

None of this brings us any nearer to an acquaintance with Rupert Deakin himself, and he remains virtually unknown to us. There was one occasion, many years ago, when a very old Old Boy, recalling his days at school in Deakin's time, delivered his own rather severe judgment: "I am sorry to say, headmaster, that I did not like Mr. Deakin. He was a sneak!" The reason which he went on to give for this condemnation was that Rupert Deakin deliberately wore slippers or soft boots on his patrols of the school premises, for the purpose of catching out his charges in the act of misdemeanours which they would have been careful to eschew if they had known he was on the prowl. This was clearly regarded as 'not fair', and for all those years it had rankled. But lest it be recorded as the last word, or anything like the last word, let us recall a much more favourable and much pleasanter reminiscence.

This came from yet another old Old Boy, and apart from anything else it established a very remarkable fact about Rupert Deakin.

After being headmaster as we know from 1885 to 1905 he lived on, in full possession of all his faculties, until the 1940's! This is what we read:

Stourbridge Feb. 17th 1959.

Dear Mr. Chambers,

As promised, I enclose a letter I had from Mr. Deakin. My letter in reply must have reached him just before he died.

He was very kind to me when I lost most of my sight in 1911 and was told that I should never be able to see properly again. I wrote him to ask if he could advise me where I could get educated as a partially blind man. He replied that he regretted he could not, but asked me to accept a cheque for £5 as a mark of his deep regret at my plight.

I bought a portable typewriter with the money, learnt touch-typing on it and wrote him a letter of thanks.

Like most schoolmasters he was not popular with all his old boys, and I have been pleased to show several the kind side of his nature. We remained good friends till his death ...

Yours sincerely

Perhaps those who had to be shown the better side of their old headmaster had been the victims of his gumshoe approach! Be that as it may, his own letter to my correspondent throws a very warm and genial light upon him.

13, Burlington Street,
Brighton.

October 18th 1943.

My dear Fred,

Your letter came this morning and was a great delight to me. Often have I wondered how you fared, and I am glad to hear that you have retained sufficient sight to get about and to do some reading. I had heard from Howard Baugh about your brother Hollis at Carisbrooke. For several years Baugh has called to see me but now that he has settled at Farnham he cannot get petrol, and so I do not see him and his wife.

It is one of the penalties of living to old age that we must see many of our intimate friends depart ... I keep up acquaintance with many Stourbridge people. Walter Brooks comes from Haywards Heath to see me every few weeks; and his brother

Arthur writes to me from Maidenhead. H.M. Pittaway is my most regular correspondent. He is rector of Rodden, near Frome ... I remember quite well the three Hingleys. Clement I knew intimately. I should like you to congratulate Norman for me on his success. Please also remember me to Rhodes and Will. Bailey. I remember Guttery, and also Yeates. Mr. Ball used to visit me every year and I grieve much for his death. His children have both kept in touch with me ... Do you remember Walker? He is teaching at Lancaster school and Guy Bartindale is mathematical master at Wakefield. A.R. Smith writes to me every Christmas, and so does Professor T.H. Sanders from Cambridge, U.S.A.

Of course at 92 years of age I am quite an old man. Nevertheless I manage to get out every day and I am able to do much reading. I feel thankful that I have retained the full use of all my faculties. Until last year I went daily to help at the Food Office. ...Of course, too, I get letters from Watson.

Every October I send to the Midland Bank at Stourbridge a subscription of 10/- for the Old Edwardian Club, and so I get news about their activities.

I hope you will keep well, for doctors are scarce now in England, and nurses are unobtainable.

Ever yours sincerely,
Rupert Deakin.

For those who like cross-checking it may be of interest that W.H. Brooks took the Cambridge Locals in 1893 and 1894, and A.E. Brooks in 1901. W.J. Walker's name appears in 1893 and 1894, G.C. Bartindale's in 1897 and 1898, and T.H. Sanders' in 1900. So the old man's visitors and correspondents came mainly from the school of the last decade of the nineteenth century. It hardly needs saying that men do not take the trouble to seek out their old teachers after fifty years unless they have pleasant memories of them. The one dissentient ("He was a sneak!"), let it be added, appears in the lists of 1893 and 1894; but he is in a minority of one. Our conclusion must be that Rupert Deakin was a kindly man who got on well with his boys, was genuinely interested in them and knew a lot about them. J.E. Boyt spoke of the high standards of his teaching and foresight. He remains a shadow, but it is now the shadow not of a nonentity but of quite a man! He raised the numbers from about 80 to about 150: he established more than the beginnings of a powerful academic tradition; he built the Science Block; he brought in the first specialist subject-masters and the first playing-field. In brief, he was a worthy successor to W.J.J. Welch; he was even a worthy predecessor to J.E. Boyt himself. But Boyt cast so gigantic a shadow that Rupert Deakin still lurks in it, almost invisible in the darkness.

As for the Boyt era of 1905 to 1934, it is very difficult to know where to begin and it may prove even harder to know where to stop. The incipient increase and expansion now really 'took off', and in the course of 29 years there was seemingly no intermission in the unrelenting process of enlargement and success. For it would be foolish to blink the fact that, though it may not be axiomatic that in schools "bigger is better", nevertheless Boyt himself was following commonsense when he took numbers as his prime criterion of achievement. The simple fact was that the school's size was a precise reflection of its public esteem and the demand for places. There was no 'ideal' size: the process of enlargement was what is called in the modern jargon 'open-ended'; theoretically there was no end to it! In J.E. Boyt's time as headmaster the theory was translated inexorably into practice, and the enlargement was still going on in 1934, when Boyt came to the end of his term of office. There used to be a story (and it is often impossible in the case of a man who has become a legend in his lifetime to separate fact from fiction and truth from invention in the tales that are told of him) — there was a story that his known desire to make the school bigger and bigger was at one stage focussed on the possibility of its passing the 600 mark: he was reputed to have declared that he would make a formal and public presentation of a gold watch to the first boy to be numbered as the 600th in the school. He was further reputed to have trumpeted the achievement of passing the magic number in due course, but then to have quietly shelved the promised presentation. However, to show how legends develop as "extensions of the truth" let us turn to the school magazine of Autumn, 1933. There we find an article entitled THE SCHOOL ROLL, which tells us what really happened.

"The official number of boys in the School this term is 608. Counting every boy who has been in attendance at some time or other during the term, the number has been 611. The following table brings up to date the figures given in Vol. 1 of the Stourbridge Edwardian.

Year	No. of Boys on School Roll	Year	No. of Boys on School Roll	Year	No. of Boys on School Roll	Year	No. of Boys on School Roll
1808	"Near 50"	1855	33	1896	123	1916	228
1814-1820	0	1856	25	1897	130	1917	251
		1857	25	1898	118	1918	277
1832	8	1858	37	1899	129	1919	332
1840	17	1859	38	1901	111	1920	340
1841	25	(No records)		1902	117	1921	361
1842	24	1868	69	1903	127	1922	393
1843	31	1869	75	1904	139	1923	397
1844	27	1870	77	1905	143	1924	418
1845	22	1871	75	1906	161	1925	432
1846	23	1872	68	1907	176	1926	463
1847	22	(No records)		1908	188	1927	478
1848	30	1887	83	1909	206	1928	496
1849	26	1888	81	1910	213	1929	539
1850	41	1890	96	1911	233	1930	540
1851	23	1891	105	1912	240	1931	575
1852	29	1892	101	1913	227	1932	593
1853	53	1894	129	1914	231	1933	608
1854	51	1895	129	1915	236		

*From the year 1905 the numbers are usually those for the Autumn Term.

"At the Prize Distribution of 1st December 1931, when Lieut. Col. Sir Percival Heywood distributed the prizes, The Rev. H.H. Williams announced that a gentleman had offered a Gold Medal for the boy who should bring the numbers up to 600. The fortunate boy is R. A. Edwards of Form I, and we now have permission to mention the name of the donor. He is Alderman H.E. Palfrey, J.P., then Mayor of Stourbridge and now Chairman of the Governors.

It will be remembered that in 1929 D.R. Leeson was the recipient of a similar Gold Medal offered by Mr. J.S. Williams-Thomas, O.B.E., J.P., Chairman of the Governors, to the 500th boy."

So much for the unflattering, and entirely inaccurate, legend! The most interesting point here, however, is the speed with which the numbers were increasing at the time in question. It had taken 25 years from 1904 for the school to grow from about 150 to 600: the next hundred came up only four years later. The general impression which King Edward's Stourbridge gave to its neighbours and acquaintances in the academic world of the years before and after the last war was one of a school where the boys were "rather thick on the ground". Most schools of its kind and status, of course, had moved at least once from their original sites, and always moved outwards from the town centres and usually onto pleasant and open positions, often surrounded by their own playing-fields. Not so Stourbridge. The site of 1950 was the site of 1430: it was totally urban, entirely hemmed in by streets and main roads, and exceedingly cramped. The remarkable thing was that in face of all these disadvantages, which must have been discouraging to the parents of prospective pupils, it flourished. But flourish it did, and flourish exceedingly. The secret must have lain, during the Boyt era, in its extreme efficiency within the limits which it set itself. Academically it established the habit of success at the top, with a steady if not spectacular stream of open awards at Oxford and Cambridge, mainly in the anciently traditional fields of mathematics and the Classics. J.E. Boyt himself we have described as a formidable scholar. He saw to it that any of his pupils in whom a mathematical bent could be fostered or forced was given expert teaching and brought on and up to the most exacting of standards. In the Middle School too the regime was designed to do exceedingly well what it set out to do. At the level of the School Certificate (later to become the G.C.E. at Ordinary level) the diet was plain fare without much in the way of extra trimmings. The bias was unashamedly academic and *ad hoc,* — and the *hoc* was the acquisition of a good certificate in basic subjects. Specialisation was deemed to be the way to efficiency, and the targets were adjusted to the individual's presumed capacity. The bias was towards mathematics and the sciences, and much was sacrificed to serve their purposes. No-one worried much about "the two cultures" or "the illiterate scientist". Success bred success, and the academic reputation of the school as it spread steadily wider and wider, brought in more and more eager aspirants to be the future beneficiaries of the system. If Mr. Bryce, the writer of the 1864 report for the Taunton Commissioners — ("Although it is not now and is not likely to become a grammar school of the first order, sending boys to the universities ...") — had come back to repeat his examination 60 years later, he would certainly have had to eat those words: but he could then without embarrassment or hesitation have repeated the end of his original sentence — "...this school is doing a good deal of useful work in a plain and practical way".

So it was, and on a scale vastly larger than Mr. Bryce could ever have imagined in his wildest dreams. And in order to accommodate that vast enlargement, the site and buildings of the school had grown in proportion. That growth began almost as soon as J.E. Boyt had settled into the headmaster's chair in 1905. For as early as 1906 the governors bought "No. 23, High Street, Stourbridge" — in other words, Green Close House — and proceeded to demolish it and to use the site for a large development of the building of 1860 (essentially the tower and the main school hall) into an extensive block including new classrooms, an art room, handicraft room, and so on. The cost of the Green Close was £2750, and the building took place in 1908. In 1909, as we have seen, came the acquisition of the first identifiable playing-field, in Amblecote (see page 239), for which the price paid to Lady Grey's estate was £950. It is worth noticing that these sums of money were very considerable at the time. Even at the end of J.E. Boyt's time in 1934, his successor and former pupil, T.W. Watson, was appointed on a salary of £1100 a year, rising by three increments of £50 to £1250. So the outlay for the Green Close site and the first playing-field represents about three years salary for a headmaster, if one wishes to see it in present-day terms. In 1910 came the decision to start a preparatory department for boys at the age of seven, and then the project of building the Preparatory School, later to be known as the P Block. This was financed by selling off one of the foundation's most lucrative assets. The story of the Great Wyrley mine, situated near Cannock, is an interesting one. Originally it was the Riddings Farm, and it was no part of the original King Edward's endowment property. In fact it came into the hands of the governors in the eighteenth century, and then only in their capacity as the trustees of the Glover Charity School. It was only when the Glover Charity was consolidated with the King Edward's Foundation by the Scheme of 1876 that the income from the Great Wyrley mine, as it had then become, was available to the general funds of the Grammar School. The governors now sold the Great Wyrley property for £7000, and were enabled to 'top up' their contribution towards building expenses out of this sum, and still to leave £5000 of it to be invested — in Railway Stock! In the course of this period of expansion and expenditure on the site and buildings they sold off virtually the whole of the endowment property — mainly land and buildings in Evesham and Worcester — and put the proceeds into stocks. It is to be remembered that all these financial manoeuvres were subject to the approval of the Charity Commissioners, in whose possession the endowment property was legally vested. It seems remarkable that they were allowed, even encouraged, to get rid of the only assets that were infallibly proof against the effects of inevitable inflation, and to replace them with investments which were inevitably speculative and which proved in the course of time to be anything but a good speculation.

Be that as it may, the same period saw the piecemeal acquisition of land to consolidate the school site — plot by plot and garden by garden, from the backs of the High Street, Coventry Street and Duke Street, until eventually the whole of the original Green Close, or Elcoxe's Close, was reunited in the governors' hands. In 1925 they bought the old Vine Hotel, next above the school buildings on the High Street front. It was ancient and ramshackle, and they never developed it for school purposes, but used it as what they called 'the Club Room', apparently for such after-school activities as debating and the like. In years long afterwards it proved to be a considerable asset, when in the 1960's it was sold for commerical development.

In 1926 the first steps were taken towards the replacement of the 1860 schoolroom, long since outgrown as a place of assembly for the enlarged school. The site chosen for the new Assembly Hall was that of the headmaster's house, the left-hand and lower of the two masters' houses which fronted onto the High Street. Originally of a basically primitive 'cruck' structure, made of wattle and daub, they had been rebuilt in brick, as we have seen, in about 1700, and refaced again, in the high Victorian fashion, in the great rebuilding of 1860. Since then they had had gables and blue-brick string-courses, large Victorian sash windows, grained and varnished front doors, and a railed and raised terrace along their fronts, with flights of stairs ,the longer one at the lower end, to provide access. It was on this terrace that another tradition (no doubt as apocryphal as the last one quoted) credited J.E. Boyt at some stage in his headmastership with the practice of presenting himself on fine evenings in his dinner-jacket to the admiring and astonished gaze of the natives — carrying, as it were, said the tradition, "the white man's burden".

Ignoring that story, as it doubtless deserves to be ignored, we arrive at the time in 1926 when the governors prepared for the great change by buying a residence for the headmaster away from the school premises. The house they bought was in the town, not very far away, in Brook Street, where a very substantial residence, with very adequate surrounding grounds, was available. So Longlands House became the home of the Boyt family, and the way was open for the demolition of the old house and the erection on its site of the great new Assembly Hall. It was a large project and an impressive building, as it remains, with its fine War-Memorial windows by Camm of Smethwick, its Tudor emblems as decorative features, its coffered ceiling and large proscenium arch disclosing the stage. It was a fitting climax to the building programme of the Boyt era, and it would be difficult to deny that it represented in itself very well the Boyt *persona*. It was substantial, solid, traditional and dignified. At long last the school could present itself formally in a setting which was worthy of its size and status, its venerable antiquity and its modern achievement.

The story of the immediate origins of the new Assembly Hall and a detailed description of it appeared in the pages of the school magazine at the time of its opening in 1931. Perhaps an extensive quotation from this contemporary source will serve better than a modern commentary to bring out the feeling of pride in achievement and tradition which pervaded the school and all who lived and worked within its walls in those closing years of the great expansion.

THE NEW ASSEMBLY HALL

The erection of the Assembly Hall is the completion of the scheme of extension which had become necessary owing to the great increase in the number of boys at the School. In 1905 there were 143 boys. This year there are 575, a quadruple increase in a period of 26 years. The original schoolroom, which was built probably on the site of Philip Hareby's chapel, was demolished in 1861, when the School Hall, familiar to Old Boys until 1908, was erected, its accommodation being for about 140 boys. At the latter date a bay was built on the north within the space formerly occupied by Green Close House the residence of the late Dr. Alfred Freer. The hall, thus extended, provided accommodation for 220 boys, but in the rapid growth of numbers which took place after the war this became much too limited. Recourse was therefore had to the expedient of holding a senior and junior assembly of the boys daily. When the numbers passed 440 these two assemblies were both again overcrowded ... . At the inspection of the school by the Board of Education in 1926, the provision of a new Assembly Hall was one of the recommendations of H.M. Inspectors. At first it was thought that the space occupied by the Headmaster's house might be used for a further extension of the existing hall. Longlands House was purchased by the governors as a residence for the Headmaster, which he commenced to occupy in 1927 ...

It was, however, finally agreed that the architectural difficulties of extending the old hall were practically insurmountable, and that it would ultimately be less expensive and more satisfactory to build an entirely new hall on the site of the School House and lawn. The plans of Messrs. Webb and Gray, Architects of Dudley and Stourbridge were chosen by the governors, and the contract was given to Messrs. J.M. Tate and Sons of Cradley. The demolition of the old School House was carried out in August of last year and evidence of the existence of a Priest's House and Chantry was discovered. It is very interesting to note that the site of the new Hall covers: (1) The old Chantry of the Holy Trinity, including its altar; (2) The Priest's House; (3) The Schoolroom which existed until 1861; and (4) The Headmaster's house and lawn. In the old Schoolroom the famous Dr. Samuel Johnson studied, and his initials are preserved, carved on the old oak panelling which was removed from the old hall and is now in one of the classrooms (A1). There are at least two old boys of the school alive who studied in the old schoolroom, namely Mr. J.S. Williams-Thomas, the Chairman of Governors, and Mr. Henry Webb, of the Laurels, Oldswinford.

The description of the new Assembly Hall . . . is as follows: It occupies the site of the old Headmaster's house, and is planned with its main axis at right angles to the High Street . . . . It is 90 feet long and 40 feet wide . . . . The main floor of the new Hall is level with the old hall, and is approached from a crush lobby and cloisters . . . . The old Assembly Hall has been converted into a library, which is cut off from the entrance hall by a carved oak lead-glazed screen, the remaining space being utilised for the School Office and Stationery Room.

The new buildings have been designed and detailed in the Tudor style, in keeping with the old work. The windows are stone-mullioned with lead glazing; the whole of the joinery, wall panelling, floors, etc., are in oak. A feature has been made of the ceiling, which is segmental and constructed of special 'acoustic' board, with moulded and modelled plaster ribs and bosses.

Carved on the upper parts of the three bays to the front elevation are the crowned portcullis in the centre, and on the side bays the Tudor rose and the sun in splendour — the royal badges of Edward VI. On the lower part of the bays, between the lower and upper windows, further carving has been carried out. In the central bay are the royal arms of King Edward VI, with the heads of that monarch and our present king carved in corbel form supporting the columns and entablature surrounding the arms.

The Worcestershire and Staffordshire County Arms are on the right and left hand bays respectively. Below the Worcestershire arms are carved heads of Mr. J.S. Williams-Thomas, Chairman of the Governors, and of His Worship the Mayor of Stourbridge, Alderman H.E. Palfrey, J.P. In corresponding positions below the Staffordshire arms are portraits of the late Randle L. Mathews, J.P., Vice-Chairman of the Governors, and of Mr. J.E. Boyt, M.A., Headmaster of the School.

The last paragraph of that description suggests to us that we might well remember Sir Christopher Wren's anonymous epitaph in St. Paul's Cathedral: — *Si monumentum requiris, circumspice*! We are bound to add that Wren did not think it appropriate to have his head carved on the exterior of St. Paul's. *Autres gens, autres moeurs*! Nor did J.E. Boyt's achievement *need* any such bodying forth to provide its monument. The school itself, — not just the buildings but the corporate living and working institution — stood as his undisputed creation and his legacy for the future. But the Boyt personality demanded expression and required recognition. In part his greatness must have sprung from that insatiable and inexorable drive. He loved the school and he loved success: this flower of his creation he did not mean should be born to blush unseen, certainly not to waste its sweetness on the desert air. So his head is carved on the front elevation of the great Assembly Hall, and no man ever deserved such an honour more.

He was born in 1869, the son of a Hampshire farmer; his school was King Edward VI, Southampton, and he went up to St. John's College, Cambridge in 1895 (once again, curiously enough, a very late under-graduate). He became a Scholar of his college and graduated in 1898 as 14th Wrangler. He taught in his old school for nine years — doubtless *before* he went to Cambridge — and at Bedford School from 1898 to 1905. Then he came to Stourbridge. After that it was a case of "Cometh the hour, cometh the man". All was set for the school's great game with its destiny: the board was set up, the pieces were ready, all was prepared for the great, sweeping drive which would carry the school to the zenith of its prosperity and achievement. All that was required was "a heart to resolve, a head to contrive, and a hand to execute". All three came together in the person of J.E. Boyt.

Let our last words on Boyt be those of his last Deputy, or more properly his last Second Master, — another great man at his own level and in his own right, H.E. Halliday. They were published in the school magazine in the summer of 1934.

THE RETIRING HEADMASTER

Mr. Boyt was appointed Headmaster in June 1905. His high scholastic attainments, his wide range of knowledge and interests, his athletic prowess, and his proved efficiency as a House Tutor at Bedford School, made him just the man the school required. From the moment of his arrival it was evident that he was determined that the reputation which under his predecessors the school had already acquired should be more than maintained.

The effect of his energy and his careful organisation was soon evident. The numbers increased and have steadily continued to increase. On his arrival Mr. Boyt found a school of 143 boys; last September there were 608 names on the roll. These statistics tell their own story.

Naturally the problem of accommodation speedily become acute, and the last 29 years have seen a series of extensions of the school premises. No sooner has increased accommodation been provided than it has been filled .... Here we can only summarise the extensions which have so transformed the school that one who had not seen it for thirty years would scarcely recognise it.

The erection of the A Block and the extension of the old hall to accommodate 220 boys (1908) was followed in 1911 by the building of the Preparatory School; the laboratories were re-arranged and duplicated, resulting in the splendidly-equipped Science Block (1927) which we now possess. Rooms A4 and A5 were added in 1925 and the B Block in 1928. Nor must we forget the acquisition of the school field, on which the present handsome pavilion was erected in 1925. Finally in 1931 came the gymnasium and the present Assembly Hall with its War Memorial window, of which not only we but also our fellow-townsmen are justifiably proud.

But it is not merely in numbers that the school has developed under Mr. Boyt. Its scholastic successes have been remarkable. The progress of the advanced work has been especially noteworthy. Before Mr. Boyt's time many striking university successes were obtained. But when he came, the number of boys doing advanced work was comparatively few, whereas we began the last school year with a Sixth form of some 90 boys, all of whom had won the School Certificate...

Further, the full and varied life which is now available for every boy is very largely the creation of Mr. Boyt. To him we owe our monitorial system, our House system, our method of managing the athletic sports, the swimming sports, the steeplechases, the Cadet Corps, and not least the institution of Charter Day. Other institutions which may not have been actually initiated by Mr. Boyt have received his constant encouragement and practical help. Hence the large number of successful school societies, and hence, we may be pardoned for adding, the continued and flourishing existence of the Stourbridge Edwardian. It would be hard to find a single aspect of our school life which has not benefited by his interest and help. This has been extended also to the Old Boys, who well know what the Old Edwardian Club owes to his unvarying support...

To the question "What is the secret of Mr. Boyt's success?" it would not be easy to give a simple answer, so many qualities go to the making of a successful Headmaster. Perhaps, however, we should come somewhere near the truth if we were to say simply that for 29 years he lived almost exclusively for the school; and his devotion to it has resulted in a thoroughness which has neglected no detail as too unimportant for his notice. He has neglected no opportunity of impressing upon the boys the necessity for making the most of their time, and his careful organisation, while giving every chance to those who are willing to profit from their opportunities, has left no loophole for the lazy and the shiftless. The result is that there has been a tradition of industry which many a boy has found invaluable in after life.

There was something symbolic about one of Mr. Boyt's first actions as headmaster. He began by shaking hands with every member of the school.... He has been a living refutation of the theory that a headmaster of a large school cannot know all his boys. He manages to see every boy personally at least once a week, and his remarkable memory and almost uncanny knowledge of what is going on must often have amazed the boys who thought themselves too insignificant for his personal notice.

H.E.H.

The Boyt 'apocrypha' of which we have spoken (an inevitable concomitant of the fame of a man like him) had one story of an occasion when he did make a mistake in identification. It should be noted, first, that he was a great exponent of the cane, and possessed of a *histrionic* temper. So there came the day when he went "off the top", and seized an unfortunate boy who was committing the unpardonable crime of whistling along the corridor. Off he was hauled to the study, down he bent, down came the cane! But justice, alas, had not been done. In the moment's pause after action the awful truth dawned. The criminal was not a member of the school at all, but the butcher's boy going about his lawful avocations. That cost J.E.B. the not inconsiderable sum of half-a-crown.

That story may quite well be another creation of the apocryphal imagination. Nevertheless it has something to tell us of the man behind the myth.

Finale and Dedication

Artistically, though not historically, that must be the end of our story of King Edward's School Stourbridge. In only the second paragraph of its first page I wrote that I was very reluctant, and genuinely so, to embark upon it. I was prevailed upon by the governors of the King Edward College to do it, for reasons which it is unnecessary to go into now. But I reminded the governors that I had myself served as headmaster of the school from 1951 to 1975, and that in consequence I felt unable to carry the history beyond the year 1950. The reasons for that are self-evident, and the governors respected them. So the tale of the end of the grammar school and the inauguration of the sixth-form college remains to be told by some other historian, probably one who was not himself concerned in the long and trying years of mounting threat, leading to their distressing conclusion — someone, it is to be hoped, who will be sufficiently detached to paint a less jaundiced picture and to write in less embittered terms than I ever could about the political act of social engineering which brought to an end the long chapter in English education represented by the history of King Edward's School, Stourbridge. That chapter was started by Philip and Joan Hayley's gift in the year 1430 and continued through five centuries and more of vicissitude, — through the period of Tudor exploitation and spoliation, the Stuart peace and progress in time of national calamity and civil war, past the eighteenth-century age of stagnation and on to Joseph Taylor's regime of total disaster; then from that nadir, as we have seen, it moved by an astonishing feat of progress and recovery, upward and ever upward to its heights, like that acme of the Victorian spirit of endeavour, "The youth who bore midst snow and ice That banner with the strange device, Excelsior!" The grammar of the Victorian ballad-writer was execrable, but his sentiment expressed precisely the spirit of our Victorian reformers — Collis, Welch, Lord Lyttelton and the Taunton Commissioners, Rupert Deakin and the rest, not forgetting the hosts of Stourbridge Edwardians — boys, masters, governors, parents — whose united aspirations towards excellence of achievement were eventually subsumed in the person and the performance of the great J.E. Boyt.

That is one reason why, if I had to go back now to the college governors and their request for a history of the school, I should seriously consider stipulating for it to conclude in the year 1934. There is another reason, — that I was myself as headmaster too near to the Watson era for me to make detailed comments about it without running the risk of stepping out of the strictly professional line. But mainly I have felt that practically everything that could be said of the years 1934-1951 has in fact already been set down in the story of J.E. Boyt.

It is not that the seventeen years under T.W. Watson were in any sense a period of stagnation or anti-climax, or a non-event: far from it! But what T.W. Watson did was what he was uniquely equipped to do: he *extended* the Boyt era and the Boyt system from 1934 to 1951. He was himself a product of that system — a pupil of Boyt, a mathematician, a Cambridge Wrangler, an accomplished games-player and a practical, substantial, solid and determined schoolmaster. His headmastership saw the erection of several new buildings, a continuation of the academic successes of his predecessor's time, and the persistence of the Boyt ethos through the medium of the Boyt system and the Boyt organisation of the school. There was little innovation, on the principle that you do not, if you have any sense, change a winning game. There was no point in innovation when change could hardly be for the better.

So the school went forward — not now upward and ever upward, since that process had in the fulness of its time achieved its proper level — but onward and steadily onward at that same level. So it was that the School which I inherited in 1951 was very much a 'going concern', possessed of enormous potential for development. For the essential foundations had been well and truly laid down by Boyt and reinforced on the same plan by Watson. It was hardly surprising that there were some Stourbridge Old Edwardians in 1951 who looked upon the appointment of a non-mathematical headmaster, trained in the now alien discipline of the ancient Classics, as something of a calamity for the school. Nor did they shrink from making their feelings known!

However, time that brings all things brought also in due course acceptance, warm and ungrudging, of the 'new boy': and he now, almost forty years on, is happy to dedicate this book to

THE STOURBRIDGE OLD EDWARDIANS

10th April, 1987

Index

Addenbrooke, Dorothy 74
Addenbrooke, Jeremiah 142
Addenbrooke, Jno. A 121, 123, 127, 128, 137, 142
Addenbrooke, John Addenbrooke (formerly Homfray) 142, 156
Addenbrooke, John Addenbrooke Jr. 156
Addenbrooke, Mary 142
Addenbrooke, Nicholas 64, 73, 74, 81
Addison, John 229, 235
Al(l) church(e), Richard 28, 29, 30, 33, 54, 61, 63, 80, 110, 130, 209.
Amblecote, site of playing field 239, 245
Amending Scheme (1900) 234
Andrew, J. B. (Assistant Master) 235, 236
Anniversary (400th) Celebration 2, 4
Ash, Edward (pupil) 123
Assembly Hall 246, 247
Augmentation Office 21, 33

Bach, Richard 34
Bailey, Will. 241
Baker family 66–68
Baker, John 62
Baker, Joseph 62
Baker, Richard 89
Baker, William 186
Ball, G. H. 235, 236, 241
Barney, Richard 185
Bartindale, Guy 241
Batchelor, Thomas 82
Bate, George 155, 169
Bate, Thos. 154, 155, 169
Bate, Prof. W. J. 38, 40, 146
Baugh 240
Baxter, Richard 80
Baylies (Usher) 107

Bedcote (Bedcott) 51, 64
Beesley, Michael (writing-master) 137, 138, 139, 150
Bell replacement 147, 148
Bentley's Worcestershire Directory 141
Best, Joseph (Governor) 100, 107
Biddle, Edward 169
Biggs, John 43, 99, 100, 101
"Billy the Blower" 229, 231
"Black Box" 2, 3, 4, 5, 9, 10, 12, 18, 58, 148, 158, 159
Bland, John N. 169
Bland, T. F. 16
Blond's Encyclopedia of Education 171
Blount, Thomas (bull-baiter) 97
Boldero, Rev. John Simon 225
Bowen, J. P. (Drawing Master) 225
Bowen, William (Assistant Master) 208
Boyle, Rev. G. D. 15, 16, 152
Boyle, Mary 152
Boyt, J. E. 20, 23, 158, 159, 197, 199, 200, 206, 210, 226, 236, 237, 241, 242, 244, 249, 250, 251, 252, 254
Bradley, Capt. 97, 110
Bradley, John (Governor) 107
Brierley Hill Advertiser 235
Brookes, Rev. John (Usher) 114
Brooks, A. E. 241
Brooks, Walter 240, 241
Broomhall, Robert 18, 224
Browne, John 35, 36, 39, 80, 83, 84, 85, 86, 120, 146
Bruce, Hon. W. N. 231
Bryce, Mr. (Assistant Commissioner, Taunton Commission) 244
Burley, George 2, 3, 18, 19, 27, 28, 32, 146, 147, 158

Butler, John (Trustee of Baker's Exhibtion) 67

Calamy — Account of the Ejected Ministers 66, 67
Camm of Smethwick 247
Canons 15, 17
Cardell, Thomas 49
Carlisle's 'Endowed Schools' 181
Caswell, Jeremiah 142
Causer, Edward 154
Causer, John 121, 123, 126, 137
Chancery proceedings (1704) 33, 34, 35
Chancery suit (1851) 45, 178, 184, 188, 234
Chandos, Duke of 15, 17
Chantry of The Holy Trinity 6, 21, 22, 23, 25, 26, 50, 51, 248
Chapman, Marmaduke 55, 61
Chappell (best junior boy in Cambridge locals) 238
Charities in England & Wales — Report of Commission 139, 141, 153, 159
Charity Commissioners 198
Charter of Stourbridge Free Grammar School (Translation of) 134
Charter Day 251
Clare, Francis 88
Clarendon Commission 200
Clarke, Daniel (Talbot Hotel) 97, 109, 112
Clarke, Mrs Mary 109
Class Lists 228, 235, 237
Clifford, Dr. J. L. 38
Cockin, Rev. W. 206
Cole, John (headmaster 1558) 55
Cole, Judith (probably an innkeeper) 73
Colebrookdale Company 146, 147
Collector 7
Collis, Bernard & King 12
Collis, George (1741–1811) 234
Collis, John 154, 169
Collis, William Blow (1) (1722–89) 118, 234
Collis, William Blow (2) (1778–1855) 234
Collis, William Blow (3) (1809–58) 133, 169, 187, 190, 234
Collis, William Blow (4) (1839–1922) 225, 229, 231, 233, 234, 235, 238 (see also 'Billy the Blower')
conjuror 28, 29
'Continuation Warrant' 21
Cooper, Thomas (surgeon) 188
Corff, Thomas (Hayley trustee) 49
Corns, J 14
Courthouse 9
Cox, Joseph (Governor) 118, 121, 123

Cranages's Royal Turf Cafe 8
Crane, Martin 35, 36, 39, 84, 120, 146
Craufurd, Rev. C. H. (Rector of Oldswinford) 171, 173, 186, 205
Cuckow Oak House 109
cupola (cast iron) 39, 146, 147, 148, 149
cupola (original) 38, 39

Dale, Robert 62
Dallyber-Poole Charity 42
Dalton, James 62, 69, 70, 72, 77, 78, 79, 204
Dalton, Thomas 69
Davenport, Edward 61
Day-book of E. H. Freer 10, 11, 12
'Dead Hand' 112, 113, 127, 141, 216
Deakin, Andrew 236
Deakin's, Mrs —'blanket box' 6, 7, 10, 236
Deakin, Rupert 6, 12, 175, 197, 226, 227, 235, 236, 237, 239, 240, 241, 242
Dean, Arthur 97
Deputy Collector 7, 115, 116
Dissolving of Corporation of Governors (1876) 219
Digbye, George 58
Dill, Dr. 195
Dixon. J. H. 154, 169
Doughty, Mr. (First Assistant Master) 207, 208, 211, 214, 225
Downey, Sgt.-Instructor 236
Downing, J 169
Duke Street 238, 246
Dyson, Edward 82, 90

Eaton, Richard (miller, of Lutley) 165
Edward the Sixth, King 13, 14, 15, 16, 17, 248
Edwards, R. A. (pupil) 243
Edwards, Sylvia 102, 104, 105, 114, 132, 161
Elcoxe, Thomas 26
Elcoxe's Close 26, 49, 246
Eldon, Lord (Leeds G. S. Judgement) 127, 128, 172
Ellis, John 39
Endowed Schools Act 1869 200, 216, 218
Endowed Schools Commission 200, 218, 220, 223
Evans, Francis 35
Everdon, William (Hayley trustee, 1430) 49
Evers, Bryan 2

Fee books 206
Fire of 1813 146, 147
Firmstone, Henry Onions JP 225, 230

Fisher, Master Frederick (pupil) 68, 165, 166
Flemyng, Richard (Hayley trustee 1430) 49
Fletcher, Col. T. W. 17, 225, 234
Foley, Alice 42
Foley, Lord 15, 17, 101, 102, 103, 104
Foley, North 89, 96
Foley, Paul 81
Foley, Philip 81
Foley, Richard 42, 58, 80, 81
Foley, Robert 70, 82, 83, 87, 88, 89, 104
Foley, Robert Jr. 81, 85, 86
Foley, Robert 118, 121, 123
Foley, Thomas (1617–1676) 80, 81
Foley, Thomas Jr. 81
Foley, Rev. Thomas P 126, 128, 150
Ford, Anne 95
Ford, Cornelius 94, 96, 98
Ford, Dr. Joseph 95, 96, 97
Ford, Nathaniel 95
Ford, Phoebe 95
Fotheringhay, College of 44
Freer, Alfred 247
Freer, E. H. 8, 10, 11, 12, 146, 223, 225
Freer & Perry (Solicitors) 8, 10
Freer, Richard Leacock 225
Freer, William Leacock 147
Freer, W. H. 154, 169
Freer, William M. 155

Gaine, C 169
Gardiner, George 9
Gaunt, John 114, 115
Gibson, Richard 186, 190
Girdlestone, James 11
Glover Charity School 41, 245
Glover, Henry 81, 219
Goddard, William Gruncell 204, 207, 208, 211, 214, 225, 235, 236
Godding, Rev. John 205
Goldsborough, Godfrey, Archdeacon of Worcester, later Bishop of Gloucester 28, 29, 54, 61
Goodacre, Rev. R. H. 182
Goppe, William (Hayley trustee) 49
Governors, List of 1688–1792 135
Governors, List of 1876 225
Grazebrook, George 171, 173
Grazebrook, 'Heraldry of Worcestershire' 72, 75
Great Wyrley Mine 245
Green Close 49, 51, 66, 88, 95, 96, 98, 99, 109, 147, 238, 245, 246
Green Close House 95, 244, 247
Grew, Jonathan 62
Grey, Lady 239, 245
Griffiths, William (1851 Petitioner) 184, 189, 190

Guttery 241

Haden, H. J. (Jack) 145, 197
Hagley Hall MSS 51
Haket, William of Lye, Jr. 49
Haket, William of Stourbridge 49
Hallifax, Rev. William 88, 90
Hall, Rev. Edmund 183, 184, 192
Hall Dr. John (m. Susannah Shakespeare) 192
Halliday, H. E. 250
Hancox, John 104, 108, 109, 114
Hareby, Philip & Joan 23, 24, 247 (see also Hayley)
Harris, Rev. Charles 104, 109, 114, 116, 117, 118, 119
Harris, John 114
Hart, Dr. A. Tindal 35
Harward & Evers 2, 8, 9, 10, 18, 25, 26, 34, 43, 44, 68, 158, 197, 227
Harward, John 8, 194, 195, 225
Hayles' Ground 26, 49
Hayley, John 49
Hayley, Philip & Joan 25, 26, 48, 49, 50, 253
Henzey, John 96, 97
Heywood, Lt. Col. Sir Percivial 243
Hickman, Alice 73, 75, 78
Hickman, Edward 74, 88, 118, 121
Hickman, Gregory (1) 95, 99
Hickman, Gregory (2) 95, 96, 97, 99, 100, 102
Hickman, Henry 71, 72, 73, 77
Hickman, Henry, of London 72, 73, 76, 77, 78
Hickman, Honor 95
Hickman, Jane 95
Hickman, Joseph 170
Hickman Library 71, 147
Hickman, Margaret 75
Hickman, Mary 95, 219
Hickman, Richard 72, 73, 82, 99, 154, 169, 170
Hickman, Walter 99, 101, 104
Hickman, W. H. 154
Hicks, John Moreton 186, 189
Hill, Mr. (Coroner) 131
Hill, John 115
Hill, Thomas 118, 123, 126, 137, 159
Hogarth 'Midnight Modern Conversation' 96, 98
Holbein 16
Homfray, John Addenbrooke (later John Addenbrooke Addenbrooke — by Royal Licence in 1798) 142, 156
Homfray, Rev. Jeremiah Caswell 151, 152, 153, 155, 156, 157, 170
Homfray, Thomas 127, 128, 137, 140, 142
Hondy, John 49

Hornblower, Sophia 169
Hottofte, Richard 62
Hough, Charlie 5, 6
Hough, (Old) 'Arbin' 5
Hughes, Henry 225
Hull, John 49
Hull, Thomas 49
Hunt, Samuel 73, 88
Hunt, Thomas 92
Hunt William 8, 160, 171, 173, 182
Hunt, William Jr. 154
Hurd, Dr., Bishop of Worcester 132
Hyde, Mrs Mary 38

James, Henry 186, 190
Jervoise, Thomas of Bedcote/
 Herriard/Stourbridge 53
Jervoises 64
Jeston, Humphrey 82, 88
Jeston, John 96
Johnson, Dr. Samuel 16, 32, 36, 71,
 80, 91, 93, 94, 95, 96, 146, 210, 237
Jones, H. P. 20, 175
Jukes, Mr. (Surgeon) 131

Kennedy, Jos. (Assistant Master) 208
Kent, John 62
Kidderminster Churchwardens 16
Kidderminster Times 16
King Edward's School, Camp Hill,
 Birmingham 234
King, Henry 186, 190
King, Joseph 154, 169, 193
Kirby, Rev. J. Malsbury 105, 155,
 157, 161, 162, 166, 167, 168, 170,
 171
Kynnersley, Clement 34
Kynnersley, Thomas of Loxley 34
Kynnersley, Thomas of Sneyd 34

Leach, A. F. 22
leases 18, 19
Leeche, William 49
Leeds Headmaster 128
Leeds Grammar School Judgment given
 by Lord Eldon 1805 127, 135
Leeson, D. R 243
Lewis, Edward George 190
Lincoln, City of 24, 25, 48, 221
Lister, Mr. 161
Lloyd, Bishop 35
Longlands House 246, 247
Lord Keeper of the Great Seal of
 England 35
Loverock, Robert 169
Lyttelton, Bishop Charles 27
Lyttelton, George 28
Lyttelton, Gilbert 28, 54, 61, 209
Lyttelton, Thomas, Bart. 27,
Lyttelton, Lord 201, 203, 218

Madstard Case 28, 29, 30, 40, 54
Madstard, Richard 28, 30, 55, 61, 63,
 80, 209
Madstard Volume 25, 30, 32
Maginnis, Rev. David 225
Mainwaring, A. J 212, 213, 215, 233
Mansell, Thomas, 154
Mark & Moody 102
Mathews, James 233
Mathews, Jeremiah 154, 155
Mathews, Paul 154, 212, 233
Mathews, Randle L 233, 249
Mathews, M 169
Meatyard, 230
Medwin, Thomas Peirce 181, 183,
 184, 185, 188, 191, 192
Milward, Edward 82, 88, 92, 100, 107
Milward Evidences 131, 154
Milward, Thomas 93, 96, 97, 98, 100,
 102, 103, 105, 110, 114
Minute Books (1688–1838) 4
 (1688–1849) 4
 (1698–1837) 4
 (1850–1876) 197
Moehring, Herr 208
Morgan, C (1833 petitioner) 169
Morley, Rev. John 143, 144, 145, 159
Moseley, Humphrey 7, 115
Moseley, William 7, 115, 116, 119,
 121, 128, 139, 142, 143, 147, 151,
 152
Mountfort, Samuel 62

Nash — History of Worcestershire 27,
 28, 71, 80
Nash, Thomas 186
National Register of Archives 18
Newbrough, Elizabeth 76
Newbrough, Joshua 81
Newcastle Commission 200
Nichols, Miss 68
Norris, William, MD 188
Nubrough, Benjamin 74
Nubrough, Jasper 58

Oldswinford 21, 22, 42, 48, 51, 52, 72,
 103, 104, 125, 154, 168, 173, 184,
 186, 222
Oldswinford Hospital School 41, 80,
 81
Oliver's Charity 42
Oliver, Edward 123
Oliver, Thomas 89, 219
Onslow, Archdeacon 15
Orme, William 154, 155, 169
Osborn Sergt. 208
'Ouldswynford' 22
Owen, Thomas 61

Palfrey, H. E. 10, 20, 33, 131, 144,
 159, 229, 243, 249

Panting, William   61
Parker, Nicholas   115
Parkes Trustees   233
Parry's Lands   49
Pattinson, Rev. John   104, 105, 114, 117, 118, 119, 122, 124, 125, 127, 128, 129, 130, 131, 132, 136, 137, 139
Payton, James   169
Penley, Rev. L. B.   236
Penn, Thomas   154
Penney, Benjamin   185, 190
Percy, Dr., Bishop of Dromore   94
Perkin, Godfrey Rowley   225
Perks, Francis   169
Perot, William   49
Perrens, Charles Skidmore   184, 189
Perrett, A. J.   16
Perring, William   169
Perry, George   10
Perry, John   150
Perry & Travis   10
Petition of 1851   193
Pettifogger   28, 29
Pidcock, Jno   118
Pidcock, John   126, 128, 135, 137, 139, 147, 181
Pitman, Joseph   154, 169, 170
Pittaway, Rev. H. M.   241
Plowman, Will   97
Pollard, Thomas   68
Polvoe, Elizabeth   75
Polvoe, Gload   75
Prattinton, Peter   93, 96
Price, Rowland   8, 11, 45, 164, 187
Purefoy, Arthur   54, 61
Puritan Document of 1652   59

Read, Rev. Joseph   142
Reade, Aleyn Leyell   71, 72
Reades of Blackwood Hill & Dr Johnson's Ancestry   71
Reed (Usher)   129, 130
Regulations of 1876   221
Report of the Commission for Inquiring Concerning Charities in England and Wales   139
Resolution of 1857   194
Reygnalds, William   49
Rhodes   241
Richards, R (Counsel 22.10.1807)   135, 138
Roberts, Henry   8, 145, 152
Robertson, Rev. Dr.   16, 17, 225
Robins, Jos.   126, 128, 137, 152, 189
Robins, William, banker & High Sheriff   152, 155, 189
Rocke, John   50, 62, 69, 70
Rocke, Nicholas   50, 53, 55
Rok, Stephen   49, 50
Rogers, Thomas   183

Royal Commission of 1819   171
Royal Turf Cafe   8
Royalist document of 1645   58
Rufford, Francis Jr.   154, 171
Rules & Orders (1702)   37
Russell Edw.   115
Ryemarket   109

Sanders, Pro. T. H.   241
Saunders, Thomas   100, 107, 115
Sawtell, W. W.   214, 215
Scamell, Prof. Ernest   50
School roll   242, 243
Schemes, Management   218, 219
Scott, Daniel   95
Scott, John   148
Scott, Robert   154, 155, 169
Scrots, Guillim   14 (see also Streets)
Sebright Charity of Wolverley   42
Secretary   7
Sedgeley, Ralph   50, 51
Sheldon   10
Shutt, Walter Witton   7, 11
Shutt, William   7
Simms, E. J.   236
Simms, Hy.   208
Skilbeck & Hall   164
Smith, A. R.   241
Smith, Henry   49
Smith, William   49
Somerset, A. F   38
South Luffenham Rectory   96
Sparry, Ambrose   62, 81
Sparry family   63, 64, 65
Sparry, John   61, 74, 88, 91
Sparry, Nicholas   50
Sparry, Roger   61
Staffordshire C. C. Grants 1899   232
Stamford, Earl of   160
Stansbie, J. H.   231, 236
Statutes & Orders (1841)   172–179, 181, 200
    (1862)   201–204
    (1876)   234
Stillingfleet, Bishop   85
Stokes, Fran.   118, 121, 123
Stourbridge Free Grammar School Report   139, 154
Stourbridge Observer   146
Stourbridge & Dudley Messenger   146
'Strangers'   167, 207
Streets, Guillim (Scrots)   14, 17
Styler, John   49
Styler, Richard   49
Swann, Dr.   194
Swinfen, John   68

Talbot, The   97, 109, 112
Talbott, Mr. (of Solicitor General's Office)   107
Task and Lesson Book   192

261

Tate, J. M. & Sons 248
Taunton Commission's Report on Endowed Schools 110, 200, 204, 216, 217, 218, 244
Taylor, George 132
Taylor, Rev. Joseph 104, 105, 114, 128, 129, 131, 132, 133, 135, 136, 137, 138, 139, 141, 142, 143, 144, 145, 146, 150, 151, 153, 157, 174, 220
Thomas, Mr. (Kidderminster & Stourbridge Banking Company) 16
St Thomas's Church, Stourbridge 42, 43, 94, 99, 100, 101, 105, 109, 132, 161
Thornton, G. R. 235, 236
Tommeson, William 49
Tookey, Rev. Charles 157
Travis & Sheldon (Solicitors) 10, 158
Travis, William 10
Tristram, John 75
Tristram, William 75, 82, 88, 89
Tristram, William Jr. 89, 96
Turner, Thomas (Staffordshire Technical Education Officer) 231, 232
Twittey, Thomas (gent., Commissioner in Chaucery) 73

Venn (Cambridge Lists) 132
Vernon, William (Governor of the School) 107
Vine Hotel 246
de Vit, Monsieur C. A. 208, 225

Waldron, Roger 97
Waldron, William 97
Walker, Agnes Mary Aston (nee Welch) 213
Walker, Capt. 208
Walker, Francis (School Governor) 126, 128, 137
Walker, Major James (School Governor) 225
Walker, Sergeant 208, 213, 214, 225
Walker, W. J. (pupil in the 1890's) 241
Wall, John 185
Wall, Mr (Tenant of school property) 120
Wall, Thomas (pupil) 193
Warner's Lands 49
Wasperton, Parish of 144
Wats, Thomas (trustee of 1430) 49
Watson, T. W. (Headmaster 1934–51) 192, 197, 226, 227, 241, 254

Watson, Mrs. 192
Webb & Gray (architects) 248
Webb, Henry (Old Boy) 248
Welch, William Gylby 204
Welch, Rev. William John Joseph 15, 16, 18, 194, 196, 197, 198, 199, 202, 203, 204, 205, 206, 207, 209, 210, 213, 215, 225, 227
Wells, Rev. Giffard 104, 105, 114, 118, 158, 159, 161, 163, 165, 166, 167, 171, 173, 174, 175, 176, 177, 178, 179, 180, 182, 184, 185, 191, 193, 194, 195, 196
Wells, John (Governor) 118
Wentworth, John 32, 33, 35, 80, 82, 83, 87, 90, 91, 92, 94, 106, 107, 108, 109, 110, 11, 112, 130, 176, 177
Westwood, Edward (Governor) 225
Wheeler Charity School 41, 223, 224
Wheeler, Emma 74, 75
Wheeler, John 34, 82, 88, 89, 90
Wheeler, John 91, 99
Wheeler-Kynnersley Papers 35, 82, 83, 87, 168
Wheeler, Richard 92
Wigan, Rev. George 100, 101, 102, 103, 107
Willetts, James R (son of Richard) 182
Willetts, Richard of Wollaston Jr. 115, 117, 118, 120, 121, 122, 123, 123, 124, 125, 128, 130, 138, 162
Willetts, Richard & Jane 115
Williams-Thomas J. S, OBE, JP 243, 248, 249
Wilmot's Act (1840) 172, 174, 188
Winshurst, George 62
Winshurst, Susannah 69
Winshurst, William 69, 81
Withers, Joseph 62
Witley Church 15
Wollaston Hall 95
Wolverley free school 42
Woods, Richard 184, 191, 192, 193, 194, 196, 197, 204
Woodward, John (Keeper of the Dept. of Art, Birmingham) 14
Worcester, Lord Bishop of 126, 128, 132, 137, 140, 144, 153, 162, 172, 173, 181, 182, 183, 201, 230
Wragge, Chas. John 154, 187
Wren, Sir Christopher 249

Yeates (former pupil) 241
York, Thos. (Governor) 115